Dividing Boundaries Contours of Indo-China Conflict

DIVIDING BOUNDARIES CONTOURS OF INDO-CHINA CONFLICT

Dr. (Prof.) Anil K. Saxena

Gaurav Book Centre Pvt Ltd

Delhi

Publisher
GAURAV BOOK CENTRE PVT LTD
ISO 9001:2008
4832/24, Prahlad Lane, S-207
Ansari Road, Daryaganj, Delhi-110002
Ph.: 011-43570976, 23278261
Email: gauravbookcentre@gmail.com

Edition: 2023

ISBN: 978-93-83316-14-4

Laser Typesetting
JEE-VEE Graphics, Delhi

Price: 1195/-

Printed
Vikas Computers, Delhi

Contents

Preface

The final settlement of the Sino-Indian territorial and boundary dispute is not a question of 'if' but 'when'. Four pertinent reasons suggest that China can be ultimately trusted to settle the dispute.

In 1962, the Chinese had a claim on what India deemed its own territory called Arunachal Pradesh. China sent many well-trained and well-armed troops to the disputed region. On the other hand, India had only ill-equipped troops there, which made them more difficult to beat Chinese troops. The Sino-Indian (Indo-China) War was started by China on October 16, 1962 on account of the territorial dispute against India. Chinese attacked India on October 20, 1962 because it was unable to reach political accommodation on disputed territory along the 3,225-kilometer-long Himalayan border.

The Chinese did not invade farther, and on November 21, 1962 declared a unilateral cease-fire. They had accomplished all of their territorial objectives, and any attempt to press farther into the plains of Assam would have stretched their logistical capabilities and their lines of communication to a breaking point. Finally, the Chinese defeated India in 1962, which as a result led to the retreat of Indian Army in terms of doctrine, training, organization and equipment from the disputed area.

Recently, the Sino-Indian border dispute once again became a focus of for the world's mass media. A "tent confrontation" between the Chinese and Indian armies took place and continued near the Line of Actual Control (LAC) for several days. From the Indian point of view, the Chinese army invaded Indian territory, and this incident was "the most serious one in the past 25 years". Level-headed analysis will indicate, however, that China would not wish to provoke simultaneous conflicts with Japan and India, two major Asian powers.

As the book addresses this crucial issue quite deftly, it is hoped that it would prove to be a source of great information for the reader. It an essential reading for the students taking courses on this book.

—*Editor*

Preface

1

Sino-Indian Border Dispute

Sovereignty over two large and various smaller separated pieces of territory are contested between China and India. The westernmost, Aksai Chin, is claimed by India as part of the state of Jammu and Kashmir and region of Ladakh but is controlled and administered as part of the Chinese autonomous region of Xinjiang. It is a virtually uninhabited high altitude wasteland crossed by the Xinjiang-Tibet Highway. The other large disputed territory, the easternmost, lies south of the McMahon Line. It was formerly referred to as the North East Frontier Agency, and is now called Arunachal Pradesh. The McMahon Line was part of the 1914 Simla Convention between British India and Tibet, an agreement rejected by China.

The 1962 Sino-Indian War was fought in both of these areas. An agreement to resolve the dispute was concluded in 1996, including "confidence-building measures" and a mutually agreed Line of Actual Control. In 2006, the Chinese ambassador to India claimed that all of Arunachal Pradesh is Chinese territory amidst a military build up. At the time, both countries claimed incursions as much as a kilometre at the northern tip of Sikkim. In 2009, India announced it would deploy additional military forces along the border.

AKSAI CHIN

From the area's lowest point (on the Karakash River at about 14,000 feet (4,300 m) to the glaciated peaks up to 22,500 feet (6,900 m) above sea level, this is a desolate, largely uninhabited area. It covers an area of about 37,244 square kilometres (14,380 sq mi). The desolation of Aksai Chin meant that it had no significant human importance other than ancient trade routes crossing it, providing brief passage during summer for caravans of yaks from Xinjiang and Tibet.

One of the earliest treaties regarding the boundaries in the western sector was issued in 1842. The Sikh Confederacy of the Punjab region in India had annexed Ladakh into the state of Jammu in 1834. In 1841, they invaded Tibet with an army. Chinese forces defeated the Sikh army and in turn entered Ladakh and besieged Leh. After being checked by the Sikh forces, the Chinese and the Sikhs signed a treaty in September 1842, which stipulated no transgressions or interference in the other country's frontiers. The British defeat of the Sikhs in 1846 resulted in transfer of sovereignty over Ladakh to the British, and British commissioners attempted to meet with Chinese officials to discuss the border they now shared. However, both sides were apparently sufficiently satisfied that a traditional border was recognised and defined by natural elements, and the border was not demarcated. The boundaries at the two extremities, Pangong Lakeand Karakoram Pass, were reasonably well-defined, but the Aksai Chin area in between lay largely undefined.

THE MACARTNEY-MACDONALD LINE

In 1893, Hung Ta-chen, a senior Chinese official at Kashgar, handed a map of the boundary proposed by China toGeorge Macartney, the British consul-general at Kashgar. This boundary placed the Lingzi Tang plains, which are south of the Laktsang range, in India, and Aksai Chin proper, which is north of the Laktsang range, in China. Macartney agreed with the proposal and forwarded it to the British Indian government. This border, along theKarakoram Mountains, was proposed and supported by British officials for a number of reasons. The Karakoram Mountains formed a natural boundary, which would set the British borders up to the Indus River watershed while leaving the Tarim River watershed in Chinese control, and Chinese control of this tract would present a further obstacle to Russian advance in Central

Asia. The British presented this line, known as the Macartney-MacDonald Line, to the Chinese in 1899 in a note by Sir Claude MacDonald. The Qing government did not respond to the note, and the British took that as Chinese acquiescence. Although no official boundary had ever been negotiated, China believed that this had been the accepted boundary.

1899 to 1947

Both the Johnson-Ardagh and the Macartney-MacDonald lines were used on British maps of India. Until at least 1908, the British took the Macdonald line to be the boundary, but in 1911, the Xinhai Revolution resulted in the collapse of central power in China, and by the end of World War I, the British officially used the Johnson Line. However they took no steps to establish outposts or assert actual control on the ground. In 1927, the line was adjusted again as the government of British India abandoned the Johnson line in favour of a line along the Karakoram range further south. However, the maps were not updated and still showed the Johnson Line.

From 1917 to 1933, the "Postal Atlas of China", published by the Government of China in Peking had shown the boundary in Aksai Chin as per the Johnson line, which runs along the Kunlun mountains. When British officials learned of Soviet officials surveying the Aksai Chin for Sheng Shicai, warlord of Xinjiang in 1940–1941, they again advocated the Johnson Line. At this point the British had still made no attempts to establish outposts or control over the Aksai Chin, nor was the issue ever discussed with the governments of China or Tibet, and the boundary remained undemarcated at India's independence.

Since 1947

Upon independence in 1947, the government of India used the Johnson Line as the basis for its official boundary in the west, encompassing Aksai Chin. However, India did not claim the northern areas nearShahidulla and Khotan, for including which in Indian territory, among other things, Johnson had been criticised. From the Karakoram Pass (which is not under dispute), the Indian claim line extends northeast of the Karakoram Mountains north of the salt flats of the Aksai Chin, to set a boundary at the Kunlun Mountains, and incorporating part of the Karakash River and Yarkand River watersheds. From there, it runs east along the Kunlun Mountains, before turning southwest through the Aksai Chin salt flats, through the Karakoram Mountains, and then to Pangong Lake.

On 1 July 1954 Prime Minister Nehru wrote a memo directing that the maps of India be revised to show definite boundaries on all frontiers. Up to this point, the boundary in the Aksai Chin sector, based on the Johnson Line, had been described as "undemarcated."

During the 1950s, the People's Republic of China built a 1,200 kilometres (750 mi) road connecting Xinjiang and western Tibet, of which 179 kilometres (111 mi) ran south of the Johnson Line through the Aksai Chin region claimed by India. Aksai Chin was easily accessible from China, but was more difficult for the Indians on the other side of the Karakorams to reach. The Indians did not learn of the existence of the road until 1957, which was confirmed when the road was shown in Chinese maps published in 1958.

The Indian position, as stated by prime minister Jawaharlal Nehru, was that the Aksai Chin was "part of the Ladakh region of India for centuries" and that this northern border was a "firm and definite one which was not open to discussion with anybody".

The Chinese minister, Zhou Enlai argued that the western border had never been delimited, that the Macartney-MacDonald Line, which left the Aksai Chin within Chinese borders was the only line ever proposed to a Chinese government, and that the Aksai Chin was already under Chinese jurisdiction, and that negotiations should take into account the status quo.

In April 2013 India claimed, referencing their own perception of the Line of Actual Control (LAC) location, that Chinese troops had established a camp in the Daulat Beg Oldi sector, 10 km on their side of the Line of Actual Control. This figure was later revised to a 19 km claim. According to Indian media, the incursion included Chinese military helicopters entering Indian airspace to drop supplies to the troops. However, Chinese officials denied any trespassing having taken place. Soldiers from both countries briefly set up camps on the ill-defined frontier facing each other, but the tension was defused when both sides pulled back soldiers in early May.

Trans Karakoram Tract

The Johnson Line is not used west of the Karakoram Pass, where China adjoins Pakistan-administered Gilgit–Baltistan. On 13 October 1962, China and Pakistan began negotiations over the boundary west of the Karakoram Pass. In 1963, the two countries settled their boundaries largely on the basis of the Macartney-MacDonald Line, which left the Trans Karakoram Tract in China, although the agreement provided for renegotiation in the event of a settlement of the Kashmir dispute. India does not recognise that Pakistan and China have a common border, and claims the tract as part of the domains of the pre-1947 state of Kashmir and Jammu. However, India's claim line in that area does not extend as far north of the Karakoram Mountains as the Johnson Line

THE MCMAHON LINE

British India and China gained a common border in 1826, with British annexation of Assam in the Treaty of Yandabo at the conclusion of the First Anglo-Burmese War (1824–1826). Subsequent annexations in further Anglo-Burmese Wars expanded China's borders with British India eastwards, to include the border with what is now Myanmar.

In 1913–14, representatives of Britain, China, and Tibet attended a conference in Simla, India and drew up an agreement concerning Tibet's status and borders. The McMahon Line, a proposed boundary between Tibet and India for the eastern sector, was drawn by British negotiator Henry McMahon on a map attached to the agreement. All three representatives initiated the agreement, but Beijing soon objected to the proposed Sino-Tibet boundary and repudiated the agreement, refusing to sign the final. After approving a note which stated that China could not enjoy rights under the agreement unless she ratified it, the British and Tibetan negotiators signed the Simla Convention. Neville Maxwell states that McMahon had been instructed not to sign bilaterally with Tibetans if China refused, but he did so without the Chinese representative present and then kept the declaration secret.

V.K. Singh argues that the basis of these boundaries, accepted by British India and Tibet, were that the historical boundaries of India were the Himalayas and the areas south of the Himalayas were traditionally Indian and associated with India. The high watershed of the Himalayas was proposed as the border between India and its northern neighbours. India's government held the view that the Himalayas were the ancient boundaries of the Indian subcontinent and thus should be the modern boundaries of British India and later the Republic of India.

Chinese boundary markers, including one set up by the newly created Chinese Republic, stood near Walong until January 1914, when T. O'Callaghan, an assistant administrator of North East Frontier Agency (NEFA)'s eastern sector, relocated them north to locations closer to the McMahon Line (albeit still South of the Line). He then went to Rima, met with Tibetan officials, and saw no Chinese influence in the area.

By signing the Simla Agreement with Tibet, the British had violated the Anglo-Russian Convention of 1907, in which both parties were not to negotiate with Tibet, "except through the intermediary of the Chinese Government", as well as the Anglo-Chinese Convention of 1906, which bound the British government "not to annex Tibetan territory." Because of doubts concerning the legal status of the accord, the British did not put the McMahon Line on their maps until 1937, nor did they publish the Simla Convention in the treaty record until 1938. Rejecting Tibet's 1913 declaration of independence, China argued that the Simla Convention and McMahon Line were illegal and that Tibetan government was merely a local government without treaty-making powers. In 1947, Tibet requested that India recognise Tibetan authority in the trading town of Tawang, south of the McMahon Line. Tibet did not object to any other portion of the McMahon line. In reply, the Indians asked Tibet to continue the relationship on the basis of the previous British Government.

Tibetan officials continued to administer Tawang and refused to concede territory during negotiations in 1938. The governor of Assam asserted that Tawang was "undoubtedly British" but noted that it was "controlled by Tibet, and none of its inhabitants have any idea that they are not Tibetan." During World War II, with India's east threatened by Japanese troops and with the threat of Chinese expansionism, British troops secured Tawang for extra defence.

China's claim on areas south of the McMahon Line, encompassed in the NEFA, were based on the traditional boundaries. India believes that the boundaries China proposed in Ladakh and Arunachal Pradesh have no written basis and no documentation of acceptance by anyone apart from China. Indians argue that China claims the territory on the basis that it was under Chinese imperial control in the past, while Chinese argue that India claims the territory on the basis that it was under British imperial control in the past. The last Qing emperor's 1912 edict of abdication authorised its succeeding republican government to form a union of "five peoples, namely, Manchus, Han Chinese,Mongols, Muslims, and Tibetans *together with their territory in its integrity*" However, V.K. Singh cites the presence of the Mauryan Empire and Chola Dynasty in regions India does not place a claim to but which were heavily influenced by Indian culture.

India's claim line in the eastern sector follows the McMahon Line. The line drawn by McMahon on the detailed 24–25 March 1914 Simla Treaty maps clearly starts at 27°45′40"N, a trijunction between Bhutan, China, and India, and from there, extends eastwards. Most of the fighting in the eastern sector before the start of the war would take place immediately north of this line. However, India claimed that the *intent* of the treaty was to follow the main watershed ridge divide of the Himalayas based on memos from McMahon and the fact that over 90% of the McMahon Line does in fact follow the main watershed ridge divide of the Himalayas. They claimed that territory south of the high ridges here near Bhutan (as elsewhere along most of the McMahon Line) should be Indian territory and north of the high ridges should be

Chinese territory. In the Indian claim, the two armies would be separated from each other by the highest mountains in the world.

During and after the 1950s, when India began patrolling this area and mapping in greater detail, they confirmed what the 1914 Simla agreement map depicted: six river crossings that interrupted the main Himalayan watershed ridge. At the westernmost location near Bhutan north of Tawang, they modified their maps to extend their claim line northwards to include features such as Thag La ridge, Longju, and Khinzemane as Indian territory. Thus, the Indian version of the McMahon Line moves the Bhutan-China-India trijunction north to 27°51′30"N. India would claim that the treaty map ran along features such as Thag La ridge, though the actual treaty map itself is topographically vague (as the treaty was not accompanied with demarcation) in places, shows a straight line (not a watershed ridge) near Bhutan and near Thag La, and the treaty includes no verbal description of geographic features nor description of the highest ridges.

Sikkim

India's annexation of Sikkim in 1975 was rejected by China at the time. The Sino-Indian Memorandum of 2003 was hailed as a *de facto* Chinese acceptance of the annexation. China published a map showing Sikkim as a part of India and the Foreign Ministry deleted it from the list of China's "countries and regions". However, the Sikkim-China border's northernmost point, "The Finger", continues to be the subject of dispute and military activity.

CHINA SPRINGS A SURPRISE AT BORDER TALKS WITH INDIA

China wants a code of conduct for troops on the India-China border areas. While the Indian side has reacted cautiously, it is not clear what effective additional protocols that the current proposed code will bring forth to usher stability in the border areas, says Srikanth Kondapalli. China surprised India once again with a formal suggestion for implementing a 'code of conduct' between the armed forces of both countries at the recently held 17th Special Representative meeting in New Delhi on February 10-11.

While the Special Representative meetings were instituted to resolve the territorial dispute, initially to clarify the Line of Actual Control between the two countries, these interactions have expanded to include issues not just on the dispute per se but also on others aspects affecting the bilateral relations. China's new proposal for modulating the behaviour of the troops on the borders comes as a surprise despite a series of arrangements between the two armies since the 1970s when confidence building measures were put in place across the undefined borders. These include the first CBMs at Chushul in Ladakh sector in the 1970s.

Subsequently, the 1993 "Peace & Tranquility" agreement, 1996 CBMs in the military field, April 2005 proposals and the 2012 Border Defence Cooperation agreement. While China had suggested such a code of conduct for the maritime areas in the disputed South China Sea islands in November 2002, this is perhaps the first time that Beijing suggested such proposals on the land domain with India. With Russia and central Asia, China did conclude CBMs in the military field, including demilitarisation, prior to the resolution of the territorial disputes with these states since the 1990s, yet the current code of conduct proposal is different with India.

Firstly, unlike with Russia, central Asia or Vietnam with which China had resolved the land territorial disputes in a time-bound manner with deadlines fixed by the civilian leadership in Beijing, no such time-frame for resolved the territorial dispute exists with India. Indeed, for various reasons — including rising nationalism and pressures on the new leadership in China, coalition era in India, etc — both sides have not provided for a time frame for the final resolution of the dispute even though both were engaged in such discussions thrice in 1960, eight times in 1980s and 15 times under the Joint Working Group meetings in 1990s and now in the 17 Special Representative mechanisms since 2003.

Two phases of the Special Representative meetings were identified with the early five discussions from 2003 to 2005 as knowing each other's positions on the border dispute, while the meetings from sixth through ninth as more intensive in nature. After five meetings between the SRs both countries, in a joint statement in April 2005 between the two premiers, decided to solve the border dispute based on "political parameters and guiding principles".

The second phase from the sixth meeting in September 2005 explored possibilities for initiating an "agreed framework" on the boundary dispute settlement. At the 15th Special Representative meeting in New Delhi in January 2012, the framework was exchanged. Interestingly, during the August 2009 13th Special Representative Meeting between M K Narayanan and Dai Bingguo, the Hong Kong based newspaper *Ming Pao* reported that China is prepared to settle for 28 percent of the disputed territory between the two countries, though denied by the Chinese foreign ministry spokesman. The Indian side, however, is tight-lipped on the details of this deal.

Secondly, the code of conduct with southeast Asian countries, specifically with Vietnam and the Philippines, has not been successful and the regional countries have demanded that the code be made enforceable. No such provisions — that no country should seize more islands or build military infrastructure — were accepted by Beijing, resulting in tensions in the last one decade.

It is not clear what provisions are including in the code suggested by Beijing to India last week but the experience on such a code is not so encouraging — at least in the southeast Asian context. Although the 17th SR talks were termed as being held in "candid, friendly and constructive atmosphere" the official statement did not mention about the status of the code. It indicates that the Indian side is cautious, but looking at the provisions of the code.

Thirdly, it was suggested that the proposed code of conduct aims at reducing/eliminating chances of conflict between the patrolling troops in the border areas. However, these were part of the earlier CBMs agreed to between the two sides including the recent Border Defence Cooperation Agreement. It is not clear what effective additional protocols that the current proposed code will bring forth to usher stability in the border areas.

The fact that China had not explained why its troops intruded 19 kilometers in the Indian claimed areas in the Depsang plains incident in Ladakh from April 15 to May 6 last year, despite a "strategic partnership and cooperation" between the two since 2005 indicates that even if the proposed code of conduct between the troops is accepted and implemented by India, there is no guarantee that Depsang plains incident will never recur.

Indeed as the code of conduct proposals were being made by the Chinese side, transgressions in the border areas were reported. This indicates to the limitations of the proposed code.

Fourthly, more significantly, the proposed code of conduct appears to be more a ploy to distract the Indian attention, although every measure needs to be taken to maintain stability in the border areas by both the troops. While the Depsang plains incident was aimed at lowering the image of the Indian Army and the Indo-Tibetan Border Police forces — as a process of "perturbing the enemy lines" — the proposed code appears to create differences in the civil-military relations in India. India then needs to take a firm call on the proposed code of conduct.

FACTS BEHIND CHINA-INDIA BORDER DISPUTE

If a general of the Chinese imperial government representing the Manchu dynasty had, by force of arms, pillage and plunder, succeeded in subjugating the North American continent and on that basis had artificially created a border line between the United States and Canada called, let us say, The Manchu Line, would a sovereign U.S. government abide by thus border line? Let us suppose further that the boundary line demarcated by this general included, for the Canadian side, parts of Buffalo, Detroit, Seattle and Duluth. Let us suppose again that the treaty between Canada and the U.S. dictated by this general had never been accepted by any government of the United States, and that in truth the people of the U.S. regarded this treaty and its boundary line as illegal, null and void, and as the imposition of a foreign power at a time when the U.S. was weak, divided and under the domination of a foreign imperialist power. All we have to do with this analogy is to just change the name — Canada to India, United States to China and China to Great Britain — and the picture becomes immeasurably clearer than it is represented in the U.S. press.

The Mcmahon Line

It is the position of the Chinese People's Republic that the so-called McMahon Line — named after the British General McMahon — is illegal, null and void, and the result of a predatory, imperialist imposition of the British government in the year 1914. No Chinese government ever accepted the McMahon Line.

Neither did the Imperial Government of China in 1914, nor the Chiang Kai-Shek government ever agree to it. The very fact that even the Chiang Kai-Shek clique, which is nothing but a tool of U.S. imperialism, has not dared to dispute the Chinese People's Republic's position of the China-India border dispute, it in itself the most eloquent testimony to the correctness of the Chinese position. Nevertheless, the Chinese People's Republic has made every effort to achieve a reasonable and just settlement of the territory in dispute. It has consistently shunned the use of arms.

Proposals For Negotiations

Although the border dispute is almost three years old now, and the Chinese have made innumerable other approaches to the Indian government to settle it on some amicable and acceptable basis the Nehru government has invariably turned them down. In the past two months alone the Chinese government made several proposals for negotiations. It made a notable effort on August 4, and another one on September 13. In neither of these proposals did the Chinese government lay down any preconditions for the negotiations. Nor did the Chinese government resort to the type of language which could in any way be construed as a threat to India.

On the contrary, the diplomatic notes directed to the Indian government were couched in the most conciliatory language, and were calculated to effectuate a reasonable settlement which would safeguard the territorial integrity of China as well as India. As a matter of fact, the London Times, certainly no friend of the Chinese revolutionary government, had to publicly admit on October 8 that if military operations were resumed on the Sino-Indian border, "onlookers will have to note that it was New Dehli.., that declined to embark upon them (talks)..."

The position of the London Times is of exceptional importance because it has always sided with India as against China. The London Times was obliged to make the above statement only after the Indian paper, Tribune, had reported that at a cabinet meeting the Indian government had decided to use armed force to deal with China.

Nehru's "Limited Offensive"

It was also reported in the world press on October 8, that Nehru had authorized India's new commander-in chief of the eastern border area to "fight a limited offensive operation."

These are the incontrovertible facts. As to what lies behind the aggressive attitude of the Nehru government, it must be borne in mind first of all that the imperialist world, particularly the U.S. would like nothing better than to see the two principal Asiatic powers, the two powers which hold the greatest revolutionary promise for mankind in the east, locked in military combat, shedding the blood of thousands, absorbing the resources and energies of millions of people, which should be used to construct a revolutionary way of life.

The efforts of the U.S. government, it must be noted, have been directed, insofar as India is concerned, not only to make it economically and financially dependent upon U.S. monopoly interests, but also to inflame the Indian bourgeoisie, particularly its right-wing extremist elements, against the Chinese People's Republic.

Four Billion U.S. Aid

According to The New York Times of October 22(1969), the U.S. has poured into India more than four billion dollars. A substantial section of this money has gone to line the pockets of Indian businessmen, government officials, and especially the extremist elements who are interested in diverting the mass discontent of the Indian peasants and workers into other channels. U.S. diplomats, State Department planners, and military figures in the Pentagon have for a long time felt that the biggest diversionary tactic that imperialism could employ to disrupt the revolutionary anti-imperialist front was to continually stir up, bribe and corrupt as many of the representatives of the Indian bourgeoisie as it could to fan the flames of an India-China war.

Nehru himself was subjected to unremitting pressure when he was in the U.S. More U.S. aid was used as bait to lure Nehru into the trap of a protracted India-China war, which can only result in further detriment to India, China and the cause of all oppressed people.

Since Nehru's Visit

Since the Indian Prime Minister left the shores of the U.S. there have been only rare intervals in which there has been a let up in the war fever fanned by the Indian bourgeoisie and its agent Nehru. For a long time Nehru played the role of moderator between left and right in the Indian-China border dispute, cautioning the extremist elements of the bourgeoisie in Parliament, and repudiating suggestions for offensive operations by his military advisers.

But his October 4 decision, taken after a cabinet meeting, made it clear beyond any shadow of a doubt that he had completely capitulated to the right wing on this issue and was kowtowing to U.S. imperialist interests. The present military efforts of the Chinese are merely a response to the offensive action taken after the Indian cabinet session.

A Defensive Battle

The Chinese government is fighting a defensive battle. It is only too well aware that U.S. imperialism is ready at all times to take advantage of any preoccupation that China may have with India to open another front against China wherever and whenever it finds it feasible, whether it be in the Pescadores, the Taiwan strait or new harassments over the air space of China. There are those who say China should give in — give up what belongs to China in the interest of peace. These are the people who are always ready to give, especially things that do not belong to them.

When to give — or whether to give — is a question which only the Chinese can decide, as it as *their* territory. Surely the Chinese, who have gone through hell and fire in the course of 22 years of civil war, in which they have had to trade many times — space for time — and in fact have endured many retreats, need no reminders on this score.

Solidarity Of Asian People

The workers of the world and the progressive anti-imperialist countries in particular, are most deeply concerned in a speedy, reasonable and honorable settlement on the part of China and India. Such a settlement can only be arrived at if the ruling group in New Delhi accepts China's offer for the resumption of talks on a high level between the two governments without any pre conditions. A border settlement would remove a tremendous obstacle to the solidarity of the Asian people who are struggling for a new life, and would be a tremendous rebuff to imperialism and its servants and underlings.

ARUNACHAL PRADESH TERRITORIAL DISPUTE BETWEEN INDIA AND CHINA

International law never supports a country or a state which attempts to plunder the territory from other countries or states by threatening or warfare. Article 2 of The UN Charter clearly defines that "all Members shall refrain in their international relations from the threat or use of force against the territorial integrity or political independence of any state" (Reynolds 2004.) It is so-called a territorial dispute, which is "a disagreement over the possession or control of land between two or more countries" ("Territorial Dispute.") What leads the territorial dispute is not only relevant to the possession or control of natural resources such as oil, coals, fertile land or rivers, but also culture and religion. In addition, it has been said that "in many cases territorial disputes result from vague and unclear language in a treaty that set up the original boundary" ("Territorial Dispute".) Consequently, many territorial disputes possibly generate some conflicts between countries, and even worse, they can become a primary cause of wars and/or terrorism.

A long time ago, before the territorial dispute between China and India emerged in Arunachal Pradesh, the first ancestors of the tribal groups migrated from Tibet during pre-historic period. Even though ancestors were there, little is known about the history of Arunachal Pradesh. Recorded history is only available in the Ahom chronicles from the sixteenth century: the British Christened, originally known as northeast Frontiers Agency (NEFA,) took administrative control of Arunachal Pradesh and it remained under this rule until 1948. Arunachal Pradesh is northeast India's largest and remotest state, as it has railways and air services connecting only three of its town. Natives in Arunachal Pradesh used to eat "their food in uncooked condition ignorant about the discovery of fire" (WebDigitech.) They were really isolated and not aware of the development and revolution which was occurring in this globalized world. The major cause of China-India territorial dispute, which deprived peace from Arunachal Pradesh, is from immediately after Chinese Revolution in 1911. At that time, Qing Dynasty, the last Chinese Dynasty, fell and the Emperor of Qing Dynasty resigned. As a result, China, Tibet and Mongolia became equal and separate countries. In these three countries, Tibet and Mongol tried to be approved internationally as independent states, and undertook to international society. However, on the other hand, Han Chinese Republicans started small war to subjugate reins of government of Tibet and Mongol. Therefore, they could not be independent states at that time.

In 1912-13, the British Raj made agreements with tribal leaders that defined the area that was known as NEFA. British rule could have very small impact on the isolated, self-sufficient in terms of economy and militarily uncontrollable tribal peoples. In order to arrange this conflict, in 1913 and 1914, the British administrator, Sir Henry McMahon, drew up the 550-mile McMahon Line as the border between India and China in Shimla, during a conference which also discussed the Tibetan and Chinese borders ("McMahon Line.") This conference is called Shimla Conference. Regardless of this reconciliation, the McMahon Line was rejected by the Chinese government in 1947 ("Arunachal Pradesh.")

Following this dispute, the Chinese troops crossed the McMahon Line on the August 26th, 1959 ("Arunachal Pradesh.") They abandoned this in 1961, but in October 1962 crossed the line once again with force ("McMahon Line.") As a result, Sino-Indian War broke out. The Chinese extended their frontier as they intruded deeper and deeper. However, this war did not go on for a long time. In 1963, the Chinese agreed to withdraw back to the McMahon Line, and also returned Indian prisoners of this war at that time.

Environment Aspects

By losing Arunachal Pradesh located on the northeastern tip of India, bordering Bhutan on the west, China on the north, Myanmar on the east and the states of Assam on the south, either China or India would receive some damage in terms of economy. Both China and India are able to run good business because Arunachal Pradesh is a very good place for tourists from all over the world to visit. Evergreen forest, which covers more than 60 percent of the state area, certainly makes people feel comfortable to stay there.

From this fact, Arunachal Pradesh is known for its forest resources. Forest products and industries are considered as a lifeline in Arunachal Pradesh. In fact, 75 percent of its total workforce is engaged in agriculture (mainly shifting cultivation.) Therefore, if either China or India could obtain Arunachal Pradesh, it would be able to improve its economy by taking advantage of agriculture and tourism.

In addition to it, there are many fairs and festivals there such as Losar, the New Year's Celebration of the Monpas. Another famous festival there is called Reh, which is associated with the Idu Mishmis, the six-day celebrations' special attraction is the Priest dance. Fairs or festivals are held every month, thus tourists can visit there any time for sightseeing.

Conflict Aspects

In 1962, the Chinese had a claim on what India deemed its own territory called Arunachal Pradesh. China sent many well-trained and well-armed troops to the disputed region. On the other hand, India had only ill-equipped troops there, which made them more difficult to beat Chinese troops. The Sino-Indian (Indo-China) War was started by China on October 16, 1962 on account of the territorial dispute against India. Chinese attacked India on October 20, 1962 because it was unable to reach political accommodation on disputed territory along the 3,225-kilometer-long Himalayan border.

The Chinese did not invade farther, and on November 21, 1962 declared a unilateral cease-fire. They had accomplished all of their territorial objectives, and any attempt to press farther into the plains of Assam would have stretched their logistical capabilities and their lines of communication to a breaking point. Finally, the Chinese defeated India in 1962, which as a result led to the retreat of Indian Army in terms of doctrine, training, organization and equipment from the disputed area.

Environment and Conflict Overlap

Arunachal Pradesh dispute was classified as a territorial dispute, but both China and India had big enough territories on their own. Thus, this dispute was not really caused by a decline of resources (territory.) Therefore, the dispute is direct more likely than not even it has been argued for about one century long.

China and India had a direct conflict over the fertile land which certainly supports their economy by agriculture. Major crops in the area are, for example, rice, maize, ginger and potato. These major crops yielded 134,807, 48,346, 34,890 and 32,434 in hectare respectively (Gov't of Arunachal Pradesh.)

Because Sir Henry McMahon, the British administrator, clearly established the McMahon Line as the border, which could establish buffer zones around its colony in South Asia, between British India and Tibet in 1913-14, the British have also something to do with Arunachal Pradesh dispute in terms of strategic interest.

China is also relevant to the territorial dispute. On account of various disagreements with the British, China refused to accept the terms imposed by Britain. As a result, China did not recognize the validity of the McMahon Line. China probably was mostly concerned about the loss of their essential resources such as land from losing Arunachal Pradesh. Therefore, British India and China were major countries in this territorial dispute with respect to strategic interest.

Even though both India and China found a peaceful solution to the border dispute in late 1980s, officials from two countries have met more than 15 times to argue the Arunachal Pradesh.

Chinese Foreign Ministry spokesman Kong Quan said that "As far as the incident mentioned, after investigations, we have found that the Indian side crossed the eastern sector of the Line of Actual Control (LAC).

At the request of the Chinese side, the Indian people who crossed the LAC, returned to the Indian side of the LAC" (Joseph 2003.) Thus, China still claims that "90,000 square kilometers of land in Arunachal Pradesh and does not recognize the northeastern state as part of Indian Territory" (Joseph 2003.)

Outcome of Dispute: Compromise

Arunachal Pradesh was part of the state of Assam until 1987 and was previously called NEFA. However, Arunachal Pradesh finally could gain statehood status on Feb. 20th, 1987 after making allowances for the security consideration in the east and Sino-Indian tensions ("Arunachal Pradesh.") India was satisfied with this outcome of dispute while China still does not admit the result.

Smoothening the India-China Border Wrinkles

The 17th round of India-China border talks (Feb. 10-11) in New Delhi passed off without any "free and frank" exchanges, that is, there was no disagreement. The first meeting was at the joint secretary level with military experts on both sides. The situation on the border was reviewed and apparently was found satisfactory. The meeting it appears, was constructed by both sides to ensure no negative vibration emerged.

The main meeting, the 17th round of talks between the Special Representatives (SRs) of the two sides was much wider in scale because matters outside the border issue were discussed. The Indian Ministry of External Affairs (MEA) statement said the talks were held in a "candid, friendly and constructive atmosphere". Mr. Shivshankar Menon, the Indian SR and Mr. Yang Jiechi, the Chinese SR are veterans in the foreign policy game and India-China relations. On the Chinese side they know the stakes they are playing with. They have in their pocket "something to give" on the border issue if need be. But no one can say for sure what that is.

It must be kept in mind that the old Chinese position "if India makes concessions in the east" has not become irrelevant. In China's foreign policy dealings, nothing once stated becomes irrelevant unless it is stated so officially.

The three-step process agreed to by both sides to resolve the boundary question was reiterated. The process has arrived at step-2 to reach a framework for a resolution of this question. This will be based on the Agreement on the Political Parameters and Guiding Principles for the settlement of the India-China Boundary Question. The SRs discussed possible additional Confidence Building Measures (CBM). Other issues discussed, according to the MEA release included areas of mutual interest including cooperation in the East Asia Summit process as well as developments in West Asia and Afghanistan. Pakistan should have figured in the discussions, but it appears that the Chinese do not want it to be seriously included in the "India-China strategic partnership and co-operation". It is too sensitive a subject.

China made its general position on the border clear when reacting to Indian President Pranab Mukherjee's visit to Arunachal Pradesh in November last year. Chinese foreign ministry spokesman Qin Gang urged *(Xinhua, Nov.30 2013)* India not to indulge in acts that complicate the boundary issue and work with China to create conditions for talks and preserve peace and tranquility on the border.

The *Xinhua* commentary went on to say "The so-called Arunachal Pradesh was established largely on three areas of China's Tibet-Monyul, Loyul and Lower Tsayul currently under Indian illegal occupation. These three areas, located between the illegal MacMahon Line and the traditional customary boundary between China and India, have always been Chinese territory." The commentary added that in February 1987, Indian authorities declared the founding of the so-called Arunachal Pradesh.

Before further meetings on the border issue the Chinese side drew the lines. That is, the basic Chinese position that the border lay along the northern banks of the river Bramhaputra; India set up Arunachal Pradesh illegally; and if India did not work with China and on its directions, China could revert to a hard-line position. This is China's position on the eastern sector of the India-China border. It is, therefore, not surprising that even Chinese incursion into India's Depsung area in the western sector last year was generally kept outside the main agenda.

The focus is now testing out the Border Defense cooperation agreement signed during Prime Minister Manmohan Singh's visit to China last October. With national elections in India barely two months away and opinion surveys emphatically suggesting that UPA government led by the Congress has little or no hope to return to power for the third time in a row, it was only right for Prime Minister Singh and National Security Advisor (NSA) Menon to take no new initiatives on the border and analyze the efficacy of Border Defence Agreement signed between the two countries last October.

The new hierarchy in New Delhi will be well advised to consider relations with China on a much bigger canvas. While getting played by China on the boundary question, New Delhi must not lose sight of other strategic interests regionally and globally.

The Chinese leadership including the People's Liberation Army (PLA) are full of hubris as the next global super power. On the India-China border, the Chinese attained confidence of military superiority, and would continue to play mind games. The Border Defence Agreement was proposed by China, and India agreed to it only after some critical amendments. China went through with it but was not satisfied. The agreement could not put the Indian forces and border development in a strait jacket. It is going to come up with more CBMs on the border in due course. This is something Indian experts must look out for.

There was some speculation that because of support to Uighur separatists from extremist elements in Pakistan, China-Pakistan relations was becoming weaker. True, the Chinese were furious with Pakistan especially during the 2008 Beijing Olympics. But weak relationship? Emphatically no. Beijing is determined to crush the Uighur separatists as evidenced by the hard crackdown in Xinjiang.

Pakistan is of immense importance to China. It concerns Chinese interests in the Gulf and the Middle East with Pakistan being a Muslim nation. Afghanistan now looms on the horizon, but it is a tricky issue.

Certainly, China is discussing Afghanistan with India but all its cards on the burning issue remain hidden. China's support to Pakistan on Pakistan's issues with India continues to be as strong as ever. On Kashmir, there has been no change in position though statements are deliberately muted. It has done nothing and said nothing on Pakistan sponsored and Pakistani based terrorism against India. Yet it high profiles the so-called "three evils" terrorism, separatism and religious extremism. China's cooperation against terrorism and extremism across the world remains a hollow trumpet till date.

A new worrisome development has taken place. The BBC reported recently that Pakistan had manufactured nuclear weapons exclusively for Saudi Arabia. There were denials but not convincing enough. It is well known that China had supplied Saudi Arabia CSS-2 nuclear capable missiles in the 1980s. Obviously, these were meant for regional use. But nuclear capable missiles without nuclear warheads is an incongruous military doctrine. China has been modernizing Pakistan's nuclear weapons capability and fissile material production facilities. The three countries tie up very nicely as the Saudis remain the mainstay not only of Pakistan's economy but of its military modernization. After all Pakistan, a Sunni majority country like Saudi Arabia, owns the "Islamic bomb"!

The above scenario is not an idle thought. The world is aware of the Pakistani nuclear scientist Dr. A. Q. Khan's nuclear trade network leading to major proliferation. China was a self-effasive but root player in this. The west let both China and Pakistan off lightly for their own geostrategic reasons. After Saudi Arabia and the US differed on the approach to the Syrian crisis the Saudis are moving back to engage China and Pakistan with more resolve. The Saudi crown prince was in Pakistan recently and his agenda included defence cooperation.

On the other end of the Indian Ocean is the issue of freedom of navigation in the South China Sea. China is increasingly trying to force control of the international maritime route through which around 50 percent of global trade passes. Using vague historical evidence mainly manipulated, China claims sovereignty of the Spratly group of Islands in the South China Sea. It is using the naval flag march here to intimidate other claimants. India is likely to get into conflict with China on its oil exploration with Vietnam in Vietnam's waters claimed by China. There are a whole range of issues that are likely to come up in India-China interface in the next five years. The new dispensation in New Delhi will have to deal with them.

How these issues are dealt with is another question. Prime Minister Manmohan Singh made non-conflict and warm relations with China and Pakistan his top priorities. He failed because such a relationship does not exist in the minds of either of these two countries. In the course of his policies, Dr. Singh bent over too much.

The foregoing are only illustrative examples of issues that India will come to face. It is not suggested that India should adopt aggressive postures against China. But at the same time, India should get out of the habit of rolling over to achieve what is not achievable. Firmness on issues of national and strategic importance is imperative. Prime Minister Singh did this in the case of the nuclear deal with the US at the Nuclear Suppliers Group (NSG) despite China's opposition till the last moment. Unfortunately, the Chinese official criticism on President Pranab Mukherjee's visit to Arunanchal Pradesh did not elicit a suitable demarche from India.

INDIA-CHINA RIVALRY EXPOSED IN ONGOING BORDER DISPUTES

As a consequence, the 4,056-kilometer (2,520 miles) frontier between India and China, one of the longest inter-state borders in the world, remains the only one of China's land borders not defined, let alone demarcated, on maps or delineated on the ground. While Indians doubt China's sincerity in border negotiations, Chinese question India's leaders' will and capacity to settle the dispute in a "give-and-take" spirit. Up until 2005, there was a great deal of optimism about a possible breakthrough. Evidence of this came during Prime Minister Vajpayee's China visit in June 2003 when New Delhi's readiness to address Chinese concerns on Tibet was matched by Beijing's willingness to resolve the Sikkim issue by recognizing the trade route through the Nathu La Pass on the China-Sikkim frontier with India and later showing Sikkim as part of India in its maps.

For its fraction, New Delhi reiterated its stance on the Tibetan Autonomous Region as part of China. This visit also paved the way for border talks to be held through special representatives of the leaders to find an early "political solution" to the boundary question, rather than going only by the legal and historical claims of the two sides. India indicated its willingness to settle for the territorial status quo by giving up claims to the Aksai Chin in Ladakh and hoped China would give up its claims to Arunachal Pradesh in the eastern sector and recognize the McMahon Line just as Beijing had accepted Tibet's British-drawn boundaries with Afghanistan and Myanmar (formerly known as Burma).

In order to give a new thrust to the ongoing border negotiations, an "Agreement on the Political Parameters and Guiding Principles for the Settlement of the Boundary Question" was signed during Chinese Prime Minister Wen Jiabao's visit to India in April 2005. The joint statement issued at the end of the visit talked of a "Strategic and Cooperative Partnership" between India and China.

No Group

Since then, though, Beijing has upped the ante by demanding major territorial concessions in populated areas of Arunachal Pradesh on terms that many in New Delhi see as "humiliating and non-negotiable." Tawang, in particular, has emerged as a sticking point since the Chinese claim it to be central to Tibetan Buddhism given that the sixth Dalai Lama was born there. Ties between China and India were strained even further in May 2007 when the Chinese government refused a visa to an Indian official from disputed Arunachal Pradesh to visit China, and the Indian government's invitation soon thereafter to Taiwan's opposition

Kuomintang (K.M.T.) party presidential candidate, Ma Ying-jeou, to visit India in June 2007 to hold talks with senior Indian officials. China voiced its opposition to Ma's visit and called on India to abide by the "One China policy."

Thereafter came media reports of the People's Liberation Army (P.L.A.) encroachments across the Line of Actual Control (L.A.C.) and Chinese small arms supplies to insurgents in India's volatile northeast via Bangladesh and Myanmar. Then, in August 2007, Beijing demanded the removal of two old Indian Army bunkers near the tri-junction of Sikkim, Bhutan and Tibet, claiming that these were located on their territory. This move raised questions about China's declared policy of treating Sikkim as part of Indian territory. Not surprisingly, China's increasing assertiveness over the disputed borders has led to a rapid meltdown in the Sino-Indian border talks and a "mini-Cold War" has quietly taken hold at the diplomatic level during the past two years, despite public protestations of amity.

Some observers argue that Hu Jintao's desire to control the choice of the next Dalai Lama has led to pressuring India to concede access to the Tawang Monastery, which is crucial to this choice. The deterioration in Sino-Indian relations under Hu, however, should not have come as a surprise given his reputation as a hardliner over Tibet. (After all, Deng Xiaoping had groomed him for the Chinese Communist Party leadership because of his prominent role in the successful suppression of the Tibetan revolt in 1988.) In this context, the rapid pace development of road, rail and military infrastructure in Tibet close to its borders with India and Nepal is seen as preempting any possible destabilization of Tibet post-Dalai Lama.

Others, however, do not see any sinister designs in western China's development. Instead, they attribute the recent downturn in Sino-Indian relations more to domestic power struggles within the Chinese Communist Party (C.C.P.) than to the Dalai Lama succession issue or to Chinese concerns about India's growing tilt toward the United States. While there may be an element of truth in all these arguments, there are other more fundamental reasons behind the recent chill in Sino-Indian relations. Apparently, the strategic consequences of India's economic resurgence coupled with U.S. Secretary of State Condoleezza Rice's offer in March 2005 to "help make India a major world power in the 21st century" have greatly bothered the Chinese. This offer, and the long-term India-U.S. defense cooperation framework and the July 2005 U.S.-India nuclear energy deal that followed soon after, have been compared by Chinese strategic analysts to "the strategic tilt" toward China executed by former U.S. President Richard Nixon in 1971 to contain the common Soviet threat. Claiming that these developments have "destabilizing" and "negative implications" for their country's future, China's India-watchers have started warning their government that Beijing "should not take India lightly any longer."

Chinese leaders be led to believe that China's growing economic and military might would eventually enable Beijing to re-establish the Sino-centric hierarchy of Asia's past as the U.S. saps its energies in fighting small wars in the Islamic world, Japan shrinks economically and demographically while India remains subdued by virtue of Beijing's "special relationships" with its South Asian neighbours. However, a number of "negative developments," from Beijing's perspective, since early 2005 — the Indian and Japanese bids for permanent seats on the U.N. Security Council, the formation of the East Asia Summit that includes India, Australia and New Zealand, the Indo-U.S. nuclear deal, India's ability to sustain a high economic growth rate of eight to nine percent and the strategic implications of India's "Look East" policy — have apparently upset Chinese calculations.

Therefore, after a hiatus of a few years, Chinese media commentaries have resumed their criticism of Washington's "hegemonic ideas" and for drawing "India in as a tool for its global strategic pattern." Some Chinese analysts express serious reservations about U.S. efforts to draw "India in as a tool for its global strategic pattern," arguing that "India's DNA doesn't allow itself to become an ally subordinate to the U.S., like Japan or Britain." Nonetheless, most see India as a "future strategic competitor" that would be an active member of an anti-China grouping due to the structural power shifts in the international system and advocate putting together a comprehensive "contain India" strategy based on both economic tools (aid, trade, infrastructural development) and enhanced military cooperation with "pro-China" countries.

INDIA-WARY CHINA INTERNAL DISCUSSION

An internal learn on India undertaken in mid-2005 (with inputs from China's South Asia watchers such as Cheng Ruisheng, Ma Jiali, Sun Shihai, Rong Ying, Shen Dingli, among others) at the behest of the Chinese leadership's "Foreign Affairs Cell" recommended that Beijing take all measures to maintain its current strategic leverage (in terms of territory, membership of the exclusive Permanent Five and Nuclear Five clubs); diplomatic advantages (special relationships, membership of regional and international organizations); and economic lead over India. Although the evidence is inconclusive, the most plausible deduction is that this internal re-assessment of India lies behind the recent hardening of China's stance on the territorial dispute and a whole range of other issues in China-India relations.

The Chinese are concerned that the U.S.-India nuclear deal and related agreements would bring about a major shift in the power balance in South Asia that is currently tilted in China's favor. The recent strengthening of China's strategic presence in Pakistan, Sri Lanka, Bangladesh, Myanmar and overtures to the Maldives should, therefore, be seen against this backdrop. Despite protestations to the contrary from India and the United States that New Delhi is unwilling and unlikely to play the role of a closely aligned U.S. surrogate such as Japan or Britain, China's Asia strategy is based upon the premise that maritime powers such as the U.S., Japan, Australia, and India would eventually form an informal quadrilateral alliance to countervail continental China.

As a commentary in *Huanqiu Shibao* noted: "The fact is that Japan, Australia, and India are respectively located at China's northeast, southeast, and southwest, and all are Asian powers, while U.S. power in the Pacific is still unchallengeable. Hence, should the "alliance of values" concentrating military and ideological flavors in one body take shape, it will have a very great impact on China's security environment." From Beijing's perspective, the responsibility for this "negative development" lies solely at New Delhi's door. In their writings, Chinese analysts seem upset over their southern neighbor's all-consuming passion to become "a big power," and see the nuclear deal as its key to unlocking the door leading to the big league in world politics.

As a *Renmin Ribao* commentary noted in August: The U.S.-Indian nuclear agreement has strong symbolic significance for India in achieving its dream of a powerful nation...In recent years, it introduced and implemented a 'Look-East' policy and joined most regional organizations in the East Asian region... In fact, the purpose of the United States to sign a civilian nuclear energy cooperation agreement with India is to enclose India into its global partners' camp, so as to balance the forces of Asia [read, China]. This fits in exactly with India's wishes.

Once the nuclear deal crosses all the "big four hurdles" (opposition from pro-Chinese Communist parties in India; negotiations on I.A.E.A. safeguards; approval by the Nuclear Suppliers Group (N.S.G.); and its passage by the U.S. Congress), Beijing believes that it would end the nuclear symmetry between New Delhi and Islamabad (or, de-hyphenate the sub-continental rivals) and put India on par with nuclear China (re-hyphenate China with India).

This, from Beijing's perspective, is quite disconcerting because a major objective of China's South Asia policy has been to perpetuate parity between India and Pakistan. Add to this India's military exercises with the U.S., Japan and Australia, support for the concept of "concert of democracies," and attempts to establish strategic ties with countries that fall within China's sphere of influence (Mongolia, South Korea, Vietnam, the Philippines, Taiwan, and Myanmar) – all of these reinforce Beijing's fears about its containment. However, despite its strong disapproval of a pact that would narrow the power gap between India and China, Beijing would not want to take a stance that pushes India further into Washington's camp. Most likely, Beijing would use its N.S.G. membership to further its own and its allies' interests by: Using the "double standards" argument to question Washington's commitment to non-proliferation goals in light of its decision to back India's nuclear industry while opposing the right to nuclear energy for Iran and Pakistan;

Insisting that any changes to the N.S.G. guidelines to accommodate the deal must not be "country [i.e., India]-specific" but "universal criteria-based" so that "all countries [read, Pakistan] can benefit from the peaceful use of atomic energy under the I.A.E.A. safeguards." This formulation, outlined by Foreign Minister Yang Jiechi, would pave the way for the Chinese construction of the Chashma III and IV nuclear reactors in Pakistan; Using the deal to extract major concessions from Washington, including an end to the arms embargo and the lifting of bans on high-tech dual-use technology exports to China;

TIBET IS THE INPUT

Tibet remains the key to China's policymaking on the India-China boundary dispute. The Chinese still suspect that India prefers an independent Tibet and covertly supports Tibetan separatists. Unless and until Tibet is totally pacified and completely Sinicized as Inner Mongolia has been, Beijing would not want to give up the "bargaining chip" that an unsettled boundary vis-à-vis India provides it with.

An unsettled border provides China the strategic leverage to keep India uncertain about its intentions, and nervous about its capabilities, while exposing India's vulnerabilities and weaknesses, and ensuring New Delhi's "good behavior" on issues of vital concern to China. Several recent commentaries in Chinese language sources confirm a shift toward a tougher Chinese stance on the territorial dispute with India. Articles on "Future Directions of the Sino-Indian Border Dispute" published in *Guogji Zhanlue* in November 2006, Liu Silu's "Beijing Should Not Lose Patience in Chinese-Indian Border Talks" in *Wen Wei Po* on June 1, 2007, and Professor Wang Yiwei's interview "Helping U.S. May Derail Border Talks" with the *Asian Age* on July 25, 2007 are broadly representative of the official thinking in China's national security establishment on this subject. The key arguments and major themes presented in these and other writings.

First, since India controls 90,000 square kilometers of the richest part of Tibet and the Himalayan region, equivalent to two and a half Taiwans and as large as Jiangsu Province, "the Chinese government will not easily give up its territory." *Wen Wei Po* commentator Liu Silu contends that as "it is equally difficult to get India to spit out the fatty meat it is chewing...Beijing had better be patient at the negotiation table [because] time is on China's side." Apparently, many Chinese strategic thinkers believe that China's comprehensive national power vis-à-vis India is likely to increase over time, and that would enable Beijing to drive a better bargain on the boundary question in the future.

Second, as Professor Wang Yiwei puts it, "China showed 'greatness' once, after the 1962 Indo-China war, when it gave up the land it controlled [in Arunachal Pradesh] and it could not be expected to show magnanimity again...India 'lost an opportunity' to settle the boundary question when Deng Xiaoping and Mao Zedong were alive. President Hu Jintao is not Deng or Mao. He is strong but cannot be compared with them." In other words, the ball is in India's court. If New Delhi wants a settlement, it must hand over a large chunk of territory in Arunachal Pradesh to China.

Third, the Sino-Indian border issue is linked with sovereignty, territorial integrity, and the respective status of the two countries in the global hierarchy. Hence, a *Guogji Zhanlue* commentary advises that Beijing "should not adopt any hasty step or make big compromises on principles" because this issue, "if approached in a hurry, could impact the respective rise of the two nuclear powers." One Chinese concern is that a border settlement, without major Indian territorial concessions, could potentially augment India's power position and thus impact negatively China's rise. An unsettled boundary suits Chinese interests for the present because China's claims in the western sector are complicated by the Indo-Pakistan dispute over Kashmir, Pakistan's interests in the Sino-Indian territorial dispute, and Beijing's interest in keeping India under strategic pressure on two fronts.

Fourth, a "fair and reasonable settlement" implies that "India will need to give up something to get something." Ideally speaking,

Wen Wei Po argues that China should "recover the entire area. But it is negotiable for the disputed territory to be split equally between China and India, as was the case of Heixiazi [Bolshoy Ussuriysky] Island in the northeast [on the Russian border]. A third option would be for Beijing to recover at least the 2,000 square kilometers covering Tawang and Takpa Shiri. It is believed that this is Beijing's last resort and it will not accept any deal worse than this." Having wrested substantial territorial concessions from Russia, Vietnam, and Tajikistan in their land border disputes with China, Beijing is now expecting the same from India.

Fifth, China should economically harmonize/integrate Tibet, Nepal and the border regions with India into China's economic sphere through increased economic links and infrastructure projects, such as the Qinghai-Tibet railway, before proceeding for a boundary settlement with India. Underlying this is the belief that economic interdependence would soften India's position, leading to a settlement on China's terms.

Last, if negotiations, coercive diplomacy and economic harmonization (a carrot and stick policy) fail to produce the desired outcome, the use of force at an appropriate time in the future to recover "China's Southern Tibet" (a new Chinese term for Arunachal Pradesh) is not ruled out. Many Chinese analysts believe that the military balance has shifted in their favor with the completion of the 1,118-kilometer (695 miles) Qinghai-Tibet railway and other military infrastructure projects in Tibet and that negates the need for any territorial concession to India in the eastern sector.

2

Sino-Indian Relations: A Growing Unease

The dramatic rise of two Asian giants set against the backdrop of a troubled diplomatic history has propelled India and China into a trajectory that will likely prove difficult to navigate in the coming years. With the world riveted by Chinese aggression against Japan and Southeast Asian states in recent months, one country was not surprised: India.

After all, New Delhi has been grappling with the challenge of China's rapid rise for some time. Bilateral ties between China and India nosedived so dramatically last year that Indian strategists were even predicting 'the year of the Chinese attack on India'; it was suggested that China would attack India by 2012 primarily to divert attention from its growing domestic troubles. This suggestion received widespread coverage in the Indian media, which was more interested in sensationalizing the issue than interrogating the claims.

Meanwhile, the official Chinese media picked up the story and gave it another spin. It argued that while a Chinese attack on India is highly unlikely, a conflict between the two neighbours could occur in one scenario: an aggressive Indian policy toward China about their border dispute, forcing China to take military action. The Chinese media went on to speculate that the 'China will attack India' line might just be a pretext for India to deploy more troops to the border areas.

A GROWING UNEASE

This curious exchange reflects an uneasiness that exists between the two Asian giants as they continue their ascent in the global inter-state hierarchy. Even as they sign loftily worded documents year after year, the distrust between the two is actually growing at an alarming rate. True, economic cooperation and bilateral political, as well as socio-cultural exchanges are at an all time high; China is India's largest trading partner. Yet this cooperation has done little to assuage each country's concerns about the other's intentions. The two sides are locked in a classic security dilemma, where any action taken by one is immediately interpreted by the other as a threat to its interests.

At the global level, the rhetoric is all about cooperation, and indeed the two sides have worked together on climate change, global trade negotiations and demanding a restructuring of global financial institutions in view of the global economy's shifting centre of gravity. At the bilateral level, however, mounting tensions reached an impasse last year, when China took its territorial dispute with India all the way to the Asian Development Bank.

There China blocked India's application for a loan that included money for development projects in the Indian state of Arunachal Pradesh, which China continues to claim as part of its own territory. Also, the suggestion by the Chinese to the US Pacific fleet commander last year that the Indian Ocean should be recognized as a Chinese sphere of influence has raised hackles in New Delhi. China's lack of support for the US-India civilian nuclear energy cooperation pact, which it tried to block at the Nuclear Suppliers Group (NSG), and its pro-Pakistan position on anti-India terrorist groups operating on Pakistani soil, including the orchestrators of the November 2008 Mumbai attacks, have further strained ties.

Sino-Indian frictions are growing, and the potential for conflict remains high. Alarm is rising in India because of frequent and strident Chinese claims about the Line of Actual Control in Arunachal Pradesh and Sikkim, where Indians have complained of a dramatic rise in Chinese intrusions into Indian territory over the last few years, most along the border in Arunachal Pradesh, which China refers to as "Southern Tibet". China has recently upped the ante on the border issue. It has been regularly protesting against the Indian prime minister's visit to Arunachal Pradesh, asserting its claims over the territory. What has caught most observers of Sino-Indian ties by surprise, however, is the vehemence with which Beijing has contested recent Indian administrative and political actions in the state, even denying visas to Indian citizens of Arunachal Pradesh.

The recent rounds of boundary negotiations have been a disappointing failure, with a growing perception in India that China is less willing to adhere to earlier political understandings about how to address the boundary dispute. Even the rhetoric has degenerated to such an extent that a Chinese analyst connected to China's Ministry of National Defence claimed in an article last year that China could "dismember the so-called 'Indian Union' with one little move" into as many as 30 states. Pakistan, of course, has always been a crucial foreign policy asset for China, but with India's rise and US-India rapprochement, its role in China's grand strategy is bound to grow even further. Not surprisingly, recent revelations about China's shift away from a three-decades' old cautious approach on Jammu and Kashmir, its increasing military presence in Pakistan, planned infrastructure linking Xinjiang and Gwadar, issuing stapled visas to residents of Jammu and Kashmir and supplying nuclear reactors to Pakistan, all confirm a new intensity behind China's old strategy of using Pakistan to secure its interests in the region.

INDIA-CHINA RELATIONS

There is a growing perception now that the global economic gravity has shifted to Asia and that India and China, the emerging economic powerhouses in the region, will shape the Twenty-first century. In making such feelings a reality however, the nature of the future dynamics of domestic conditions as well as external relations of the two nations appears a crucial factor; this article attempts to focus in particular on the future prospects for India-China ties on the premise that this, along with the roles of other Asian powers like Japan, is going to be important in the matter of guaranteeing the stability and prosperity of the region as well as rest of the world.

The article tries to present the Chinese side with Indian perspectives of key developments. Chinese perspectives are already being made available in India in a similar manner. The writer feels that put together, such exchanges will facilitate creation of a better mutual understanding between the two sides, impacting favourably on the overall India-China relationship.

Growing Optimism

Broadly speaking, India-China ties at government levels remain stable at this juncture; New Delhi and Beijing have established a 'strategic and cooperative partnership for peace and prosperity' and signed a document on 'shared vision for the 21st century', signifying that the Sino-Indian ties have gone beyond the bilateral context and acquired a global character. Accordingly, India and China are cooperating on international issues related to the diversification of global energy mix, climate change, arms control and disarmament, non-traditional security threats, counter-terrorism, WTO, WMD, human rights and South-South Co-operation.

Bilaterally, the two sides now aim at building 'a relationship of friendship and trust, based on equality, in which each is sensitive to the concerns and aspirations of the other'. They are not viewing each other as a security threat and are by and large satisfactorily implementing confidence building measures in the disputed border, besides carrying out joint military exercises. Special Representatives of India and China have so far held thirteen rounds of border talks, though with no tangible results. Most important is that with an attitude of promoting ties looking beyond the unsolved and 'complex' border dispute, India and China are speeding up their trade and economic contacts. Bilateral trade is fast gathering momentum, with the volume to the tune of US$ 40 billion now and projections for US$ 60 billion by 2010.

China has emerged as India's largest trading partner, replacing the US, in April 2008- February 2009 period. Also significant is the ongoing momentum in their exchanges of high level visits reflecting the desire of each party to forge stronger ties, of which the recently concluded state visit of Indian President Ms Patil to China is a prominent example. Notwithstanding the encouraging picture brought out above, there are issues deeply dividing India and China; resolving them once for all is of utmost necessity, to further strengthen their relations. There are some talks in India about the past civilisational contacts helping resolution of the issues; they however lack substance. As modern nation states, the India and China have developed geo-political interests, which often tend to clash. What follows is a discussion on the conditions contributing to India-China frictions and the likely scenario in bilateral ties in future.

Problem Areas—Boundary Issue

As this writer sees, the boundary issue comes foremost in the list of problem areas. It is most sensitive one for both India and China as it relates closely to territorial integrity and sovereignty in respect of each side. It therefore needs to be handled carefully by the two nations. China's understanding of Indian perspectives on the boundary issue will remain incomplete if it does not take into account the traditional doubts prevailing in India on China having been territorially ambitious. Examples being quoted in India in this regard include Mao's description of China's 'palm' (Tibet) and 'five fingers' (Nepal, Sikkim, Bhutan, NEFA and Ladakh); references are also being made in India to the PRC's sense of 'historical loss' of territories expressed through their maps and atlas series, published in eighties. Such maps had even been seen claiming that India's Assam, even Andamans, were 'historically' parts of China.

Proceeding from 'doubts' to substantive points, it is being seen in India that the border positions of India and China are in conflict with each other and hence are difficult to solve. China's claims are based on its historical stand – all its borders, including with India, are as defined during the Qing dynasty period which ended in 1912.The root of the border problem with India lies in Beijing's position that a large chunk of its territory, especially the 90,000 Sq km area in the Eastern sector, were illegally taken away by the

British India, after the 1914 Simla Convention and that India inherited the British legacy. This has provided the rationale for Beijing in rejecting the McMahon line, a product of the Convention and in claiming the entire Arunachal Pradesh state of India as part of Chinese territory, called by it as 'Southern Tibet' Authoritative scholars in China have categorically stated that Beijing cannot recognize the McMahon line; if it did so, it would amount to Chinese admission of the 1962 conflict as a 'war of aggression' as well as an implicit acknowledgement that Tibet was once independent of China. On the other hand, for India, McMahon line remains the 'de facto' border with China.

The Sino-Indian border problem remains complicated with the Chinese claiming recently the 2.1 Sq km 'finger area' of Sikkim, the status of which as an Indian state has already been recognized by Beijing 'de facto'. On the current scenario, meriting attention are India's concerns arising from various factors – the reported Chinese intrusions, said to number 270 in 2008, into the Indian border, the adverse reaction of Beijing to the visit of the Indian Prime Minister Dr. Manmohan Singh to Arunachal Pradesh, China's bid to stop the loans for Arunachal Pradesh from the Asian Development Bank and strong Chinese state-controlled media criticisms of India's dispatch of additional troops to and positioning of advanced fighter aircraft in its Eastern border. Adding to India's discomfort has also been the rise in the level of Chinese media rhetoric against India, noticed in 2009; this has however subsided now.

Sino-Indian border talks, despite thirteen rounds of talks so far between two Special representatives, have not led to any tangible result in finalising a 'frame work' for a boundary settlement in accordance with the Agreement on Political Parameters, reached in 2005. While Beijing's stand is to approach the border issue in the spirit of 'mutual understanding and mutual accommodation', India wants 'ground realities' to be taken into account. About the reported Chinese claim over Tawang, an interesting argument is that besides strategic factors, the same has been due to the China's fears that Buddhist monasteries in the border including the one in Tawang have been centres of Tibetan resistance to the Chinese authority and as such, they should be taken over by it. Interestingly, the Chinese have introduced some new elements to the border question by questioning the already agreed position of keeping areas with settled populations out of the dispute. Is China ready for accommodation on the border issue? The statement made by the PRC Ambassador to India in November 2006 that both sides should make compromises on the 'disputed' Arunachal may be meaningful in this regard.

China's general stand is to 'shelve' the difficult border issues like the one with India and instead work for 'common development'. For e.g the PRC wants to 'shelve' the South China Sea territorial dispute, leave the Senkaku issue with Japan for 'future generations' to solve and 'put aside the Sino-Indian border dispute waiting for a suitable climate for solution' (Deng Xiaoping to the then Indian leader Vajpayee, Beijing, 1979). What is being noticed in India is that China never gives up its claims on sovereignty over disputed areas. An example is Japan-China settlement on exploring the disputed Chunxiao gas field in the East China Sea.

Though Beijing has agreed for joint development of the field, it has declared that China's sovereignty over the field is indisputable. The Chinese 'shelving' formula needs close scrutiny of India in particular. As this writer views, this formula has inherent flaws – for some at least, the projected completion of China's military modernization in 2050 may create new pressures on the leaders in Beijing at that time to become aggressive on all border issues. What are therefore needed are serious efforts from India and China at their border talks, leading to a 'compromise' based solution to the issue, much sooner than later.

Other Bilateral Issues —Tibet Issue

Tibet issue is prominent among other problems. It can be said that with India accepting the Tibet Autonomous Region as an integral part of China and standing firmly against any anti-China activity of the Dalai Lama from India's soil, this issue does not figure in Sino-Indian state to state relations. However, Beijing appears to be having reservations on India's motives with respect to the Dalai Lama. The State-controlled media allegation, made on the eve of Manmohan Singh – Wen Jiabao meeting in Thailand, that the Dalai Lama is colluding with India whenever Sino-Indian border talks are held, along with the Chinese official view that the proposed visit to Arunachal Pradesh by the Dalai Lama in November 2009, 'further exposes the anti-China and separatist nature of the Dalai clique' and a subsequent authoritative comment that such visits cast a new shadow on Sino-Indian relations, firmly point to Beijing's approach linking the Dalai Lama factor with the Sino-Indian border question.

China's fears need to be understood in the context of March 2008 unrest in Tibet, posing a challenge to China's sovereignty over that territory, even weakening Beijing's position in its border negotiations with India. Also, the question as to why India is tolerating the Tibetan Government in Exile in its soil, seems to be bothering China. Premier Wen Jiabao's description of the Tibet issue as a 'sensitive' one in relations with India, assumes significance in the context of what has been said above. The writer feels that Chinese suspicions on India-Dalai Lama relations are not going to disappear soon; the picture may change if talks between Beijing and the exiled spiritual leader succeed, but chances in this regard appear to be bleak at least for the moment.

China-Pakistan Nexus

China-Pakistan nexus is the next major bilateral issue. A better understanding is required in China about India's sensitivities on this account. The Chinese military, missiles and nuclear help to Pakistan continues, but Beijing is not in a position to give a guarantee to India that Pakistan will not leverage such support from China, to fight against India. Not surprisingly, New Delhi perceives that China's military assistance to Pakistan has direct implications for India.

China's Defence Modernisation

On the third issue of China's military modernization programme, India's concerns are being expressed through its important government documents, for e.g. the Defence Ministry's

Annual Report (2008-2009) has said that the programme has implications for India's defence and security. Asking Beijing to show greater transparency in its defence policy and postures, particularly on the double-digit growth in defence spending in last two decades, it has observed that China's stated aim in its Defence White Paper for 2008 to develop missiles, space based assets and blue water naval capabilities will have an effect on the overall military environment in the neighbourhood of India. The Chinese side should properly address such concerns of India.

China's Policy towards India's Neighbourhood

India's concerns also relate to China's attempts to establish a strategic presence in India's neighbourhood, for e.g port projects like Gwadar (Pakistan), Hambantota(Sri Lanka), Chittagong (Bangladesh). They are giving rise to fears in India of a Chinese encirclement of the country, under what has come to be known as a 'string of pearls strategy'. The PRC has taken care to officially repudiate such concerns, by asserting that it has no plans to try for domination of the shipping lanes in the Indian Ocean and has no intentions to establish a chain to encircle India. An India-China understanding on the issue is a must for further improving bilateral relations.

India-US Relations

Chinese critical positions on the India-US relations are also a matter of India's concern. The Chinese have welcomed the India-US Strategic Dialogue and are themselves promoting ties with the US. Still, China seems to nurture fears about US-India collusion against it. Its official media description of India's policy as one 'befriending the far and attacking the near' is unmistakably an indirect, but strong criticism of the developing strategic relations between India and the US.

East Asia Integration

It would be necessary for China to pay attention to the Indian perception that it hesitates to accept India's leading role in the East Asian regional integration process on the plea that the process should only be based on ASEAN+3 (China, Japan and South Korea) cooperation, and that ' outsiders' like India, Australia and New Zealand have no place in it.

India's Defence Strategy

Reports in India about the country's defence strategy visualizing war on two fronts- Pakistan and China, have been commented upon in China. A Chinese comment (China Youth Daily) has said that India's real target is China, not Pakistan. Indian strategic planners have only done a scenario building; war is not an option for India, which wants to settle its historic problems with its two neighbours peacefully. Under the strategy, both land and sea power are getting emphasis in India, which reflects a logical consideration of the country's geopolitical position.

How to Read Chinese Media?

The Indian public does not understand the reasons for appearance of hawkish views on India in some of China's strategic journals/websites. Global Times and writers like Colonel Dai Xu, have often given controversial views on India. How far such views reflect official thinking remains a question in India. Is the People's Liberation army (PLA) influencing China's foreign policy making? Even the US Defence Secretary Robert Gates has hinted to such possibilities (Shangrila Dialogue, Singapore, 2010).The answer to such misgivings may lie in the need for reporting transparency in China.

Economy

Questions are being asked in China on how India will use its economic power. They are similar to doubts in India and abroad about China's intentions once its modernization programme gets completed, say in 2050. China has announced peaceful development as its goal. India's objectives are on the same lines – enriching the entrepreneurial and economic potential of the country through a suitable reform strategy as well as integrating the country with the world's economic system under a new order. India's increasing role in G-20 mechanism speaks for the latter in particular. Another basic point relates to attempts to compare the development models of India and China. Which one is the better? A debate may be unending in this regard- generally, the Indian model based on democracy is being viewed favourably from a long term point of view than that of China which rests on a one-party system. The main difference is that while China has been following a model based on investment flow from abroad and exports. India has been giving a boost to entrepreneurship and free enterprise. In the opinion of the writer, the Indian superiority in the service sector notwithstanding, it will not be easy for India to catch up fast with China, which has already emerged as a manufacturing giant.

What will be India's global interests as an emerging power is another topic getting focus in China. As Dr Manmohan Singh, the Indian Prime Minister puts it, India's goal is to gain its rightful place in the comity of nations, making full use of the opportunities offered by a globalised world, operating on the frontiers of modern science and technology and using modern science and technology as important instruments of national economic and social development. The emerging India's partnerships with the US, China and other powers, India's role in the G-20 mechanism etc stand to explain its interests in the 21st century. Realising its responsibilities as a growing power, India is cooperating with other nations on addressing issues of global concern like terrorism, climate change, disarmament, world trade etc. In conclusion, it can be said that there are mixed views on China in India; Indians are noticing the prevailing good atmosphere in bilateral relations at state levels, but their concerns are continuing on China's strategic intentions vis-à-vis India. More and more people to people contacts between the two sides can bring a beneficial change to such conditions.

THE CURRENT RELATIONSHIP BETWEEN INDIA AND CHINA

There is an overall positive trend in Sino-Indian relations, as seen in supporting statistics. In 2004-2005, total trade figures jumped from 13 billion dollars to 20 billion. In 2008, China became India's largest trade partner, and last year trade between the two countries reached $62 billion annually. In the field of defence, China and India have also established an annual defence dialogue and hold regular joint counterterrorism exercises. Setbacks in the relationship do occur but it is difficult to say how much of this is due to real concerns and how much is a tit-for-tat game. The border clearly remains an unresolved dispute. China, for its part, still lays claim to most of the Indian state of Arunachal Pradesh, which China asserts is part of Tibet and since 2007 has referred to the area as "South Tibet." Similarly, while India has acknowledged China's sovereignty over Tibet, it has not changed its stance on the McMahon Line as the boundary.

Since 2003, fourteen rounds of talks have been held on the border issue and, while no breakthrough has been reached, the mechanism provides a forum through which the two countries can address complaints about incursions and the build-up of defenses. Despite the occasional flaring up of bilateral tensions and acrimony in the press, policy in India toward China has so far been highly pragmatic and driven primarily by economic concerns, leading to an issue-based attitude toward coalition building within multilateral fora like the World Trade Organization. A key concern for India, however, is the large Indian trade deficit. In 2010 alone, India's exports to China were $20 billion lower than those of China to India. The concerns over the trade deficit are compounded by the fact that a huge proportion of Indian exports to China are raw commodities—ores, slag, ash, and cotton—with little value adding capacity. India's imports from China are much higher value-added manufacturing items which is in part due to China's greater manufacturing efficiency but also due to Chinese non-tariff barriers.

China Perceived by The Indian People

The living memory of the Indian forces' traumatic defeat in the 1962 border war with China continues to affect Indians' opinion of China. When George Fernandes, former Indian defence minister, described the Chinese as "India's enemy number one" in the 1970s, the statement drew a sympathetic chord among many Indians. However, more recent surveys reveal a picture that is more nuanced and complex.

A Pew Global Survey in 2010 showed that 42 percent of Indians see Lashkar-e-Taiba as the greatest threat to India, followed by

Pakistan at 33 percent, then the Naxalites at 16. Only 3 percent of Indians see China as the greatest threat. The report also notes that the United States enjoys a largely positive image, with nearly two-thirds expressing a favorable opinion, although this was down from 76 percent in 2009. By contrast, only 34 percent see China favorably.

While opinion surveys have their shortcomings, when several surveys concur, even partially, they help build a trend. The Pew findings have a distinct echo in polling from BBC World Service. There has been a steady decline of mutual positive perception between China and India over the years. The most significant fall is in Chinese opinions of India, where between 2009 and 2010, approval fell by 14 percent. Indian opinion of China has risen from a low of 22 percent in 2008 to 30 percent in 2010. Both are now roughly at the same level of around 30 percent approval, which is lower than the high point of 2005. In regards to India's opinion of China, the trends can perhaps be explained by growing anxiety about China's rise, especially in terms of the competition for energy resources and manufacturing capabilities. While a strong lobby in India argues that China's growing economy is good for the region and for India, the Indian government has been cautious regarding Chinese foreign direct investment. China's expanding military might is also viewed with a growing sense of wariness that has manifested publicly, including in a 2009 statement by Admiral Suresh Mehta, India's naval chief, warning that India was no match for China militarily.

SINO-INDIAN RELATIONS: A CHRONOLOGY

On the eve of the 11th meeting of the Sino-Indian Joint Working Group (JWG) to discuss bilateral relations, with special reference to the pending border dispute, it would be useful to analyse the set-back to the bilateral relations since May, 1998, and the Chinese perception of its relations with India in the bilateral and global context after the Pokhran II nuclear tests. An attempt has been made to cover all important Chinese statements since May 1998 in this chronology. From the chronology, one could notice three phases in the Chinese reactions. In the first phase (May to July, 1998), there was a strong barrage of criticism of the statements of

George Fernandes, the Indian Defence Minister, and Prime Minister Atal Behari Vajpayee's letter to President Clinton portraying the threat from China as a motivating factor for the Pokhran II nuclear tests.

The characterisation of the Chinese threat was condemned by China as hurting the Chinese people and projected as a mere pretext to cover India's hegemonistic ambitions. The tests were viewed as also indicative of India's desire to acquire a new political status through the possession of nuclear weapons. During this phase, the Chinese criticism of India related to the bilateral (damage to Sino-Indian relations) as well as global (damage to the global non-proliferation regime) aspects. There was rigidity in the Chinese attitude to both these aspects. In the second phase (July-middle to December, 1998), there were signs of a mellowing down of the Chinese rigidity on the bilateral aspect. There was once again stress on the importance of Sino-Indian relations and repeated calls to India to make amends in a suitable manner so that the bilateral relations could be put back on track. After the initial hard-line comments on Kashmir suggesting a multilateral conference on the issue, Beijing reverted back to its 1996 and pre-1996 stance of neutrality as between India and Pakistan on this issue.

In the third phase (since January, 1999), while welcoming the Indian initiatives for mending the damage to bilateral relations, Beijing continued to be rigid in its insistence that the international community should not accept India's concept of a minimum nuclear deterrence and that India and Pakistan should sign the NPT and the CTBT unconditionally and immediately. There was also a note of concern in Chinese pronouncements that other permanent members of the UN Security Council might ultimately accept India's need for a minimum nuclear deterrence.

During all these phases, Chinese inconsistencies in possessing a nuclear and missile capability for itself and opposing a similar capability for India were sought to be explained as follows:

- The Chinese capability was acquired in self-defence in the context of the cold war. China did not view the capability as conferring a political status on it. Moreover, China was already a permanent member of the Security Council.

- On the other hand, the Indian capability was acquired after the cold war was over when the contemporary trend was towards peace, harmony and non-proliferation. The Indian nuclear aspirations marked a revival of its hegemonistic designs and had the ulterior motive of seeking a new political status in the international community.

It is evident from the chronology that China's two-pronged policy is to continue to oppose India's nuclear aspirations and deny it any new political status at par with that of China through its emergence as a de facto nuclear weapon power, while at the same time not allowing this to affect the bilateral relations.

The Chronology

The setback process started with a statement by George Fernandes, the Indian Defence Minister, in the beginning of May 1998, in which he reportedly described China as a major military threat to India. However, he subsequently claimed that his observation made to a private TV channel was distorted.

On May 5,1998, Zhu Bangzao, a spokesman of the Chinese Foreign Office, described Mr.Fernandes' remarks as "absolutely ridiculous and unworthy of refutation" and added that China had noted with the "utmost regret and resentment" his statements on China since coming to office.

He said:" The remarks by the Indian Defence Minister George Fernandes have seriously sabotaged the friendly atmosphere for improving bilateral relations between China and India…China does not pose any threat to neighbouring countries. His accusation concerning China's relations with relevant countries is utterly fictitious and has no basis in facts...His statement that China has built a sophisticated electronic surveillance base in Myanmar's Coco Islands and has installed missiles in Tibet targeting India is absolutely fictitious and entirely baseless…. It is extremely irresponsible."

On May 8,1998, an unidentified spokesman of the Chinese Foreign Office told pressmen that China had twice protested to India through the Indian Embassy in Beijing over the "ridiculous and fragile" statements of Fernandes.

On May 12,1998, Lin Shanglin, the Chinese CDA in New Delhi, issued a written statement at New Delhi stating as follows:" The so-called issue that China has been building a naval base in Myanmar is utterly fictitious, whose aim is to find grounds to the so-called China threat...Allegations of Chinese involvement in the development of Pakistan's Ghauri missile are a fabrication. It is irresponsible to assume that China is engaged in nuclear proliferation. The co-operation between China and Pakistan in the peaceful utilisation of nuclear energy is under the safeguards and supervision of the International Atomic Energy Agency (IAEA) and conforms to the international general practices."

After the suspected leakage to the "New York Times" by the US State Department of the letter written by Indian Prime Minister Atal Behari Vajpayee to President Clinton citing India's perception of a possible threat from China as one of the reasons for Pokhran II, Chinese Government spokesmen, govt-controlled media and strategic analysts started a barrage of vigorous criticism of India.

The Xinhua news agency said on May 18,1998: "Political analysts are of the view that with the nuclear explosion, India seeks to develop nuclear weapons, barge into the world's club of nuclear powers and then seek regional hegemony."

Ye Zhengjia, a former Chinese diplomat posted at New Delhi and subsequently posted to the Chinese Foreign Ministry's Institute of International Studies, told Japan's Kyodo news service on May 18,1998: " By presenting a China threat scenario, India is trying to extract mileage out of ideological differences between China and the West while New Delhi is actually masking its own contradictions with the West to lessen the blow of sanctions." He denied that China's nuclear tests were carried out to raise the country's political status in the new world order. He added: " In any case, a country's international standing does not depend upon its capability to do a nuclear test. That time has passed."

The official "China Daily" wrote on May 20,1998: " India's improper move of attributing its nuclear tests at Pokhran to potential threat from China has made the international community realise that the new Indian Government is not only irresponsible, but also immoral. This is the first time in history that a nuclear country has denied its own responsibility for its nuclear tests and shifted the blame to others..To justify its series of nuclear tests, India uses the political tactic of making India-China ties tense....China had been taking a reserved attitude towards provocative statements from India in order to push forward Sino-Indian ties. However, India took China's forbearance as weakness."

Xinhua reported on June 2,1998, that at a meeting between the Chinese Vice-Premier Qian Qichen and the US National Security Adviser Sandy Berger both sides "believed that the international community must take effective and feasible measures to halt the nuclear arms race in the South Asian region and prevent nuclear proliferation in order to restore and safeguard peace and stability in the region." Sandy Berger had gone to Beijing to prepare the ground for Clinton's visit.

In an interview to the AFP news agency on June 3,1998, President Jiang Zemin denied that China had helped Pakistan make nuclear bombs and said: "The nuclear co-operation between the two countries is strictly peaceful in the area of technology of nuclear reactors and all the installations concerned are under the control of the IAEA."

He recalled his historic visit to India in 1996 "after a number of signals of friendship from New Delhi" and said he had received a warm welcome, " but the Prime Minister then was not the same person as the one today."

Jiang further said that Pokhran II which clearly showed that "India is targeting China and Pakistan" surprised him He added: "China hopes that Pakistan will not respond and will make a wise decision. But the Pakistani Government is faced with strong public pressure on the subject."

In an article on June 5,1998, the "Liberation Army Daily", the journal of the PLA, accused George Fernandes of recklessly using China's name as an excuse for India's nuclear ambitions and warned: " If this arrogant boast and military expansionism are not effectively checked, the consequences will be serious."

A signed editorial in the "China Daily" of June 6,1998, urged India to show wisdom by renouncing its nuclear weapons programme and said that a 14 per cent rise in India's defence budget was an unwise decision which would further escalate the arms race in South Asia.

It added: "Such a rise in defence spending reveals the South Asian country's ambition to be a military power and is adding fuel to the already heated arms race...It is unwise for the Indian Government to develop nuclear weapons and raise defence spending with no regard for its relations with the international community." It described Fernandes' statement in the Indian Parliament about the occupation of Indian territory by China as a "concocted excuse."

In an interview to the "Newsweek" on June 21,1998, Jiang Zemin said: "In November 1996, I paid a successful visit to India. I was accorded a very friendly reception by the Government and people of India. That visit has left me with very good memories. I was very surprised that they conducted the nuclear tests. I was even more surprised that they cited China as a reason for their nuclear testing. I really don't know what kind of threat China poses."

Jiang also said that if Clinton raised the question of alleged Chinese supply of missiles to Pakistan, "the answer very simply is that we don't plan to sell missiles."

A joint statement issued by Jiang Zemin and President Clinton on June 27,1998, after the latter's visit to Beijing in the last week of June, 1998, said: "Recent nuclear tests by India and Pakistan and the resulting increase in tension between them are a source of deep and lasting concern to both of us.

"Our shared interests in a peaceful and stable South Asia in a strong global non-proliferation regime have been put at risk by these tests, which we have joined in condemning.

"We have agreed to continue to work closely together, within the P-5, the Security Council and with others, to prevent an accelerating nuclear and missile arms race in South Asia, strengthen international non-proliferation efforts and promote reconciliation and the peaceful resolution of differences between India and Pakistan.

"The P-5 joint communiqué of June 4, which was endorsed by UN Security Council Resolution 1172, set out clear and comprehensive objectives and a plan for action to address the threat of a South Asian nuclear and missile arms race.

"We pledge our full support for the steps outlined in the joint communiqué and again call on India and Pakistan to stop all further nuclear tests and adhere immediately and unconditionally to the CTBT, to refrain from weaponisation or deployment of nuclear weapons and from testing or deployment of missiles capable of delivering nuclear weapons and to enter into firm commitment not to weaponise or deploy nuclear weapons or missiles capable of delivering them.

"The United States and China remain firmly committed to strong and effective international co-operation on nuclear non-proliferation, with the NPT as its cornerstone.

"We will continue to bolster nuclear non-proliferation efforts and reiterate that our goal is adherence of all countries, including India and Pakistan, to the NPT as it stands, without any modification.

"States that do not adhere to the treaty cannot expect to be accorded the same benefits and international standing as are accorded to NPT parties. Notwithstanding their recent nuclear tests, India and Pakistan do not have the status of nuclear weapon states in accordance with the NPT."

Speaking at the Beijing University on June 29,1998, Clinton said: "We (the US and China) are now pursuing a common strategy to move India and Pakistan away from further testing and engage in a dialogue to resolve all outstanding issues."

Commenting the same day on the reference in the Clinton-Jiang statement to the nuclear issue in South Asia, the "China Daily" said that the US-China understanding on this subject "signified a healthy, stable China-US relationship." It added: " Such a relationship is not only in the interest of China and the US, but of the world peace and stability at large. "

Tang Guoqiang, a spokesman of the Chinese Foreign Office, rejected on June 30,1998, India's criticism of the Clinton-Jiang statement. He said that as major powers, the US and China had to act in the common interest of the international community to prevent a nuclear arms race in the region and promote reconciliation between New Delhi and Islamabad.

Accusing India of starting a nuclear arms race in South Asia, he said: "The joint statement expresses the strong determination of China and the US in further preventing nuclear proliferation and also promoting reconciliation and peaceful settlement of the differences between India and Pakistan.

"There is nothing reproachful about the joint statement on South Asia. While India opposed the joint statement, Pakistan has welcomed it. However, we have taken note of India's comments."

Writing in "The Hindu" of July 2,1998, F.J.Khergamvala, its Tokyo correspondent, quoted Robert Manning and James Przystup, former senior US State Department officials, who had visited China, as having stated in an article in the "Wall Street Journal" (date not mentioned) that during their visit a prominent Chinese analyst told them that "transferring material or technology to Iran is negotiable, but Pakistan is our Israel", implying thereby that Pakistan's security was as important to China as Israel's was to the US.

However, in an interview to the State-run China Central Television before leaving China, Clinton said that the US and China had agreed to work together to prevent the spread of nuclear and missile technologies to countries like Pakistan that might misuse it.

He added: "China has agreed to work with the US to stop the transfer of technologies to countries that might misuse it, to not assist unsafeguarded nuclear facilities like Pakistan's and to consider joining the worldwide system that prevents the exportation of dangerous technologies."

At a meeting of the leaders of China, Russia, Kazakhstan, Kyrgyzstan and Tajikistan held at Almaty in Kazakhstan on July 3, 1998, Jiang Zemin failed to have a critical reference to the nuclear and missile arms race in South Asia included in the final communiqué. However, during a joint press conference by the leaders after the summit he condemned India for starting a nuclear race in South Asia.

While briefing pressmen on July 9,1998, Tang Guoqiang, the Chinese Foreign Ministry spokesman, avoided commenting on India's offer of a pledge of no-first-use of nuclear weapons. He merely said: "The most urgent task for India is to immediately abandon its nuclear programme and sign the NPT and the CTBT unconditionally as soon as possible."

However, in an interview to K.K.Katyal and C.Raja Mohan, the New Delhi correspondents of "The Hindu" the same day, Zhou Gang, the Chinese Ambassador to India, gave the first indication of the beginning of a mellowing down of the Chinese criticism of India. He made the following points:

- "It is up to the doer to undo the knot". Beijing would like India to provide responsible explanations for totally "unreasonable and groundless" accusations against China and, thus, create a favourable atmosphere for a new beginning in bilateral relations. The initiative for this must be taken not by China, but by India. It was China's set policy to develop a "constructive and co-operative partnership" with India towards the new millennium.
- It was impossible to call for a dialogue and establish best relations while keeping up attacks on China, which had been the victim of baseless accusations. China would like these charges to stop and "actual actions" initiated. China would not like the present situation to go on. "As two big powers, the high-level political contacts between India and China should be normal."
- He hoped that India and Pakistan would peacefully resolve their differences "including the Kashmir issue" through talks. "The position of the Chinese side is consistent". After the nuclear tests by India and Pakistan, the growing tension on Kashmir and the issue of peace and security in South Asia had caused widespread concern in the international community. "We will do whatever is beneficial for the improvement of India-Pakistan relations and peace and stability in South Asia, but never do otherwise."

- China's ties with Pakistan were State-to-State relations between two sovereign countries. China had not transferred to any country equipment or technology that could be used for making nuclear weapons. Some of India's concerns over Sino-Pakistan military co-operation were caused by misunderstandings and others arose out of unnecessary misgivings. China would like to exchange views on this subject with India through diplomatic channels, as used to be done in the past. He disapproved of the resort to media and exaggerations based on "rumours from the West."
- There was peace and tranquillity on the India-China border. "We hope the two sides would make joint efforts to maintain this situation." China had taken "a series of flexible measures" on Sikkim and he hoped that the Indian side " would also adopt a positive and flexible attitude so as to create a proper atmosphere and conditions for the disposal of this issue."

In a lead article on July 14,1998, the "China Daily" called for " a multilateral meeting attended by India, Pakistan, the US, China and Russia to help resolve the Kashmir dispute, over which India and Pakistan have fought two wars since 1947."

The article, quoting Ma Jiali of the China Institute of Contemporary International Relations, said: "Indian Government officials should stop spreading the China menace theory which will create suspicion and hostility between the two peoples. The Indian Government's unreasonable attacks on China deeply hurt the feelings of the Chinese people and undermined the mutual trust the two countries have been trying to build over generations." Quoting Ouyang Liping, another expert of the same Institute, the article said that China had consistently adhered to the policy of non-proliferation of nuclear weapons and denied that China was aiding Pakistan's clandestine nuclear programme.

Commenting on the annual report of the Defence Ministry of the Government of India for 1997-98, the article said: "In the report, the Indian Government did not examine its mistake in provoking a dangerous nuclear arms race. It vilified China as the main reason for the deterioration of South Asia's security environment instead."

The article described the BJP-led Government as head strong and alleged that the real purpose of Pokhran II was to gain regional hegemony.

It further quoted Ouyang Liping as saying: "India's recent nuclear explosions reflect a dangerous ultra-nationalism and its ambition to build a regional hegemony and become a major political power."

The article added: "Continuously denying its faults and spreading lies will not win sympathy or trust from others, but will make the international community more vigilant against its ambitions. India should first abandon its nuclear development plan unconditionally so as to convince Pakistan to follow in its foot steps."

The article again quoted Ouyang Liping as saying that the international community must press India and Pakistan to completely abandon their nuclear programmes and convert South Asia into a non-nuclear area. In this connection, he cited the examples of South Africa and Ukraine and said: "They (South Africa and Ukraine) abandoned their nuclear capability in the 1990s under international pressure and for the good of their own peoples."

Despite this article, there was another indication of a possible mellowing down of the Chinese official criticism in an address by Zhou Gang, the Chinese Ambassador, in the India International Centre at New Delhi on July 25,1998. He made the following points:

- India's nuclear tests had led to "temporary difficulties" in Sino-Indian ties, but had not diluted Beijing's commitment to building a long-term friendly relationship with New Delhi." It is a firm policy of the Chinese Government to develop with India a long-term neighbourly and constructive partnership of co-operation for the 21st century.
- India and China could play an influential role in promoting

Asian stability. "As the two most populous developing countries in the world, China and India can exert important influence in the affairs of South Asia and Asia as a whole."

- China did not seek hegemony in the region though it was naturally interested in the developments between India and Pakistan. China had normal relations with Pakistan, which were based on the five principles of peaceful co-existence. Pakistani nuclear weapons programme could not be linked to China's. Pakistan had, however, received conventional weapons from China, but the quantum of these exchanges was much smaller to the defence trade between India and a "powerful country" (an apparent reference to Russia).
- "Friendly relations between China and any country are not directed at any third country." China did not pose any security threat to India. "Fictitious charges against China have gravely hurt the feelings of the Chinese people and harmed Sino-Indian relations."
- China wished India "stability, progress and development" and sought "neighbourliness, friendship and progress" from New Delhi. The Chinese pronouncements were a refutation of some wanton attack and accusations by certain personages in India. They were meant to "safeguard the friendly relations between our two countries and bring them back on track."

Co-operation between India and China must diversify and should not be held hostage to the pending resolution of the border dispute. The boundary question could be resolved on the principle of mutual understanding and mutual accommodation. The Peace and Tranquillity accord of 1993 and the subsequent agreement of 1996 on confidence-building measures continued to be the cornerstone of the Sino-Indian security relationship.

In an interview to the "Al Ahram" of Cairo on July 26,1998, Prime Minister Zhu Rongji said: "I assure there is no Chinese threat to India. I confirm our keenness on good neighbourly relations and peaceful co-existence. Beijing had no time to threaten or scare other countries, as it is busy with its own economic development. Any view on China's fearful size came only from India. No other State took this view. India has utilised this theory as a pretext to conduct its nuclear tests. However, the real target behind the nuclear tests is practice of hegemony as well as settling the internal crisis facing the ruling party. Due to limited economic capabilities, China sets aside a limited percentage of its resources for defence purposes. It is less than that allocated by India and Japan. In fact, China needs some defence capabilities."

Jaswant Singh, who attended the ASEAN meeting at Manila as the Indian Prime Minister's special representative, met Tang Jiaxuan, the Chinese Foreign Minister, on July 27,1998. A Chinese spokesman later said that "both sides conducted frank discussions on the Indian nuclear explosions and Sino-Indian relations." He added that during the discussions, the Chinese Foreign Minister stressed that India, running counter to the world trend, conducted nuclear tests and that India, "in an attempt to find an excuse for the tests, groundlessly alleged that China poses a threat to India."

A joint statement issued by Tang Jiaxuan and his Filipino counterpart, Domingo Siazon after bilateral talks on August 2,1998, expressed the support of the two countries for the Security Council Resolution 1172 of June 6,1998. The two countries expressed "their grave concern over and strongly deplored the recent nuclear tests in South Asia. These had exacerbated tensions in the region and raised the spectre of a nuclear arms race." In a statement in the Lok Sabha, the lower House of the Indian Parliament, on August 4,1998, Prime Minister Vajpayee said India was keen on improving its relations with China and asserted that his Government had never dubbed China as an enemy or a threat. He also said that India wanted to accelerate the efforts for a solution to the border problem.

Commenting on this statement on August 7,1998, Tang Guoqiang, spokesman of the Chinese Foreign Office, said: "We have taken note of the Prime Minister's statement in Parliament. We hope that the Indian side will take concrete actions so that the bilateral relations will return to normal." Replying to a question on the Kashmir issue on August 11,1998, the same spokesman distanced himself from the views mentioned in the "China Daily" article and re-stated the traditional Chinese position. He said: " Kashmir is an outstanding issue between India and Pakistan. The Chinese position on that is consistent. The Chinese side hopes that India and Pakistan will solve their dispute through peaceful negotiations and maintain calm and restraint before the solution of the problem."

Addressing a meeting of industrialists organised at New Delhi on August 12,1998, by the Federation of Indian Chambers of Commerce and Industry, Zhou Gang, the Chinese Ambassador, made yet another reassuring statement. He said that despite the setback to the Sino-Indian bilateral relations, there was scope for increased bilateral trade and economic relations "because the reforms and the opening up of the economy in both the countries have provided great opportunities for expanding trade and economic relations." He expressed his optimism that "on the eve of the next century trade and economic relations and cooperation between China and India would be pushed on to a new high." However, while talking to journalists after the meeting, he added that India's nuclear tests had severely damaged bilateral relations and "this will spill over to the economic relations also."

In reply to questions during the daily press briefing on August 13,1998, Tang Guoqiang, the Chinese Foreign Office spokesman, again evaded comments on China's reaction to India's no-first-use of nuclear weapons offer and repeated the Chinese demand that India should first give up its nuclear programme and sign unconditionally the NPT and the CTBT.

Addressing a meeting at the Bharat Chamber of Commerce at Calcutta on September 14,1998, Zhou Gang, the Chinese Ambassador, said differences between the two countries should not be seen as an obstacle to fostering trade. He added: "Expansion of economic relations, trade and technological co-operation between our two countries is beneficial for the overall development of bilateral relations and in conformity with the fundamental interests of the people of our two countries." He also claimed that China's nuclear tests were undertaken in the interest of self-defence.

China reacted sharply to a courtesy call by the Dalai Lama on Prime Minister Vajpayee in the third week of October 1998. On

October 22,1998, a Chinese Foreign Office spokesman described it as a violation of India's commitment to keep itself away from the Dalai Lama's anti-Chinese activities. Rejecting the Chinese criticism, a spokesman of the Indian Foreign Office pointed out the next day that the Dalai Lama had been received in his capacity as a religious leader by successive Indian Prime Ministers and that leaders of other countries had similarly received him too. The 11th meeting of the JWG, which should have been held in the second half of 1998, could not be held due to the misunderstanding in the bilateral relations. While talking to a group of visiting American journalists at New Delhi in the middle of November, 1998, a diplomat of the Chinese Embassy said that China had adopted an "active approach" to the subject and that the matter was under discussion through diplomatic channels.

In his briefing for the US journalists, the unnamed Chinese diplomat reportedly made the following points:

- China acquired a nuclear weapon capability in the context of the cold war. After the end of the cold war the trend was towards non-proliferation.
- The Indian tests were against the contemporary historical trend and seriously affected peace and stability in South Asia. The Indian tests had also dealt a heavy blow to international nuclear disarmament and the global non-proliferation regime.
- China did not agree that there was a nuclear apartheid. "The nuclear status of the five permanent members of the UN Security Council is a product of history. In our opinion, favouring the NPT doesn't mean that the nuclear weapon states will enjoy the permanent privilege of possessing nuclear weapons. China had all along urged countries with the largest nuclear arsenals to speed up the process of nuclear weapon reduction. As a nuclear state, China will never shirk its own responsibility for the complete prohibition and thorough destruction of nuclear weapons in the end."
- "China has always been committed, on the basis of the Five Principles of Peaceful Co-Existence, to the

development of good neighbourly and friendly relations with its neighbouring countries, including India. China has made unremitting efforts to improve and develop Sino-Indian relations. This stand of China has not changed. Before and after India's nuclear tests, the Indian Defence Minister and other senior officials preached the China threat theory and made wanton accusations against China. All this cannot but affect the normal development of the bilateral relations. The responsibility for upsetting Sino-Indian relations at present is totally on the Indian side. As the ball is now in the Indian court, we hope that apart from expressing its willingness to improve the relations in words, what is more important for the Indian side is to take concrete actions to improve the relations."

A joint declaration signed by Russian President Boris Yeltsin and Jiang Zemin, at the end of the latter's visit to Russia on November 25,1998, cited South Asia along with Kosovo, Afghanistan and Korea as regions of "the most acute conflict situations, which, if they escalate, may pose real threats to the international community." It added: "On South Asia, Russia and China confirm their position expressed in the UN and at other international fora and stress the paramount importance of the NPT and the CTBT for the global efforts to promote the non-spread of nuclear arms and nuclear disarmament. Russia and China call upon all countries which have not yet joined these treaties so far to do so without delay and without conditions."

Russian Foreign Office officials tried to play down the significance of the reference by saying that they had succeeded in toning down a harsh statement which Jiang wanted and in ruling out any reference to India by name. According to them, since Jiang insisted on some reference to it in the joint declaration they had to agree to a mild formulation which need not cause embarrassment to India.

In a letter to Jaswant Singh on December 15,1998, congratulating him on his taking over as the Minister for External Affairs, Tang Jiaxuan, the Chinese Foreign Minister, hoped that Sino-Indian relations could be consolidated and further developed during Singh's tenure. In his reply to the message, Jaswant Singh said:" India remains committed to the process of dialogue to address and resolve outstanding issues." He referred to his meeting with Tang at Manila and said that he looked forward to "continuing our interaction to further mutual understanding, co-operation and friendship, so essential for our two countries and peoples."

In his first press conference after taking office, Jaswant Singh stated that India was committed to improving its ties with China so that all outstanding issues were resolved in accordance with the five principles of peaceful co-existence.

In his daily press briefing on December 28,1998, Zhu Bangzao, the spokesman of the Chinese Foreign Office, said: " We welcome Minister for External affairs Jaswant Singh's remarks. China has always attached importance to the growth of its good neighbourly, friendly and co-operative ties with India on the basis of the five principles of peaceful co-existence. Normalisation of Sino-Indian relations complies with the fundamental interests of the people of both the countries."

The "Jane's Defence Weekly" reported in the last week of December, 1998, that the Chinese authorities had assessed that India would take at least 10 years to establish an operational nuclear strike capability and, hence, India did not pose an immediate threat to China's security.

China strongly expressed its annoyance over the remarks of Ram Jethmalani, the Indian Urban Affairs Minister, that there was a strong case for India to recognise Taiwan as an independent country. He made these remarks in an interview to "The Week" of Kerala in the last week of December 1998.

The "People's Daily" wrote on December 31,1998: "We strongly urge certain Indian politicians to stop interfering in China's internal affairs and work towards improving rather than damaging the bilateral ties. Jethmalani's remarks have further hurt the feelings of the Chinese people. "

In a despatch on January 1,1999, Xinhua described Jethmalani's remarks as "evil-minded and dangerous." In an article on January 6,1999, the "China Daily" asked Indian leaders "not to test China's patience with irresponsible comments" and to adopt a coherent policy towards China. It added: "China's goodwill and repeated patience should not be returned with vile language." The criticism came down after the Government of India, through the Indian Embassy in Beijing as well as through its press spokesman in New Delhi, assured China that there was no change in India's policy on Taiwan.

There were clear indications in January 1999, that while showing readiness to restore the pre-Pokhran II normalcy to the bilateral relations, China remained determined in its opposition to India's acquiring any nuclear deterrence capability. Addressing a meeting of non-proliferation experts in Washington in the middle of January 1999, Sha Zukang, head of the Department of Arms Control and Disarmament in China's Foreign Office, reportedly stated as follows:

- "It is a direct violation of UN Security Council Resolution 1172 to negotiate, or to even discuss, with India on India's so-called minimum nuclear deterrence capability."
- "It is also unhelpful to publicly support India's permanent membership in the UN Security Council soon after its nuclear tests."
- The South Asian tests had become a litmus test for the effectiveness of the global non-proliferation regime. The international community should do its best to stop and reverse the nuclear weapons programmes of India and Pakistan.
- There were two essential requirements for the success of the international nuclear diplomacy in the sub-continent. First, " the international community should have sufficient patience and perseverance and should not lose hope because of the lack of progress in the short run." Second, "the major powers must have a consensus view and take concerted actions in this matter."
- "If any country seeks to exploit the South Asian situation to obtain unilateral, short-term political, economic or strategic benefits at the expense of the other countries and the international solidarity, it can only further undermine

the already badly-damaged international non-proliferation regime, and, in the end, the long-term interests of that country will also be jeopardised."

- "We have noted with concern that after the Indian nuclear tests, some Nuclear Suppliers' Group members have taken a more pro-active stand on issues of nuclear co-operation with India. We hope that these countries could be more cautious in this area."

In an interview to the "Handelsblatt" of Germany on February 2,1999, Tang Jiaxuan, the Chinese Foreign Minister, rejected indirectly the idea of a Russia-India-China strategic triangle to which Prime Minister Yevgeny Primakov had referred during his visit to India in December, 1998. Tang spoke of China's "very good strategic partnership with Russia, which is full of vitality and regularly produces new elements" but clarified that Beijing's partnership with Moscow "includes neither alliances nor confrontation with third countries such as the US."

He described relations with India as far from ideal and blamed India for the deterioration in the relations. He urged India "to take practical steps towards the restoration of normal and healthy relations."

In an interview to the Press Trust of India on February 4,1999, Zhou Gang, the Chinese Ambassador to India, said: "India, instead of maintaining the so-called minimum nuclear deterrent, must accede to the CTBT and the NPT without delay and conditions."

Referring to speculation about the possible easing of sanctions against India by the US in the wake of the latest round of Jaswant Singh-Strobe Talbott discussions, he said:"Basically, China does not advocate sanctions."

On Primakov's strategic triangle idea, the Ambassador said:" China handles international affairs by proceeding from the fundamental interests of the people of China and the whole world and does not enter into alliances with any big power or group of countries. China's developing relations with any other country are not directed against another country." In his daily press briefing on February 23, 1999, a spokesman of the Chinese Foreign Ministry welcomed the Vajpayee-Nawaz Sharif summit and the resulting Lahore Declaration. He added: "We hope the two sides will keep the momentum of dialogue and solve their differences through peaceful negotiations and consultations."

In his inaugural address to the budget session of the Indian Parliament on February 22,1999, President K.R.Narayanan said that India "seeks to strengthen and deepen its historic and friendly relations with China" and "is looking forward to continuing the dialogue with that country."

Addressing a seminar on Sino-Indian relations at New Delhi on February 25,1999, Zhou Gang, the Chinese Ambassador, said as follows:

- "We have consistently believed that the problems that cropped up in the Sino-Indian relations are temporary and can be surmounted. There exist extensive common interests between China and India and our commonalties far outweigh our differences."
- 'The outstanding issue between China and India is no more than the boundary dispute left behind by history." These differences could be resolved on the basis of the five principles of peaceful co-existence and in accordance with the principle of mutual understanding and mutual accommodation.
- "We have noted that the Indian side has recently expressed its willingness to attach importance to its relations with China, not to view China as an enemy,and resume the dialogue, so as to find solutions to mutual concerns."
- China was not involved in the Pakistani nuclear and missile programmes."All co-operation between China and Pakistan in the field of peaceful uses of nuclear energy is under the safeguards of the IAEA. Non-existent is the issue of nuclear and missile proliferation to Pakistan. In fact, the Chinese side has already taken note of some concerns of the Indian side and, proceeding from the overall interests of friendly relations between China and India, it has taken a positive, flexible and pragmatic approach and made proper re-adjustment of certain policies concerned."

- The entire historical baggage of Sino-Indian differences could not be shed overnight, but only on the basis of reciprocity in a step by step manner. "All this needs a favourable atmosphere in our bilateral relations. Therefore, we hope that the Indian side will also adopt a flexible and pragmatic approach and solve the Chinese side's concerns earnestly."
- The attribution of a Chinese threat to justify India's nuclear tests by some personalities was mainly responsible for the recent deterioration in the Sino-Indian relations. "All this has deeply hurt the feelings of the Chinese people and seriously harmed the Sino-Indian relations. This is the main cause upsetting Sino-Indian relations."

The Ambassador's presentation coincided with the visit of a team of officials of India's Ministry of External Affairs to Beijing for three days from February 25,1999, to prepare the ground for holding the delayed JWG meeting.

In the daily press briefing on March 1,1999, Ms. Zhang Qiyue, a spokesperson of the Chinese Foreign Office, commented as follows on the talks with the Indian team: "Both sides discussed India's tests and their impact on Sino-Indian ties and expounded their respective positions on the issue. The two sides also focused on bilateral issues and re-affirmed their faith in the five principles of peaceful co-existence. The two sides agreed to work for the restoration and improvement of bilateral relations."

A spokesman of the Indian Embassy in Beijing said that India stoutly defended its position on the Pokhran tests and added: "We pointed out to them India's rejection of the UN Security Council resolution and our stand on the NPT and the CTBT." Addressing a press conference during the session of the National People's Congress, Tang Jiaxuan, the Chinese Foreign Minister, said on March 7.1999: "I expect, may be soon, the JWG on the boundary question between China and India will resume its activity." He again appealed to India and Pakistan to roll back their nuclear programme.

Addressing a seminar on "India, China and Russia in the 21st century" organised by the Indian Council of World Affairs at New

Delhi on March 9,1998, Zhou Gang, the Chinese Ambassador, said:

- The recent consultations in Beijing between officials of the two Foreign Offices marked a "new starting point" to improve bilateral relations.
- "We have noted that the Indian side has recently expressed its willingness to attach importance to and improve relations with China and not view China as its enemy. All this is welcome."
- China was pursuing an independent foreign policy vis-à-vis Russia, the US and India. "As powers of major influence and permanent members of the UN Security Council, China and the US share common interests on major issues related to peace and development in the Asia-Pacific region and the world as a whole. The two sides have decided to work together for the establishment of a constructive strategic partnership."
- The concept of a Sino-Russian strategic partnership did not have any military connotations. "Building a Sino-Russian strategic partnership is not aimed at forming an alliance and is not directed at any third party, but is aimed at abandoning confrontations between the two countries so as to create conditions for the broadest equal exchanges and co-operation."
- "It is the firm policy of the Chinese Government to develop with India, a long-term neighbourly, constructive and co-operative partnership into the 21st century. The two countries had the foundation and potential for evolving mutually beneficial co-operation. India and China shared similar or common views on such issues as peace and development, human rights, environmental protection and population control."
- "Strict adherence to the five principles of peaceful, co-existence, mutual trust and shedding a threat image of each other were the key for laying a credible foundation for a healthy Sino-Indian relationship."

- China hoped that "South Asian countries will treat one another on an equal footing, live in harmony, develop friendly co-operation and settle their differences and disputes through peaceful means."
- When the bilateral relations were developing without a hitch, some personalities in India accused China of posing a threat to India's security so as to justify the nuclear tests. This was the main cause for upsetting the bilateral relations. Beijing's policy was defensive in nature and any fear of a China threat was entirely "unfounded and fabricated with ulterior motives."

In an interview to the PTI on March 21,1999, Sha Zukang, Director-General of the Department of Arms Control and Disarmament in the Chinese Foreign Office, said:

- "We have never posed a threat to India and history clearly shows that...We didn't have New Delhi in mind when we decided to go nuclear."
- Since China became a nuclear power, it had never threatened any country. "On the contrary, because of our own bitter experience of being blackmailed, we have declared to the world that we would never be the first to use nuclear weapons. To say China's nuclear weapons are threatening the security of India is hurting."
- China was willing to resume dialogue with India in the post-Pokhran phase, provided New Delhi took concrete actions to normalise strained bilateral relations. "We are prepared to enhance dialogue with India so as to clear misgivings, further mutual understanding and promote the goal of establishing a constructive and co-operative partnership between China and India. We hope that the Indian side will also take concrete actions in the same direction."
- "We continue to maintain that India and Pakistan should fully implement the UN Security Council Resolution 1172. To maintain peace and stability in South Asia and establish a nuclear-weapon-free world, both South Asian neighbours

should abandon their nuclear weapons programmes and unconditionally accede to the NPT and the CTBT."

In an address to the United Services Institution (USI) of New Delhi on March 24,1999, Zhou Gang, the Chinese Ambassador, said as follows:

- "There exists profound traditional friendship between the people of the two countries. China and India sympathised and supported each other during their struggles of national independence and liberation against foreign aggression. The two countries share similar or identical views on many major issues such as economic development, human rights, environmental protection, combating drug trafficking and crime and population control."
- "There is nothing abnormal about some differences between the two countries. As long as both sides proceed from the overall interests of bilateral friendly relations and handle these concerns on the basis of mutual trust, with a positive, flexible and pragmatic approach and in a truth-seeking and forward-looking spirit, the differences will be narrowed gradually and problems resolved instead of coming in the way of the normal development of the bilateral relations."
- "Good neighbourly relations between India and China will not only conform to the fundamental interests of the two countries, but will encourage peace, stability and development in Asia and the world at large."
- "The outstanding issue between China and India is no more than the boundary dispute left behind by history. The Chinese Government has maintained that while positively seeking a solution to the boundary issue, the two sides should work hard to develop bilateral relations in various fields so as to create a favourable atmosphere for the final solution of the boundary issue. China stood for a peaceful, fair and equitable solution to the boundary issue on the basis of the five principles of peaceful co-existence, in accordance with the principle of mutual understanding and mutual accommodation through friendly talks, while taking into account the historical

background and the present reality and the national feelings of the people of the two countries."

- "China welcomed the resumption of talks between the two Foreign Office officials in February. This useful meeting provides a new starting point for the improvement of Sino-Indian ties." He hoped that the two sides trust each other and treat each other with sincerity and strictly adhere to the five principles of peaceful co-existence.

Talking to pressmen on April 2,1999, Brajesh Mishra, Principal Secretary to the Indian Prime Minister, said that an official dialogue with Beijing had already commenced and that the forthcoming JWC meeting might result in a visit to China by the Indian Minister for External Affairs.

During a meeting with a visiting delegation of the Congress (I) led by K.Natwar Singh, at Beijing on April 8,1999,Hu Jintao, the Chinese Vice-President, asked India to pursue a long-term policy on Sino-Indian relations in view of the "complex and dynamic international situations unfolding at the turn of the century." He said that under the changing international situation today, India and China should "look closely at and handle the relations between the two countries from the historical perspective and a long-term viewpoint." He noted that the bilateral relations had progressed on the normal track over the past decade "thanks to the joint efforts of the leaders of the two countries ", and regretted the chill in the bilateral relations after Pokhran II. The process of progress had consequently suffered "undesirable disturbances", he said.

Reports of Chinese reaction to the Agni II missile test available so far indicate that the spokesman of the Chinese Foreign Office expressed regret and concern at the test which, he pointed out, was a violation of the Security Resolution 1172 and added:" We have taken note of the remark by the Indian Prime Minister that this test is not directed against any country."

The annual report of the Indian Defence Ministry for 1998-99 released on April 16,1999, said as follows on Sino-Indian relations:

- Sino-Indian relations have improved in recent years and New Delhi regards China as "a great neighbour."

- India does not regard China "as an adversary and would like to develop mutually friendly relations with it."
- India has expressed its interest time and again in resolving its boundary dispute with China peacefully and through bilateral negotiations as quickly as possible.
- The September 1993 agreement on peace and tranquillity and the subsequent accord on confidence-building measures provided a reliable framework for the maintenance of peace and tranquillity in the border areas.
- Contacts between the two sides such as the meeting between Jaswant Singh and Tang Jiaxuan at Manila and the earlier visit to India by the Chinese Chief of General Staff serve the objective of furthering mutual understanding between the two countries and reassuring each other about their peaceful intentions.

SINO-INDIAN RELATIONS 1950-1959

The Sino-Indian relationship from 1950 to 1959 was particularly warm, and several reasons for these cordial relations existed. Arguably the most important was the hasty diplomatic recognition of the PRC in December 1949 by India, making them the second nation in the world after Burma to do so. This conferment of legitimacy was helpful in establishing a cooperative environment with China, as many nations chose instead to recognize the Republic of China (ROC) in Taiwan. Furthermore, India's existence as a socialist and not a capitalist state, allowed for greater cooperation with the PRC since they did not come into direct conflict with Maoist ideology like the U.S. This basis of diplomatic and ideological congruency led Prime Minister Nehru to attempt to revolutionize international affairs by producing the Panchsheel Agreement between China and India in 1954. The Panchsheel Agreement stressed five points; (1) mutual respect for each other's territorial integrity and sovereignty; (2) mutual non-aggression; (3) non-interference in each other's domestic affairs; (4) equality and mutual benefit, and finally; (5) peaceful coexistence. This agreement originates from Nehru's optimism that post-colonial nations could invalidate the precepts of a bipolar world, and that the regional powers of Asia can contradict the validity of traditional balance of power politics.

The diplomatic and ideological reasons for Sino-Indian cooperation are bolstered by shared historical experiences. Both China and India share a long and uninterrupted cultural and historical tradition. Both nations at one time were great powers. Most importantly though, both nations were invaded by Western imperialists and consummately humiliated and exploited. This occupation and exploitation by the West caused the growth of significant nationalist forces within India and China, and the desire to gain independence. The ROC received its independence in 1912, and the later consolidation of the PRC in 1949 ushered in a new era of Chinese sovereignty and independence from imperialism. Likewise, India achieved its independence from Britain in 1947.

Due to their history of Western occupation, China and India had additionally failed to develop independent industries. Their occupations meant that the Chinese and Indian economies were still largely agrarian, and dependent on the import of finished goods. This led the Indian government to implement a form of democratic socialism, while the PRC engaged in agrarian based communism, or Maoism. Regardless of their system's differences, both nations abhorred capitalism creating an ideological common ground. Their common historical experience produced a familiar perspective upon which Indian and Chinese policymakers could relate to one another.

This environment of common history and diplomatic cooperation producing positive relations would be challenged by the Chinese policy of taking back historical possessions. The 1950 invasion and takeover of Tibet by the PRC would begin to show strains in the relationship. Trepidation over Tibet's seizure by the PRC was based in the idea of a historical Indian-Tibetan relationship, but the Seventeen Points Agreement of May 1951 ironed out their differences with India recognizing China's historical sovereignty over Tibet while still preserving Indian economic and social interests in Tibet. The agreement appeared to settle a possible dispute over Tibet between the two powers, but right-wing elements in the Indian parliament expressed this viewpoint of the PRC invasion, "the final action of the Chinese, in my judgment, is a little short of perfidy". This underlying opinion of the Tibet invasion by the PRC would bring forward another issue heightening tension in the relationship.

This issue was the definition of China's border with India in the Northeast and Northwest. Maxwell argues that one of China's diplomatic priorities was defining diplomatically agreed boundaries, as "boundaries are one of the first expressions of a modern state" and the PRC sought this validation of modernity. However, to not endanger Sino-Indian relations over the border question, Nehru and Zhou Enlai agreed to leave the border issue between mid-level bureaucrats to be mediated at a later date paving the way for the 1954 Panchsheel Agreement. Thus, this issue remained on the back-burner of Indian foreign policy until the PRC began to make moves towards its historical conception of Sino-Indian boundaries south of the McMahon Line in 1957. Two years later Tibet rose up in a massive revolt against Chinese authority. China's People's Liberation Army (PLA) moved in to put down the rebellion by breaking popular will in the capital of Lhasa. March 31, 1959 the Dalai Lama fled from Tibet into India where he was granted political asylum. This course of events angered the Indian public as they saw it as a renunciation of Indian trade and cultural access to Tibet guaranteed in the Seventeen Points Agreement. PRC officials chaffed at India's meddling in their domestic affairs by granting asylum to the Dalai Lama and thereby violating the 1954 Panchsheel agreement. The Tibetan revolt combined with gradual Chinese assertion of borders in 1957 due to diplomatic impasse, are the primary factors contributing to a hostile Sino-Indian diplomatic relationship from 1959 to the outbreak of hostilities.

Important the Systems Theory

Now that a historical context for Sino-Indian relations during the 20th Century has been established, it is necessary to define the systemic level theory from which the case will be analyzed. A systemic level of analysis eschews the individualities of states and the impact of individual leaders on foreign policy outcomes. Instead it focuses on the structure of the international system, and how this structure forces states to conform to a set of probable responses regardless of their individual differences.

In Kenneth Waltz's seminal work, *Man the State and War,* he lays down the foundation for a levels-of-analysis framework for studying international relations. Waltz does not contend to have created this framework, but instead argues that different theories of international relations promote one or another level of analysis over the other. The basis of this assertion is in Waltz's take on how is politics best to be studied, "Can man in society best be understood by studying man or by studying society" ? If one believes that man in society can best be understood by studying man then you will focus on individuals and reject the influence of society on them, and vice versa. This idea is then refocused from the question of man and politics to the question of why states go to war.

Classical realists like Hans Morgenthau believe that war is driven essentially by the natural evilness of man. Essentially the "ubiquity of evil in human action arising from man's ineradicable lust for power and transforming churches into political organizations ...revolutions into dictatorships... love for country into imperialism". From this perspective, society and government are not influential forces in history, but instead magnifiers of mans collective malevolence when grouped into nations. From a classical model states cannot cooperate because "passion often obscures the true interests of states as of men," and not because "states are never honorable and peaceful". Waltzian neo-realism departs from these ideas by exploring the other half of the question. Believing that "Man is born and in his natural condition remains neither good nor bad," but is influenced by society to one extreme or the other, as states are influenced by a society of states (the international arena) to engage in war or not.

Neorealist systems theory is driven by one primary characteristic: in no matter what form the system is structured, the system is driven by the essential existence of anarchy. The source of this anarchy is the absence of an overarching international body with the power to force the conformity of the units of the structure (the states). As such the United Nations and other international organizations are not important and have no bearing on the system since they lack the capability of shaping the unit actors decisions. Acknowledging this, states are the only relevant actors, and the anarchic system leaves them with two realities. The first is that states are responsible for their own security, and secondly that threats to this security are unending.

Additionally, neo-realism departs from classical realism in that classical realists view power itself as the ultimate goal of the state, whereas neorealists view power as a means with the end being security. Peace in an anarchic system is fragile, and therefore each state must provide for its own security. However, providing for one's own security through military power or alliances often times undermines the security of neighboring states. This paradox where increasing a states security undermines the perception of security in another state is known as the "security dilemma," and is a major structural explanation for the outbreak of war. This is due to the fact that one can never be certain if additional security measures are defensive or offensive in the anarchic system. Another cause on the systemic level for the outbreak of war is the failure of deterrence. Deterrence strategy implies a buildup of military force adequate enough in perception or reality to prevent a state from threatening another states security. If any state misperceives the deterrent capability of another, or believes it has a greater offensive capability war is likely to break out.

In addition to these universal characteristics of the systemic structure is the variable concept of how power in the international system is actually divided. In the period of the Sino-Indian war the world was locked in a bipolar balance of power led by the U.S. and the Soviet Union. In a bipolar system states are rigidly aligned to either pole, but states in each camp have great flexibility of strategy. This was caused by the zero-sum nature of a bipolar system, in that the gain of one side is the loss of the other. As such, the leader of either faction is unwilling to allow client members to fail in policy endeavors. Finally, in a bipolar system states that refuse to join either faction drastically increase their security dilemma unless they have the power to challenge the international structure towards a multi-polar balance. Now that the neorealist systemic level theory is defined it shall be applied to explain the variables causing the outbreak of the Sino-Indian war.

Derivation and Events Leading to Border Dispute

The 1914 Simla Convention between Britain and Tibet established the McMahon Line as the official border between British India and China, denying the right of Chinese suzerainty over Tibet. However, the line's namesake McMahon, was ordered back to London in disgrace over the "chicanery" he exercised in border negotiations in which he presented a different map to the Chinese envoy, thus distancing Britain from the legitimacy of the negotiated border. Thirty years later British cartographers began drawing the McMahon Line as the border between British India and China, thus reviving the lines legal legitimacy.

When India gained its independence from Britain in 1947 it inherited all of the British territorial agreements, and as such inherited the McMahon Line as the border between it and China. Indian belief in the legitimacy of the McMahon line dated back to the Simla Convention of 1914, as well as to the numerous maps of British India with the line delineating its northern border. As such Nehru shrugged off Chinese insistence in border negotiation during the 1954 agreement stating that "the McMahon line marked their border with China, where was the need" ? Despite India's view of the McMahon Line's legitimacy, China had not signed the Simla Convention and under no circumstances consented to any bilateral agreement between Tibet and Britain because it violated their sovereignty.

Indian intransigence on negotiating a border acceptable to both parties led the PRC to act independently in areas south of the McMahon line. The justification for this was that in the absence of mutually negotiated borders, the true national boundary was a line of actual control represented by the extent of either nation's ability to administrate the territory.

Practical assertion of this idea was first revealed to India in 1957 when an Indian patrol discovered an all-weather road which had been constructed in the Aksai-Chin Plain connecting Xinjiang and Tibet. The Indian government launched diplomatic protests asserting a violation of their territorial integrity; however the PRC "considered [Aksai-Chin] to have long been Chinese territory". This issue was not resolved as the Indian government refused to engage in territorial negotiations until Chinese forces completely withdrew from the Aksai-Chin Plain. The PRC refused to do so, and instead of a diplomatic solution India began to pursue a more confrontational approach to assert their territorial claims.

The rebellion in Tibet helped to drastically sour relations between the PRC and India, but the border dispute widened due to a change in Indian military strategy. This change in military strategy was to create forward-posts behind the Chinese claim line, and in strategic locations to flank Chinese military positions.

These posts were constructed to assert Indian territorial claims in the Ladakh region and to threaten the Xinjian-Tibet road in Aksai-Chin. By September, 1962 a similar series of forward posts had been built beyond the Chinese claim line in Tibet, and four such posts were built even beyond the McMahon Line. This resulted in an inability to claim that these posts were simply to defend Indian territorial integrity. The territorial dispute from India's perspective, coupled with the building of forward military posts by the Indian military caused the 1954 Panchsheel Agreement to not be renewed in 1961. Crossing both the claim and McMahon lines, both nations were in violation of each other's territorial conception, and India was now physically challenging Chinese sovereignty in Tibet.

HOW CAN THEY BE IMPROVED? INDIA-CHINA RELATIONS

Despite the development that has occurred so far, however, there are still many constraints in bilateral relations between China and India, affecting political, economic and security co-operation. In economic relations, the current status of India-China co-operation does not match the economic scales of the two countries. There is a huge opportunity for them to expand the size of their markets and deepen their economic interdependence.

In 2011, the trade volume between China and India was only equal to one-sixth of that between China and the United States and one-third of that between China and South Korea. Given the large populations in each of these countries, it is obvious thatneither country has fully explored the market opportunities available in the other.

Moreover, India has been worried about a trade deficit with China; for instance, India had a US$27 billion deficit with China in 2011. Such a trade imbalance could lead to nervousness in the bilateral relationship.

According to the *Wall Street Journal,* India has been putting pressure on the Chinese Government to import more Indian products and has set high tariffs to protect Indian industries. Further, the relative backwardness of the domestic infrastructure in India is another constraint on co-operation that restricts deeper economic collaboration and personnel exchanges.

Border Issues

The India-China border and other territorial disputes, along with the issue of Tibet, restrict the establishment of political trust. Such a bilateral security dilemma is difficult to solve and is not conducive to co-operation. India has been concerned with China's infrastructure building in Tibet, which it views as a strengthening of China's strategic advantage in the region.

According to the Indian media, Prime Minister Singh agreed to station an additional 90,000 troops along India's border with China in 2012.

Although India has officially recognised that Tibet is part of China, it still hosts the Tibetan independence force. Moreover, given that China and Pakistan maintain a quasi-alliance, while India and Pakistan are still hostile to each other, the power-balance game is still being played in the region. China is also very sensitive about India's recent involvement in oil exploration in the South China Sea and its actions to strengthen maritime co-operation with Japan, which has disputes with China over islands in the region. The so-called "String of Pearls" strategy, which suggests that China is constraining India by constructing ports and bases in the Indian Ocean region, has been heavily covered by the Indian media.

Perception Problems

Finally, the peoples of China and India lack a comprehensive and rational understanding of each other. In India, China is often viewed as a dangerous competitor; the media particularly portrays China this way. In China, a few nationalists tend to express a strong dislike of India and do not recognise that the country should be viewed as a regional and global power. A recent poll showed that two-thirds of Chinese respondents had negative views of India and only 23 per cent of Indian interviewees believed that the relationship between China and India was co-operative. The mutual distrust between the two peoples has undoubtedly affected the development of the relationship between their countries and may continue to do so.

Multi-Sector Co-operation

The development of economic co-operation is the main pillar of India-China relations. The volume of India-China trade increased from US$100 million in 1988, to US$73.9 billion in 2011. China has become India's biggest trading partner and India is China's seventh largest trading partner. The two governments have set the goal of increasing their trade volume to US$100 billion by 2015. With increasingly closer trade relations, mutual investment has developed quickly as well. By December 2011, China's accumulated investment in India had reached US$57.6 million and India's investment in China had reached US$44.2 million. Their mutual investment is still booming.

In their political interaction, a multi-channel and multi-level political dialogue platform has been set up, with frequent bilateral visits for in-depth discussions to resolve difficult issues and problems. On 26 September 2011, the first Sino-Indian Strategic and Economic Dialogue was launched, in which Chinese and Indian economic and foreign affairs policymakers began frank and direct discussions. National leaders of the two countries have frequent meetings in bilateral, regional and global forums. Taking 2012 as an example, in March President Hu Jintao travelled to India to take part in a joint Brazil, Russia, India and China meeting and spoke with Prime Minister Manmohan Singh of India. Then, in June, Premier Wen Jiabao met with Prime Minister Singh at the "Rio+20" United Nations Conference on Sustainable Development in Brazil. In November, Premier Wen again met with Prime Minister Singh in Cambodia, during the East Asia Summit. The leaders' diplomacy strongly promotes the development of the relationship between their countries.

China and India have also begun co-operating on security issues, particularly on border and non-traditional security issues. In January 2012, State Councillor Dai Bingguo and Indian National Security Advisor Shivshankar Menon met to discuss border issues; this was the fifteenth meeting of its kind. The two parties agreed to build a mechanism for consultation and co-ordination on border affairs. The first meeting of the mechanism was held in March 2012. China and India have also reached a basic consensus on strengthening maritime security co-operation and a maritime affairs dialogue is currently being planned. Cultural exchanges and co-operation between China and India continue to expand. This has become an important driving force for promoting the development and deepening of relations between the two countries. For example, in 2011 and 2012, 500 Indian and 500 Chinese young people were invited to visit the other country and to participate in cultural activities. That same year, 606,000 people travelled from India to China and 118,000 travelled from China to India, illustrating how frequently the people of the two countries interact.

True Strategic Partners

We believe that China and India should become strategic partners in the true sense, rather than viewing each other as hostile competitors. Currently, it seems that a certain degree of asymmetry exists in China's and India's perceptions of each other. In particular, India does not trust China politically and views it as a competitor. In contrast, to the extent that India features in Chinese strategic thinking, it is viewed more as a development partner, rather than a competitor. These different views affect the efficiency of co-operation, which has already led to misunderstandings between the two and some estrangement. Therefore, to achieve fully the goal of co-operation based on common interests, China and India should first adjust their view of each other's role in their foreign policy, by viewing each other as real strategic partners, beyond mere rhetoric. On the regional level, China and India are stakeholders in maintaining regional peace, stability and prosperity. They should go beyond zero-sum thinking and employ a co-operative attitude to resolve their differences and address common regional challenges. Globally, they should play a greater role in the process of reforming global governance.

Prerequisites for Success

The key to achieving this partnership is to abolish both the Cold War mentality and the concept of "sphere of influence". India and China should not see South Asia or East Asia as being solely under their respective spheres of influence. For its part, India should understand that China respects the special role that India plays in South Asia and work with Beijing to promote the development and stability of the region. China's active approach in South Asia and the South Asian Association for Regional Co-operation does not aim at eliminating the influence of India; its involvement concerns the fact that it shares borders with South Asian countries. If we judge a country geographically, China could also be seen as a South Asian country, in the sense that the South Asian-influenced Tibetan Plateau comprises a quarter of China's overall territory. Historically, culturally and geographically, China has had close ties with South Asian countries and India does not need to be nervous about China's engagement with the region. Taking economic development as an example, China's south-western provinces, such as Sichuan and Yunnan, have strong interests in promoting business connections with South Asia, as they see this region as a major market and investment destination. China's investment in the ports of the region ispurely for commercial purposes. This investment is important because China needs commercial ports on the Indian Ocean for transportation across the region, which is very important for China's trade and its energy supplies.

In turn, China should also accept the reality that India is an important player in East Asia. India, as an emerging power, has been seen as an economic opportunity by many regional countries. For example, the prime minister of Singapore, Lee Hsien Loong, once commented that the historical origin of Singapore was due to trade between China and India. It now seems that history is repeating itself, as an opportunity exists for Singapore in linking the two countries. It is natural for India to pursue its interests in the region, as East Asia is the most robust economy in the world, particularly since the Global Financial Crisis.

Some Chinese intellectuals have expressed concern that India could ally with the US to constrain China. Judging from developments since 2010, however, there is no evidence that India has formed a strong alliance with the US to compete with China. For example, India refused to join in the proposed quadrilateral security mechanism comprising the US, Japan, India and Australia. Regardless of the effort the US has put into trying to draw India closer by emphasising shared values and democratic institutions, Indian policymakers have remained as neutral as possible and developed foreign policy based on India's own national interests. India has its own goal of great power status and understands that a good relationship with China is the key to achieving it. Both countries are latecomers to the international system and passive receivers of the existing international norms and rules. Hostility between these two countries will only weaken the alliance between the emerging countries in attempting to reform the global order. Based on the above, the authors recommend following measures to improve India-China relations:

- Upgrading the current Sino-Indian Strategic and Economic Dialogue meetings to a higher level – for example, by having future dialogues led by the Chinese State Councillor and Indian National Security Advisor, with the full participation of diplomatic, economic and military policymakers;
- Strengthening co-ordination and communication in regional and global institutions;
- Nurturing a more positive image of each other, both in government and society;
- Working on non-traditional security issues, such as the maritime security co-operation, and making it a basis for better mutual understanding;

- Careful handling of sensitive issues – particularly such issues as the Tibetan independence movement, the South China Sea and the so-called "String of Pearls"; and,
- Promoting open regionalism and rejecting the idea that East Asia and South Asia should be viewed as separate blocs and defined regions.

Future Prospects

Although these constraints exist, we still believe there is a positive future for the bilateral relationship, because the two countries share many common interests in a wide variety of areas. For example, their economic structures are complementary. Further, China is a manufacturing power and India is a major worldwide player in the service industry. Both countries face similar problems in domestic economic and social development and can share their experiences and support each other in approaching these. Regarding security, from China's point of view, if China cannot handle its relationship with India effectively, it will not be able to shape an ideal security environment, which is crucial for its domestic development. For India, a good relationship with China will not only benefit India's development but also be an important way to enhance its international influence.

On the regional level, China and India actively participate in multilateral co-operation processes, such as the free-trade schemes in South-East Asia. Both countries have concluded a free-trade agreement with the Association of South-East Asian Nations.

The recently launched negotiations for the Regional Comprehensive Economic Partnership also include them. If concluded by 2015, as intended, this partnership will become one of the world's largest free-trade areas. Moreover, both countries recognise that non-traditional security issues in the region, such as terrorism, transnational crime, piracy, natural disasters and other challenges, can only be tackled through joint efforts and regional co-operation. One example is the sub-regional co-operation between China, India, Burma and Bangladesh, which focuses on economic co-operation, as well as non-traditional security issues, such as narcotics. On a global level, broad common interests exist between China and India, such as reform of international financial institutions, maintenance of an open international trade system and tackling the challenge of climate change. As developing countries, China and India can strengthen coordination in global institutions to protect their national interests. China and India's strategic partnership has already had a great impact, especially in dealing with North-South relations. This is why, worldwide, an increasing number of people are beginning to talk about a possible future for "Chindia".

INDIA'S RELATIONS WITH CHINA: THE GOOD, THE BAD AND THE (POTENTIALLY) UGLY

Indian Prime Minister Manmohan Singh will travel to Beijing. The visit will cap a year that has been full of ups and downs in India's relations with China. The tale of three trips is representative. One in May by Chinese Premier Li Keqiang, his first abroad, was intended to signal the importance Beijing placed in the Sino-Indian relationship. But it took place in the aftermath of—and some would say was overshadowed by—a border standoff between the two countries' militaries. In July, the Indian defence minister visited Beijing to rebuild trust and defence ties. Media coverage, however, focused on warnings to India issued by a PLA general, which Chinese officials had to rush to dismiss.

And Singh will be travelling from a country that is largely preoccupied domestically. When discussions do turn to China, they have focused on concerns about Indian capacity vis-à-vis that country, Indian politicians accusing the government of being soft on China and Chinese scholars labeling India's border infrastructure upgrades as provocative. These and other developments have highlighted what Indian policymakers acknowledge—that there are elements of cooperation, competition and concern in the China-India relationship.

There have been good signs for those interested in stable, cooperative Sino-Indian relations.In the spring, just after he'd formally taken office, Chinese President Xi Jinping proposed a five-point formula to improve ties between the two countries. "Positive vibes" were detected at Xi's subsequent meeting with

Singh on the sidelines of the BRICS summit in Durban in March. There have been numerous public Chinese declarations of the importance of the relationship—perhaps not seen since the first half of the 1950s. The Chinese ambassador to India unusually took to the editorial pages of an Indian newspaper to emphasize, "To strengthen good-neighbourly and friendly cooperation with India is China's strategic choice and established policy which will not change." Chinese officials have indicated that greater efforts should be made toward a boundary settlement. The two countries have strategic and economic dialogues in place. They restarted their defence dialogue earlier this year and are expected to resume joint military exercises shortly. China and India also have specialized dialogues on issues like Afghanistan, Central Asia and counterterrorism. The agreement to discuss Afghanistan was considered a departure from previous Chinese policy; Beijing had earlier been reluctant to add it to the agenda because it would have likely meant talking about Chinese ally Pakistan. Along with regional discussions, China and India have also cooperated in the multilateral realm, including on issues like trade and climate change.

Premier Li chose India as his first overseas stop, with the Chinese government indicating that the choice was very deliberate. Hosting an Indian youth delegation, Li put a personal spin on the choice, noting the "the seeds of friendship sown" when he visited India 27 years ago—a trip that he said left a "lasting impact." During the May visit, he stressed the need to build trust and especially emphasized the economic benefits of greater ties.

Those economic ties have already grown. China is one of India's largest trading partners. Bilateral trade in goods has gone from less than $3 billion in 2000 to $66.57 billion in 2012. While investments haven't kept the same pace, they have also grown. In India, the interest in doing business with China is evident beyond the private sector and the central government—along with visits by a number of Indian CEOs, China has also seen visits from chief ministers of a number of Indians states, including Andhra Pradesh, Bihar, Karnataka and Madhya Pradesh. Narendra Modi, current chief minister of the state of Gujarat and prime ministerial candidate for the forthcoming national election for the BJP (India's largest opposition party), has also traveled to China. While Modi has expressed hawkish views on China on the geopolitical front, he has expressed admiration for that country's economic achievements.

The governments of both countries have reasons for wanting stable ties: the desire for a peaceful periphery in order to focus on domestic socio-economic objectives; the need for stability in South Asia, especially with the impending American drawdown of forces from Afghanistan; existing and potential economic ties; and the prospect for cooperation in the multilateral realm. For Delhi, in addition, a stable relationship with China opens up the possibility that Beijing might use its leverage with Islamabad to shape Pakistan's behaviour in a way that might benefit India. For Beijing, there's desire to limit India's burgeoning relationships with the United States and Japan, as well as with other countries in what Beijing considers its backyard. Moreover, as China is preoccupied with eastern maritime disputes and the North Korean situation, stable relations on its southern and southwestern flank would also help the Chinese leadership.

This year has, however, also shown how quickly the bad in the relationship can steal the spotlight from the good—with the potential to turn ugly. In April, less than two weeks after an Indian observer commented on the "upswing in relations" between China and India, their long-standing boundary dispute flared once again. While the two countries communicated through the crisis and resolved it diplomatically, and Li's visit proceeded as planned, the border incident reinforced the mistrust that many in India feel toward China and its intentions. Furthermore, it was a reminder that despite increased engagement, bilateral differences have the potential to stall, if not reverse, progress toward more stable relations.

Differences are not restricted to the boundary dispute. Tibet remains a key source of tension between the two countries though the two countries have found a way to manage their differences on the issue for now. In addition, China's relationship with Pakistan has been a major source of concern in India. Its role in strengthening Pakistan's conventional, missile and nuclear capabilities is especially highlighted. India also disapproves of China's assistance to Pakistan in developing projects and infrastructure in area disputed between India and Pakistan.

China's growing political and economic ties with India's neighbours are also a subject of concern. Delhi watches warily increasing Chinese interactions—political and commercial—with and involvement in countries like Afghanistan, Bangladesh, Myanmar, Nepal and Sri Lanka. Concern about a military dimension being added persists. Beijing's increasing interest in operating in the Indian Ocean, which India has traditionally considered its backyard, has also not gone unnoticed. While China emphasizes that these activities have benign goals—economic development, security for its ships, etc.—some in India who tend to take a hawkish position are not convinced; others are taking a wait-and-see attitude. Even beyond the neighborhood, there are concerns about competition with China for markets, influence and resources across the globe.

Closer to home, water is the resource that has become the subject of tension—specifically Chinese dam construction on its side of the Brahmaputra River. Indian officials have publiclycalled for Beijing to reassure India on this matter. Domestic critics, however, perceive the Indian government as being too tolerant of the construction. They argue that China has not respected information sharing agreements on this front and warn of more ambitiousChinese river diversion plans.

Economic ties, which many envisioned as the driver of good Sino-Indian ties, have also not escaped trouble. Bilateral trade in goods actually fell almost 10 percent from 2011 to 2012. In India there's much concern about the trade imbalance. The overall trade deficit has gonefrom $28 billion in 2010-2011 to $40.8 billion in 2012-2013. While investments have grown, they remain limited compared to the investment relationships that both China and India have with other countries. In India, there have also been complaints about market access in China and the treatment of Indian labor there, concern about Chinese investment in "strategic" sectors in India, accusations about visa abuses by Chinese companies and restrictions on Chinese labor. Indian companies also privately express concerns about cyber-espionage. Overall, reports of cyber-attacks on Indian government and military networks—allegedly emanating from China—have done nothing to decrease distrust that persists, especially among the public.

There is also an overall sense that China does not respect India and/or that it will seek to prevent India's rise. As evidence, critics point not only to China's relationship with Pakistan, which is seen as driven by a desire to keep India tied up in South Asia, but also note China'sreluctance to endorse India's demand for a permanent seat on the U.N. Security Council or its objections to India being given membership in the Nuclear Suppliers Group.

Another overarching problem: the lack of trust in China and its intentions. This is especially evident among the public. According to a Pew poll last year, more Indians have an unfavorable view of China than a favorable view. In a more recent Lowy Institute poll, China ranked only second to Pakistan in terms of countries that people considered threatening to India, with 60 percent indicating China would be a major threat over the next decade (an additional 22 percent identified it as a minor threat). 73 percent of those surveyed identified "war with China" as a big threat over the next ten years. Almost three-quarters believed that China wants to dominate Asia. 58 percent felt that China's growth had not been good for India. This reinforces what the Pew poll found last year. In that poll, two-thirds of urbanites who expressed an opinion on the subject believed that China's growing economy was a bad thing.

Overcoming this mistrust continues to be a major obstacle. The legacy of history remains a problem. Every time there is a border incident it reinforces the narrative that has prevailed in many quarters in India since the 1962 China-India war: that China only understands strength; that while Beijing's leaders say China and India "must shake hands," they cannot be trusted—that one hand held out might just be a precursor to the other stabbing one in the back. This problem is made worse by limited connectivity and communications, and little knowledge about the other country—even though these have improved. Media coverage about

China and the relationship can also get quite heated, with a tendency to focus on the negative. All these problems are exacerbated by the lack of transparency when it comes to Chinese decision-making. This has led to uncertainty about Chinese behaviour and motivations, which was evident in the debate about why the border incident in April occurred—and this uncertainty exists even among policymakers.

Thus, Indian governments have tried to follow a multi-pronged strategy. The emphasis might have differed somewhat, but for the last two governments in India—one a coalition led by the BJP and the current one led by the Congress—the general approach towards China has been to co-operate, if possible, and to compete, if necessary. Indian officials have joined with Chinese counterparts to increase ties, build trust and improve communications. Simultaneously, policymakers note that competition in and of itself is not all bad. As former Indian Prime Minister Vajpayee noted in Beijing, "a sense of competition between two close and equal neighbours" might indeed be natural. There is also, however, a realization that beyond cooperation and competition, there is a potential for conflict. Thus, while hoping and working for the best, there has been some attention on planning and preparing for the worst—i.e. the possibility that China will emerge as an explicit threat. There is a desire to do this cautiously, however, with policymakers quite conscious of the potential for provocation, miscalculation and exacerbation of the security dilemma.

In practice, this overall approach has meant increasing engagement with China—political, economic and even military-to-military—at the bilateral, regional and multilateral levels. Simultaneously, this approach has translated to a series of actions including strengthening India's military, as well as its border infrastructure and border regions, maintaining a nuclear deterrent, and consolidating or expanding ties and influence in India's near abroad.

India has also tried to step up its game in China's neighborhood. Indian policymakers underplay the strategic aspects and goals of India's "Look East" policy—which the Indian foreign ministry describes as "oriented towards deepening India's engagement with the countries of East and Southeast Asia"—and emphasize its cultural and economic aspects. However, these elements and the link to China have not been entirely missing in action. The Indian government and companies are increasingly interested and engaged in the region, especially focusing on countries like Indonesia, Japan, Singapore, Thailand and Vietnam. In recent months, India-Japan ties have probably been in the spotlight the most, with another round of the U.S.-India-Japan trilateral dialogue and Singh's visit to Japan in May. India has also sought to be more engaged with multilateral fora in the region. Officials from some Southeast Asian countries, however, want India to do much more. Channeling some of their frustrations, Hillary Clinton, when she led the State Department, called for "India not just to look east, but to engage East and act East as well."

Another key aspect of India's approach has been the pursuit of closer relations with the United States. Of course, these ties with the United States are not solely driven by China. India indeed has no desire to make a choice between its relations with China and the United States. However, the United States plays a useful role as an offshore balancer. Furthermore, Indian policymakers believe that a strong U.S.-India relationship gives them leverage with China and sends a signal to that country. Some also note that China takes India more seriously because the United States does. India, however, still has doubts about U.S. reliability as a potential partner, especially given the level of Sino-U.S. engagement, and prefers to maintain a diversified portfolio of partnerships.

So, where do India's relations with China go from here? In the near term, during the Prime Minister's visit, the two sides might sign a border defence cooperation agreement. The accord would essentially be a way to manage rather than resolve the boundary question, which the Indian foreign secretary has noted continues to be "a particularly difficult issue." The trans-border rivers question is also likely to be discussed. In addition, given the two countries' priorities, bilateral and global economic and financial issues will be high on the agenda. Potentially, there also might be agreements that could facilitate greater people-to-people ties, including a cultural and visa pacts. Regionally, developments vis-à-vis Afghanistan and the Middle East that concern both governments are likely to be discussed. Finally, on the multilateral front, trade and climate change issues might be on the agenda, given upcoming international summits in those two areas.

As for the longer term, the scenarios usually outlined are deepening cooperation, increasing competition that might lead to conflict, or continuity with both competition and cooperation in evidence. There is a debate in India—inside and outside government—about China, which scenario might prevail, the future of the relationship and what approach to take with China. The differences are evident in the Lowy poll—almost equal numbers of those surveyed believe that India "should join with other countries to limit China's influence" and "should cooperate with China to play a leading role in the world together."

How the relationship plays out will depend on a number of internal, bilateral, regional and global factors. In the meantime, Shyam Saran, a former foreign secretary and currently chairman of the National Security Advisory Board, has called for India to manage relations with China "with prudence but firmness." An air force chief described the way forward as "play cool and continue to develop capabilities."

SINO INDIAN RELATIONS: A POSITIVE SHIFT?

The rocky road of Sino Indian relations seems to have once again come out of the trough of the past two years with a clear signal of rapprochement after the Sanya bilateral on 13 April 2011 between Indian Prime Minister Dr Man Mohan Singh and Chinese President Hu Jintao. The statements coming out of the Summit from both the sides are all positive. It is evident that each has addressed the others concerns and thus forebodings are sanguine.

India for instance wanted the stapled visa issue for citizens of Jammu and Kashmir to be resolved, while the Chinese seem to want to restart the defence exchange programme. For India stapled visa issue contests sovereignty on Jammu and Kashmir while for China lack of defence cooperation with one of its many formidable neighbours means a perception of, "aggressive," behaviour. It appears that Beijing after the past few months of bellicosity has decided to abandon this approach. More over both sides have established an intermediate mechanism for resolving the so called transgressions on the Line of Actual Control between that of flag meetings and Special Representatives.

Significantly, it was the National Security Adviser Mr Shiv Shanker Menon who was the "Sherpa," for the bilateral thereby indicating that the talks were likely to be, "security and border," heavy. Mr Menon in the post bilateral press conference highlighted that defence exchange which he said was never called off will be a part of the, "Year of India-China Exchange in 2011," which will also include visits by senior political leaders, Strategic Economic Dialogue and people-to-people contacts.

The working mechanism for consultation and coordination on border affairs is a new initiative which Menon said was suggested during Premier Wen Jiabao's visit to New Delhi in last December and which will enhance peace and tranquillity on the border areas. The Special Representatives (SRs) on the other hand will continue their work towards a permanent boundary settlement.

At the working level meetings of commanders, flag meetings, or the border commanders' meetings are being held regularly but possibly given the rancour over the last few years over transgressions and media pressure that has been building up on the issue, "a mechanism at the official level which will consult and coordinate on border affairs relating to the maintenance of peace and tranquillity, if there are any issues; and will explore cooperation in the border areas.———— It will implement the agreements that we already have in place to maintain peace and tranquillity that is the 1993 and 1996 Border Peace and Tranquillity Agreement and the CBM agreement," has been devised as per Mr Menon.

Clearly the government is looking at an arrangement similar to that on the Line of Control in Jammu and Kashmir with Pakistan hoping that more interactions, border trade and people to people movement should open up the path for maintaining peace and getting away from the humdrum of patrol crossings that has been the main paradigm in the past couple of years. This was evident from remarks of Mr Menon, "It [border mechanism] also includes border trade which we have; it also includes the exchange of mails across the border which we do; also there is a question of whether people travel across that border; a whole series of other issues are also involved in cooperating across the border. Once the defence exchanges and formal delegations from both the sides meet each other, it is hoped that joint training and exercises will also be carried out".

The Indian government is no doubt taking a holistic view of relations with China the recent statements by Lt Gen K. T. Parnaik, India's Northern Army Commander of Chinese presence in Gilgit Baltistan not considered a dampener as possibly the talks with Beijing had moved ahead for establishing the mechanism. General Parnaik had said: "Chinese presence in Gilgit-Baltistan and the Northern Areas is increasing steadily... There are many people who are concerned about the fact that if there was to be hostility between us and Pakistan, what would be the complicity of Chinese." "Not only they are in the neighbourhood but the fact that they are actually present and stationed along the LoC," he added as per media reports.

A subsequent Times of India Report claimed that, "highly placed sources," have also indicated that US intelligence agencies have reiterated to Indian authorities increasing presence of Chinese troops all along the LoC. "We have a strong real time intelligence sharing mechanism with the US and they have conveyed the same thing to Indian agencies including RAW – that these troops are stationed all along the LoC in PoK. They conveyed this to Indian agencies independently without us seeking any confirmation from them," an official was quoted by the Times of India. Why Indian intelligence should be dependent on US sources for corroboration of information across its own land borders however remains a mystery?

The Sanya bilateral indicated that both sides discounted these intelligence and security fears and strived to establish additional structures for resolving the issue of transgressions. With China increasingly under pressure at home as well Beijing possibly did not want to confront challenges on the border or perhaps Hu

Jintao does not want to leave a legacy of confrontation with India, we will never know. Suffice to say Sanya meet offers some hope that the daily, "sniping," of transgressions may be a thing of the past and India and China and look forward to more constructive security cooperation.

'SINO-INDIAN MIRACLE' EMBARRASSES JAPANESE POLITICIANS

But what surprised the media was that China and India properly solved the issue in a short time. During Premier Li Keqiang's visit, the top leaders of both countries had sincere and candid talks and came to a series of strategic consensus and cooperation. The shift of Sino-Indian ties in such a short time is a miracle. In the development of Sino-Indian ties there are several divergence and contradictions. Some countries see these differences as an opportunity to provoke dissension.

Not long ago, Japanese Prime Minister Shinzo Abe called on Japan, India, Australia and the U.S. to jointly form a "Democratic Security Diamond" to compete with the ascendant China. He also proposed that Japan should promote "Strategic Diplomacy" and "Values Diplomacy" and made visits in countries around China. Some politicians just made themselves petty burglars on China-related issues. The so-called "Democratic Security Diamond", "Strategic Diplomacy" and "Values Diplomacy" among other new terms seem very strategic. But in fact they unveiled the narrow-minded diplomatic thoughts of Japanese government. The conspiracy of these petty burglars is doomed to fail for three reasons.

First, China and India have great vision and great wisdom. As two developing countries with ancient civilizations as well as two emerging markets, joining hands and working together have strategic significance for both countries and for the world. India's great wisdom lies in dealing with ties with China in a calm way, undisturbed by internal and international provocateurs.

Second, China has good faith. One will never lose anything when cooperating with China. China insists on bringing benefits to neighboring countries and the world through its development.

This principle also applies to Sino-Indian ties. As for trade imbalance, China is seeking a mutually beneficial resolution.

Third, it's in line with the trend of the times to transcend differences and build consensus. As long as two countries share a boundary there will be interest division and disputes between the two countries. The most important thing is that most countries realize the importance of dialogues, exchanges, peace and mutual trust and are willing to conduct win-win cooperation instead of a lose-lose game. The economic corridor among China, India, Myanmar and Bangladesh proposed by China and India reflects this trend. How can the words and acts that go against the trend of the time survive in this context?

With increased comprehensive national strength, China will use more effective ways to transmit its positive energy to the world. China's diplomacy will create more miracles. Before the miracles, the "petty burglars", like some of Japanese politicians, will bring disgrace on their own heads.

INDIA'S FORMIDABLE CHALLENGE

While it has not yet achieved the economic and political profile that China enjoys regionally and globally, India is increasingly bracketed with China as a rising or emerging power-or even a global superpower. Indian elites who have been obsessed with Pakistan for more than 60 years suddenly have found a new object of fascination. India's main security concern now is not the increasingly decrepit state of Pakistan but an ever more assertive China, a shift that is widely viewed inside India as one that can facilitate better strategic planning.

India's defeat at Chinese hands in 1962 shaped the Indian elite's perceptions of China, and they are unlikely to alter them anytime soon. China is thus viewed by India as a growing, aggressive nationalistic power whose ambitions are likely to reshape the contours of the regional and global balance of power with deleterious consequences for Indian interests. Indian policymakers, however, continue to believe that Beijing is not a short-term threat to India but needs to be watched over the long-term. However, Indian defence officials are increasingly warning in rather blunt terms about the disparity between the two Asian powers.

The Indian naval chief has warned that India neither has "the capability nor the intention to match China force for force" in military terms, while the former Indian air chief has suggested that China posed more of a threat to India than Pakistan. China's recent hardening toward India could well be a function of its own internal vulnerabilities, but that is hardly a consolation to Indian policymakers who have to respond to an Indian public that increasingly wants the country to assert itself in the region and beyond. India is rather belatedly gearing up to respond with its own diplomatic and military overtures, setting the stage for a Sino-Indian strategic rivalry.

Both India and China have a vested interest in stabilizing their relationship by seeking out issues on which their interests converge, but pursuing mutually desirable interests does not inevitably produce satisfactory solutions to strategic problems. A troubled history coupled with the structural uncertainties engendered by their simultaneous rise is propelling the two Asian giants into a trajectory that they might find rather difficult to navigate in the coming years. Sino-Indian ties have entered turbulent times, and they are likely to remain there for the foreseeable future.

THE INDIAN AND CHINESE EXPERIENCE

One of the cruel ironies of today's world is that India which is applauded as the world's largest democracy has the largest number of poor and destitute in any country, and China which has achieved, a steady rise in people's living standards and has also acquired the status of a world power has failed to develop democratic institutions and practices. It is also interesting to note that despite the absence of liberal democratic freedoms the West has a deep fascination with China which is reflected not only in the tourist inflow to China but also in the flow of foreign investment and government good will. Operation of democratic institutions such as free and fair elections, existence of competitive politics and dissent do not particularly attract either Western tourists or Western capital to India. On the contrary the geopolitics of South

Asia has been governed by the US and other Western countries as compared by India's pre-eminent position and therefore they have followed by an large a policy of containment of India vis-a-vis its neighbours. The functioning democratic system of India has had little effect on their policy. The experience of India and China have put the theory of democracy to a severe test. Two old questions need to be asked again about democracy. In addition, two new questions have to be raised. Do formal political institutions and practices constitute democracy or does it involve appropriate socio-economic conditions which enable citizens to exercise their political rights. On this issue India scores poorly with nearly forty per cent of its people below what is statistically called a "poverty line". China has asserted that it is engaged in creating better living conditions for its people after overthrowing semicolonial and semifeudal domination. Today, however, this dichotomy between economic and political conditions of democracy is seriously questioned. Their mutual dependence is emphasised. Therefore both India and China have to achieve yet more conditions of democracy.

The other familiar question relates to equality and freedom. Western liberal democratic theory asserts the priority of freedom over equality even though the radical stream in liberalism stresses that gross inequalities are detrimental to the exercise of freedom. On this criterion pre-Reform China scored higher marks than India. Social inequalities were reduced in China to a very large extent with the abolition of landlordism and formation of cooperatives and Communes and also takeover of the bourgeoisie owned industries by the state. The wage system was directed towards promoting equality and limiting income differences within the six point grade system. In India too there were a number of measures taken in the early decades following independence to curb monopoly in industry, abolish zamindari system and carry out land reforms. In both the countries the stress on equality declined in the 1980s and almost disappeared in the 1990s. In the past decade or so equality has been a low priority in both China and India. The "equalitarianism", "theory of eating from the iron rice bowl" and such ideas of the Cultural Revolution were severely criticised by the Chinese reformers as being obstacles to the development of the productive forces. The perspective of the present day leadership in China is to "allow some people to get rich first" so that the general level of growth is raised steadily. In India the introduction of the Structural Adjustment Programme promoted the ideology of profit and the egalitarian programmes of social transformation took the back seat.

The two new issues arise from the great democratic upsurges of the past few decades, namely the social movements such as the women's movements, the environmental movement, the autonomy movement and the human rights movements. One question posed by them is to concretise freedom as freedom from multiple forms of domination so that freedom to realise the potentialities of the human being is advanced. Patriarchal domination continues substantially in all the countries of the world as evident from the deliberations at the Fourth World Congress of Women in Beijing and as documents in the 1995 *Human Development Report*. China and India have only marginal difference among them. As to ethnic self-determination there has not yet been a scientific measurement. But both the countries have fairly centralised regimes and both have regions manifesting popular discontent. The caste hierarchy and disabilities in India are targets of public attention and social action. There is no comparable social problem in China though new forms of social stratification have emerged in the recent years.

The other issue is response of the modern state to these expanding democratic demands. All ruling elites would like to have an appearance of being popular and responsive to the demands of the various unprivileged groups. And they engage in innumerable measures of legitimation to create a climate of acceptability among the people. Thus the modern state is coercive, responsive and legitimative at the same time. For this purpose it has developed sophisticated systems of management of society, complex methods of propaganda and innovative techniques of manipulation. Today the technology of repression and the vast networks of communication allow the formal democracy to continue while the citizens remain helpless. There is a new authoritarianism in the modern societies including those of the

West which make the basic notion of democracy nominal. The tragedy is that while failing on the scores of either political or socio-economic freedom both India and China have fast accumulated the resources of modern authoritarianism. These tools include modern capitalist preoccupation with consumerism promoted through advertisement. Sensate entertainment that commefcialises culture in the global scale on the one hand and building up security forces of all kinds to suppress democratic movements on the other. It is this process which is strengthened by the forces of capitalist globalization. The alliance of Western capitalists and the native elites has intervened to assimilate the rest of the third world into the Western model of capitalist political economy. The alternatives which the socialist revolutions and the anticolonial struggles had presented have been defeated in course of the battles of the recent decades. The socialist experiments adopted the same economic goals as capitalist systems and failed to promote socialist democracy. The anticolonial struggles such as India's which centred on the comprehensive concept of *Swaraj* failed to institutionalise after Independence.

The result was the crisis of the state and crisis of development in the third world to tackle which the elites leaned on the West. Thus today on the one hand there is an expanding demand for multidimensional freedom while on the other hand there is a an advancing tide of global hegemony by the capitalist West. The experiments in India and China are caught in this historical conjuncture. With these comparative notes let us look at the democratic prospects in China.

3

Resolving the Boundary Dispute: China's Reasons and India's Choices

The final settlement of the Sino-Indian territorial and boundary dispute is not a question of 'if' but 'when'. Four pertinent reasons suggest that China can be ultimately trusted to settle the dispute. On its part, India can take certain steps to ensure that China's reasons do not alter and that 'compromise' is seen as mutually beneficial. One, China has steadily resolved its territorial disputes with almost all of its 15 land neighbours.

Negotiations with the Soviet Union and Vietnam began in 1964 and 1977 respectively. However, it was not until much later that the negotiation processes fructified; it was only in October 2004 that the eastern sector of the Sino-Russian border was finally resolved with the signing of the Supplementary Agreement.

With Vietnam, China signed a land boundary agreement in 1999, although they continue to meet regularly at the governmental level to thrash out details pertaining to the Beibu Gulf and the placement of border markers. Therefore, boundary negotiations between China and its other neighbours have been long and arduous affairs. The slowness of the boundary negotiations between India and China needs to be seen in this context. Two, China has settled 17 of its 23 territorial disputes since 1949, according to M. Taylor Fravel, Assistant Professor of Political Science at MIT. Fravel suggests that regime insecurity and legitimacy crises in peripheral border regions best explain why China not only made concessions but also favoured the peaceful resolution of its territorial disputes. Despite a significant rise in China's economic and military strength vis-a-vis weaker neighbours, China received less than 50 per cent of the contested land. China's 'peaceful development' and 'new security concept' are directly responsible for the gradual stabilization of its borders-both concepts demand peaceful and stable borders for sustained economic growth.

Three, the absence of territorial disputes on China's western flank is a consequence of its 'western development' strategy. Starting with Myanmar and Nepal in the 1960s, a flurry of diplomatic activity saw the resolution of China's borders with Tajikistan and Kazakhstan (in 2002), Kyrgyzstan (in September 2004), Russia (in October 2004), and Mongolia (in November 2005). The pacification of China's western border is driven by the need to build cross-border linkages for economic development as well as the suppression of the three evils-separatism, extremism and terrorism. China's two westernmost provinces that border India, Xinjiang and Tibet, are important to China not least due to the fear that an economic imbalance can potentially fuel secessionist sentiments amongst the Uighurs and Tibetans.

Four, China is likely to reserve the use of force to settle heartland disputes. The hard component of China's comprehensive national strength will continue to dictate an inflexible stance on Taiwan's reunification as well as territorial conflicts of strategic value. Therefore, China is unlikely to make concessions on approximately 30,000 square kilometres of Aksai Chin, not least due to the fact that the Karakoram highway that traverses it provides a strategic link between Pakistan, and China and a shorter route between Tibet and Xinjiang. However, even in the case of disputes over territory of great economic value, such as the South China Sea, China has emphasized the joint development and exploitation of resources, albeit without making any concessions.

As emerging powers, India and China will continue to be pitted against each other. The sheer size and altitude of the disputed area is likely to make demarcation a difficult and lengthy process. However, India can take certain steps to ensure it remains in

China's interest to settle the dispute. India must do its utmost to convince China that it is not the target of the newly sealed Indo-US strategic relationship. India must clarify that the support for Tibetans in India is humanitarian and cultural and not a challenge to China's sovereign territoriality. China's friendship with Pakistan cannot be wished away; however, India can make itself important to China by promising trade and joint border development projects that make good business sense. India's inclusion into the Shanghai Cooperation Organisation as an observer in July 2005 was an important recognition of India's commitment to curbing cross-border terrorism.

Even though there are reasons to believe that China is not a revisionist state determined to use force to uphold its territorial claims, proactive steps to create lobbies with vested interests in resolving the dispute must be taken. The seventh round of Sino-Indian border talks in March 2006 helped provide a 'constructive and friendly' atmosphere. It is time for India and China to carry that forward and focus on opening Nathu La for trade, reviving the Stilwell Road for trade across India's northeast, building border free trade zones similar to the Sino-Kazakh one and establishing independent inter-linkages between border regions through transport linkages akin to the Kashgar (Xinjiang, China)-Gilgit (Northern Areas, Pakistan) bus service. Discussion on the Sino-Indian boundary talks must therefore go beyond the rhetoric on China's 'concirclement' of India; it must emphasize the domestic constraints and foreign policy concerns of the Chinese government and the resolution of territorial disputes that such a study reveals.

BEIJING'S RESPONSE TO INDIA-PAKISTAN TENSIONS AFTER 9/11

Since the late 1990s, China had become increasingly concerned over the gradual shift in the regional balance of power in South Asia, driven by the steady rise of India coupled with the growing US-India entente and the talk of "India as a counterweight to China" in Washington's policy circles, and by Pakistan's gradual descent into the ranks of failed states. Since the end of the Cold War, a politically dysfunctional and economically bankrupt

Pakistan's flirtation with Islamic extremism and terrorism, coupled with its nuclear and missile programs, had alienated Washington.

However, the 11 September 2001 attacks changed all that. Pakistan saw an opportunity to revive its past close relations with the United States, shed its near pariah status, and enhance its economic and strategic position vis-à-vis India by instantaneously becoming a "frontline state" in the international coalition fighting global terrorism. In return, Washington lifted sanctions and agreed to provide Pakistan with billions of dollars in aid and debt rescheduling. From Washington's perspective, courting Musharraf made geopolitical sense because the Pakistani military not only knew a great deal about the Taliban, Osama bin Laden, and al Qaeda, but also because any US military operation against Afghanistan could not be successful without the bases, logistics, personnel, and airspace in neighbouring Pakistan. In Beijing, as a result, there were great expectations of a sharp downturn in US-India relations, because in many ways what happens on the Indian subcontinent is unavoidably a zero-sum game and Pakistan's new relationship with the United States did affect India negatively.

However, tensions between South Asia's nuclear-armed rivals rose sharply after the terrorist attacks at the Kashmir Assembly in October 2001 and the Indian Parliament on 13 December 2001. The attack on the Indian Parliament triggered a major deployment of Indian troops along the border with Pakistan, with Islamabad responding in kind. New Delhi warned of retaliatory, punitive military strikes against terrorist camps inside Pakistani-controlled Kashmir. Although the Chinese Foreign Ministry spokesperson condemned these attacks, Chinese leaders and South Asia watchers were much more circumspect and ambivalent while lauding Pakistan's contribution to the war against terrorism. A South Asia specialist from China's National Defence University, Wang Baofu, noted with satisfaction that under the new circumstances, "The United States, considering its own security interests, readjusted its policies toward South Asian countries and started paying more attention to the important role of Pakistan in the anti-terrorism war, therefore arousing the vigilance and jealousy of India." Wang criticized India for "defin[ing] resistance activities in Kashmir as terrorism by taking advantage of the US anti-terrorism war in Afghanistan, thus putting more pressure on Pakistan through the United States," and praised General Musharraf for his "clear-cut attitude toward fighting against international terrorism)." Such a stance was not unexpected. For almost a decade, China had rejected India's proposal to issue a joint declaration against terrorism lest it be interpreted as a condemnation of Pakistan. Pakistan President General Musharraf made three trips to Beijing in less than a year (in December 2001, January 2002, and August 2002) for urgent security consultations with President Jiang Zemin and Premier Zhu Rongji and reportedly obtained "firm assurances of support in the event of a war" with India. At the time of heightened tensions in mid-January 2002, General Zhang Wannian, Vice-Chairman of China's Central Military Commission, met with General Muhammad Aziz Khan, Chairman of Pakistan's Joint Chiefs of the Staff Committee, and was quoted as telling Khan: "For many years the militaries of our two nations have maintained exchanges and cooperation at the highest and all levels and in every field. This fully embodies the all-weather friendship our nations maintain." Zhang's reference to "cooperation... inevery field" (meaning the nuclear and missile fields) was a thinly veiled warning to India to back off. Later, Beijing matched words with deeds by rushing two dozen F-7 jet fighters, nuclear and missile components, and other weapon systems to shore up Pakistani defenses in the tense border face-off.Asecret "futuristic arms development cooperation" agreement was signed during General Musharraf's five-day visit to China in December 2001 to construct, among other weapons, an all-solid-fuel Shaheen III missile with a range of 3,500-4,000 kilometers to target all major Indian cities. The People's Liberation Army (PLA) troops from the Military Regions of Chengdu and Lanzhou and their respective subdivisions, the Xizang (Tibet) and Wulumuqi (Urumqi), along China's southern borders, were also put on alert in January to test their war preparedness should the conflict in the Indian subcontinent spill over onto Chinese soil.

The Chinese leaders had reportedly conveyed the following message to Musharraf: "China hopes Pakistan will not initiate any assault. Pakistan should not get involved in wars and instead focus on economic construction. However, if a war does break out between India and Pakistan, Beijing will firmly stand on the side of Islamabad." Soon thereafter, President Musharraf in a televised speech on 12 January 2002 announced a crackdown on extremist organizations waging jihad from Pakistani territory, and as a result, Indo-Pakistani tensions somewhat subsided. The Chinese media claimed some credit for "mediating" between the two sub-continental rivals despite the Indian government's aversion to the dreaded "m" word: "Mediated by the United States, China, Britain, and Russia, leaders of India and Pakistan recently expressed their desire to try to control the tense situation." 12 Interestingly, this stance contradicted then Indian Foreign Minister Jaswant Singh's statement during Premier Zhu's visit to New Delhi in January 2002 that "China has neither any intention, nor shall it play any mediatory role between India and Pakistan." Not only that, the Chinese Foreign Minister also succeeded in persuading his Russian counterpart to issue a "Joint Declaration on the India-Pakistan Situation," signaling to New Delhi that, for the first time, Beijing and Moscow had a unified stand on the dispute. In concrete policy terms, it meant that New Delhi could no longer count on the Russian veto in the UN Security Council in the event of a war.

Then came the 14 May 2002 terrorist attack on a military base in Jammu that killed 34 people, mostly women and children, once again escalating tensions along the border where more than one million troops backed by heavy armor, warplanes, and missiles were deployed. There was renewed tough talk of war, including nuclear war, on both sides of the border. Beijing called for restraint from both India and Pakistan and emphasized the need for peaceful dialogue to settle outstanding disputes. Chinese Defence Minister Chi Haotian also urged both countries to desist from a military conflict and not to threaten each other with nuclear weapons. Describing the US diplomatic moves (i.e., the dispatch of Deputy Secretary of State Richard Armitage and Defence Secretary Donald Rumsfeld in early June 2002) to defuse the India-Pakistan military stand-off as "too little too late," the state-run media accused Washington of showing "no genuine desire to resolve the Kashmir issue." It noted that Washington had clearly not taken the tensions very seriously when it went on with a ten-day joint military maneuver with India on 16-26 May 2002, thereby implying that the Indo-US joint military exercise had emboldened India to up the ante against Pakistan. On 15 May, a Chinese official accompanying Foreign Minister Tang Jiaxuan during his visit to Islamabad told Pakistani journalists that China would back Pakistan in any conflict with India. Concerned over the "one-sided nature of public appeals" from Washington, Moscow, London, Paris, and Tokyo to General Musharraf to halt "cross-border terrorism" into Indian Kashmir, Chinese Foreign Minister Tang Jiaxuan told US Secretary of State Colin Powell on 27 May 2002 that "the international community should encourage direct dialogue between India and Pakistan in a more balanced and fair manner, which is the most effective way to lead South Asia towards peace and stability." Apparently, the growing threat of nuclear war and the prospect of Pakistani nuclear weapons falling into the hands of Islamic terrorists have made Washington lean heavily on Islamabad. In contrast, Beijing repeatedly asked New Delhi to do more to end the military stand-off while publicly calling for restraint by both sides and claiming to be even-handed. China continued to covertly side with its long-term ally, however, and is providing military wherewithal to Pakistan.

Meanwhile, in yet another television address on 27 May, Musharraf pledged that all militant infiltration across the Line of Control (LoC) would end, and he announced the banning of Lashkar-e-Toiba, the Jaish-e-Mohammad, and the Harkat-ul-Mujahideen—the three "*jihadi*" outfits at the forefront of terrorist activity in Indian Kashmir. From New Delhi's perspective, India's military deployment had succeeded in bringing the international focus on Pakistan as the home of pan-Islamic *jihadis* after the war in Afghanistan.

At the Conference on Interaction and Confidence Building Measures in Asia held in Kazakhstan in early June 2002, Chinese President Jiang Zemin pressed Indian Prime Minister Vajpayee to enter into direct talks with Pakistani President Musharraf to prevent the Kashmir conflict from exploding into a full-scale war. But the

Indian government was so irked over Musharraf's playing of "the China card" that Vajpayee refused to budge. Later, in an interview with *The Washington Post*, the Indian Prime Minister complained that he saw "no basic change in China's policy. China continues to help Pakistan acquire weapons and equipment." In an article titled "Beijing as Guarantor of Pakistan's Security," a Russian weekly, *Nezavisimoye Voyennoye Obozreniye* (Independent Military Review), had reported that new security commitments have indeed been made to Pakistan by China since 9/11.18 New Delhi expressed its displeasure with Beijing by postponing scheduled visits by Indian Army Chief Padmanabhan and Prime Minister Vajpayee to China in October and November 2002.

The Nuclear Connection

There were other grounds for the cooling of relations between Beijing and New Delhi. In his testimony before the US Senate governmental affairs subcommittee in early June 2002, the Assistant Secretary of State for Nonproliferation, John S. Wolf, revealed that "China recently provided Islamabad with missile-related technologies, which include dual-use missile-related items, raw materials, and other accessories essential for missile manufacturing." In a sense, China's nuclear and missile assistance to a volatile Pakistan over the last two decades has now created the risk of a conventional conflict swiftly escalating into nuclear war. Beijing has not only provided Islamabad with nuclear bombs, uranium, and plants (all three Pakistani nuclear plants—Kahuta, Khushab, and Chasma— have been built with Chinese assistance) but also their delivery systems: readyto-launch M-9 (Ghaznavi/ Hatf), M-11 (Shaheen), and a number of Dong Feng 21 (Ghauri) ballistic missiles. This cooperation has continued despite Beijing's growing concerns over the "Talibanization" of the Pakistani state and society. When Islamabad carried out a series of missile tests amidst heightened tensions apparently to warn New Delhi to back off, the Indian government drew the international community's attention to the Pakistani missiles' China connection. "We are not impressed by these missile antics, particularly when all that is demonstrated is borrowed or imported ability.... The technology used in the missiles is not their own but clandestinely acquired from other countries," said a spokesperson of the Indian External Affairs Ministry.

Pakistan's test of its nuclear-capable, medium-range, Shaheen ballistic missile in early October 2002, just days before the parliamentary elections, once again provoked India to level accusations of missile technology proliferation by China. India's outspoken Defence Minister, George Fernandes, long a critic of China, said that Pakistan's military had always depended on support from China ever since it was carved out as a homeland for South Asia's Muslims in 1947 following decolonization of British India.

"Everyone knows what Pakistan will be without China. Its ego is boosted purely by the support it gets from China," Fernandes said at a party convention in Mumbai. Earlier, when India weaponized its nuclear capability through a series of tests in May 1998, Fernandes had described "China [as] the mother of Pakistan's nuclear bomb" and claimed that India's aim was to counter China's capability rather than Pakistan's, drawing protests from Beijing. When Pakistan came in the firing line following revelations in the US media about the missiles-for-nukes barter deal with North Korea, New Delhi argued that blame should also be put on China for making Pakistan a nuclear weapons state.

For New Delhi, Beijing's military alliance with Islamabad remains a sore point because the Sino-Pakistani nuclear nexus has introduced a new element of uncertainty and complexity in sub-continental strategic equations. While the attention of world leaders and the media has been focused on the nightmarish scenario of a nuclear Armageddon in South Asia and large-scale mutual assured destruction leading to the deaths of 12 to 30 million people, strategic circles in Islamabad and New Delhi have been discussing the pros and cons of a short, limited nuclear war in Kashmir. Media reports based on intelligence leaks have revealed the forward deployment by the Pakistani military of low-yield (five kilotons or less) tactical nuclear weapons (TNWs). Such small battlefield nuclear weapons have a one-mile destruction radius and could be used effectively against large troop concentrations and advancing tank formations along the LoC in Kashmir.

The Pakistanis seem to have taken a page out of China's book on tactical nuclear warfighting capability. Just as persistent Sino-Soviet disputes and the Soviet Union's conventional military superiority during the 1970s and 1980s gave China strong incentives to develop and deploy TNWs, the decade-long India-Pakistan border tensions and India's conventional superiority may have added momentum to Islamabad's efforts to deploy TNWs. Most of Pakistan's missiles acquired from China, such as the M-9, are short-range, solid-fueled, mobile, nuclear-capable missiles and can be used in a tactical mode. Asked to comment on reports that Pakistan has acquired TNWs, the Deputy Chief of the Indian Army, Lieutenant General Raj Kadyan, was quoted as saying that the "Indian Army has trained itself to cope with a tactical nuclear strike in the battlefield." Tactical nukes can be launched over an unpopulated area from field artillery guns or aircraft to halt an enemy advance or in an effort to intimidate a numerically stronger enemy. Since the damage is localized or confined to a certain area, the danger of affecting the civilian population is greatly reduced as compared to a strategic nuclear weapon of the Hiroshima kind and therefore need not evoke massive retaliation by enemy forces. The mountainous terrain in Kashmir provides the perfect setting for their use.

In addition to the United States and Russia, only China is believed to have a large stockpile of about 120 TNWs or "baby nukes." Some of these were apparently delivered to Pakistan following the visit of PLA Deputy Chief and military intelligence boss General Xiong Guangkai (arguably China's most important military figure and the man who calls Pakistan "China's Israel") to Islamabad in early March 2002.27 If the reports of China's transfer of TNWs to Pakistan are indeed true, the question then is: Would India, which does not possess TNWs but has strategic nuclear weapons in abundance, keep a nuclear conflict limited or escalate it to the strategic level and respond with massive retaliation? Though New Delhi has long maintained that even a tactical nuclear strike on its forces would be treated as a nuclear first strike, and would invite massive retaliation, some Pakistani generals believe that a tactical strike would circumvent retaliation from India, since such an attack on an advancing tank regiment or infantry battalion (in contrast to a strategic strike killing millions of civilians), would not be provocation enough for all-out retaliation. They contend that the many layers of bureaucracy surrounding India's nuclear capability, the strength of world public opinion, and the fact that strategic command remains in civilian hands places severe doubts on India's willingness and ability to retaliate with a massive nuclear strike against an opponent, particularly in the face of only a limited tactical strike from Pakistan.

Some analysts attribute the recent lessening of tensions to the belated recognition in India's strategic circles that New Delhi cannot afford to dismiss Pakistan's repeated threats of using nuclear weapons as "mere posturing" or "bluffing" on Islamabad's part. They point to the Pakistani military's strong aversion to fighting a 1965-or 1971-type conventional war with India and offer this as the rationale behind Islamabad's decision to pull back from the brink on several occasions in recent history (in 1987, 1990, 1999, and 2002). Others believe that the tendency of Indian strategic planners to discount the threat of nuclear escalation may well be based on some fundamentally erroneous assumptions:

- That the United States cannot allow Pakistan to be the first Islamic country to use nuclear weapons to settle a territorial dispute, as it would mean the end of the global nonproliferation regime and encourage other countries to go nuclear to settle their territorial disputes as well.
- That the presence of US forces in Pakistan will be a constraining factor.
- That the international community (the United States, United Kingdom, China, or the United Nations) will intervene in time to prevent such a catastrophe.
- And that India can count on American and Israeli military support to seize or take out Pakistan's nuclear and missile infrastructure. These assumptions do not seem to be based on cold, clear-headed calculations of the strategic interests and influence of major powers (especially the United States and China) and may well be a sign of wishful thinking on India's part. It is worth noting that new strategic and geopolitical realities emerging in Asia since 9/11 have put

a question mark over Beijing's older certainties, assumptions, and beliefs.

China's Concerns

Much to Jiang and his Politburo's chagrin, the US-led war on terrorism has developed in ways that could not have been foreseen, with potentially disastrous consequences for China's core strategic interests. A major unintended (and unsettling, from Beijing's standpoint) consequence has been not only to checkmate and roll back China's recent strategic expansion moves in Central, South, and Southeast Asia, thereby severely constricting the strategic latitude that China has enjoyed since the Cold War, but also to tilt the regional balance of power decisively in Washington's favour within a short period. The supposedly brief Unipolar moment in history seems to have turned into a long-lasting Imperial moment—a Pax Americana *par excellence*. More important, recent developments show how tenuous Chinese power remains when compared to that of the United States.

The fast-changing strategic scene not only undercuts Chinese ambitions to expand Beijing's power and influence in Asia, but also hems in the one country in the world with the most demonstrable capacity to act independently of the United States. Not surprisingly, the beginning of 2002 saw Chinese leaders and generals shedding their earlier inhibitions about publicly expressing concern over the growing "southern discomfort"—that is, ever-expanding US military power and presence in southern Asia after 9/11. China's Chief of the General Staff Fu Quanyou warned the United States against using the war on terrorism to dominate global affairs by saying "counter-terrorism should not be used to practice hegemony." On an official visit in April 2002 in Iran, Jiang Zemin openly repudiated the US stance against the Iranian and Iraqi regimes, saying, "Our opinion [on terrorism] is not the same as the United States." In Germany, he told the *Welt am Sonntag*: "We all want to fight terrorism. But the states involved in the fight against terror each have their own specific viewpoint." China's initial optimism that new Sino-US-Pakistan triangular cooperation in the aftermath of 11 September 2001 would wean Washington away from New Delhi turned out to be wishful thinking as Bush

Administration officials went out of their way to assure India that America's intensifying alliance with Pakistan would not come at India's expense. If anything, the current crisis has strengthened the American commitment to building stronger relations, including defence ties, with South Asia's preeminent power. However, China does not want to see India increasing its power, stature, and profile regionally or internationally. Beijing shares Islamabad's deep mistrust of India's strategic ambitions and seeks to prevent India's emergence as a peer competitor and a major strategic rival in Asia. That is why Chinese strategists have long argued that China's pursuit of great power status is a historical right and perfectly legitimate but India's pursuit of great power status is illegitimate, wrong, dangerous, and a sign of hegemonic, imperial behaviour. For its part, New Delhi has long accused Beijing of doing everything it can to undermine India's interests and using its ties with other states to contain India. Beijing is also alarmed over the growing talk in some con-servative policy circles in Washington and New Delhi of India emerging as a counterweight to China on the one hand and the fragile, radical Islamic states of West Asia on the other.

Earlier, when President Bush unveiled his missile defence plan, New Delhi responded far more positively than did most US allies. Some Indian strategic thinkers even see in the emerging US-India quasi-alliance an opportunity for "payback" to China. As G. Parthasarthy, former Indian Ambassador to Pakistan and Burma, put it: "Whether it was the Bangladesh conflict of 1971, or in the Clinton-Jiang Declaration in the aftermath of our nuclear tests, China has never hesitated to use its leverage with the Americans to undermine our security." Growing Chinese strategic pressure on the Malacca Straits has already led to maritime collaboration between India and the United States, with their navies jointly patrolling the straits. More significantly, US-India strategic engagement has scaled new heights with the announcement of a series of measures usually reserved for close US allies and friends: joint military exercises in Alaska that would boost India's high-altitude warfare capabilities in the Himalayan glaciers of northern Kashmir where it faces Pakistan and China; sale of military hardware including radars, aircraft engines, and surveillance equipment to India; joint naval exercises and the training of India's special forces; and intelligence sharing as well as the joint naval patrols in the Straits of Malacca. Washington also reportedly gave the green light for Israel to proceed with selling the Phalcon airborne early warning and control system (AWACS) to India—something that was earlier denied to China for fear of enhancing Beijing's air surveillance and early warning capabilities in the Taiwan Strait.

All of these measures send an implicit signal to China of India's growing military prowess. In a cover story in the authoritative *Beijing Review*, one of China's noted South Asia specialists expressed concern over the US sale of arms to India which "enables it to become the first country to have close military relations with the world's two big powers—the United States and Russia." To make matters worse, in early May 2002 Prime Minister Koizumi of Japan, Beijing's other Asian rival, which sees China representing a clear and future threat to its security, called for a broadening of Japan's security cooperation with India.

Many Chinese strategists believe India is using the war on terrorism as a pretext to militarily subdue Pakistan or to destabilize and dismember the country. Pakistan is the only country that stands up to India and thereby prevents Indian hegemony over the region, thus fulfilling a key objective of China's South Asia policy. 39 As South Asia watcher Ehsan Ahrari points out: "India may end up intensifying its own rivalry with China by remaining steadfast in its insistence that Musharraf kowtow to its demands, especially if China calculates that US-India ties are harming its own regional interests. China, though still concerned about the continued activism of Islamist groups in Pakistan and contiguous areas, is not at all willing to see the regional balance of power significantly tilt in favour of India." Though Beijing welcomes the new US commitment to prop up Beijing's "all-weather friend" after a decade of abandonment and estrangement, most Chinese strategists worry about the destabilizing consequences of a prolonged US military presence in Pakistan and increased influence on the future of Sino-Pakistan ties as well as on Pakistan's domestic stability. The Chinese are also believed to be "highly uncomfortable" with the four US military bases in Pakistan. Of special concern to Beijing is the US presence at Pasni in the Baluchistan region of Pakistan, where China is constructing a deep-water naval port at Gwadar, the inland Makran coastal highway linking it with Karachi, and several oil and gas pipeline projects.

Beijing has long been eyeing its construction of the naval base at Gwadar, at the mouth of the Strait of Hormuz in the Persian Gulf, as a bulwark against the US presence and India's growing naval power. Furthermore, the US military presence in Pakistan could sharpen the divide within the Pakistani military into pro-West and pro-Beijing factions, with China supporting the latter to regain ground lost since 9/11.[44] The pro-Beijing lobby within the Pakistani military is reportedly getting restive and waiting to strike if and when General Musharraf falters. The pro-China faction within the Pakistani military could also join hands with the pro-Islamic fundamentalist faction opposing the US military presence on Pakistan's soil. Alternatively, it could throw its support behind those nationalist elements that find Pakistan's loss of its "strategic depth" in Afghanistan for elusive diplomatic gains very hard to digest. The US arms sales to India and joint US-Indian military exercises may further sour China's and Pakistan's willingness to assist Washington in its war on terrorism.

War Scenarios

It is said that each conflict simply prepares the ground for the next one or every war contains the seeds of another. The AfghanWar of the 1980s against the Soviet occupation culminated in the war on terrorism in 2001. Whether the war on terrorism will lead to another war or a clash of civilizations or a nuclear jihad in South Asia, only time will tell. Pakistan is, in the words of former Italian Foreign Minister Gianni De Michelis, "the fuse of the world." The provinces close to the Afghan border and home to the US military bases are now controlled by Islamic parties that created the Taliban and are openly sympathetic to the aims and ideals of al Qaeda. The rising anti-American sentiment in Pakistan as demonstrated in the recent elections has made the country increasingly unstable. Violence levels in Indian Kashmir also continue to rise. Many observers believe that Washington may have to rethink its strategy vis-à-vis Islamabad if the war on terrorism is to be won decisively. The complete dismantling of the al Qaeda terrorist infrastructure in Pakistan seems unlikely because of the apprehension within the Pakistani military that doing so would devalue Pakistan's importance in the US security strategy and once again make the United States turn its back on the country and make the country vulnerable to Western pressure and sanctions. It would also deprive Pakistan of invaluable Western aid and leverage vis-à-vis Washington and New Delhi.

One Chinese national security analyst argues that "what worries China more is the possibility that it could be drawn into a conflict, not between Pakistan and India per se, but between Pakistan and the United States, with the latter using India as a surrogate." With the top al Qaeda and Taliban leadership fleeing into Pakistan's Wild West and Pakistani-held Kashmir, Beijing knows full well that Pakistan is no longer the "frontline state" in the war on terrorism that it once was; it is, in fact, the battlefield in the war on terror. Should the India-Pakistani conflict escalate into a nuclear one, neither the geopolitical nor the radioactive fallout will remain limited to South Asia. Indeed, the most worrisome scenario would be one where Pakistan is losing a conventional conflict and uses tactical nuclear weapons in a desperate effort to win or to salvage a face-saving defeat that would allow the regime to survive. (The risk-taking nature of the Pakistani military leadership suggests that such a scenario cannot be completely ruled out.) Should India respond by launching strategic nuclear strikes resulting in the complete destruction of the Pakistani state, China would find it difficult to sit idly by. The next India-Pakistan war also could bring the United States and Pakistan on a collision course, with or without India acting as a US partner. Such a development would obviously present China with difficult choices. Open support for its closest ally would jeopardize China's relations with the United States and India. But nonintervention on Pakistan's behalf could encourage India to solve "the Pakistan problem" once and for all, with or without a nuclear exchange, and thereby tilt the regional balance of power decisively in its favour. As Zhang Xiaodong put it: "There is the real possibility that a new Indian-Pakistani war will take place in the future. This war would be disastrous, as it would change the whole political balance in Central and South Asia," which is currently tilted in China's favour. Unrestrained Indian power could eventually threaten China's security along its soft underbelly—Tibet and Xinjiang.

Should post-Musharraf Pakistan disintegrate or be taken over by Islamic extremists, a new level of instability would rock the region and increase tensions among Pakistan, India, and China. Another dreadful scenario is one in which Chinese-made Pakistani nuclear weapons fall into the hands of the United States, Israel, or even India in the event of a civil war should al Qaeda or the Taliban declare jihad against Pakistan—the weakest ally in the US-led anti-terrorism coalition. 51 India would be tempted to militarily intervene in Pakistan if Islamists gain control over the nuclear weapons of its neighbour, either through a coup or civil war. Such a scenario could reveal information regarding China's own nuclear program and the extent of help provided by Beijing to Islamabad. The scenario of Pakistan in splinters, with one piece becoming a radical Muslim state in possession of nuclear weapons, can no longer be simply rejected as an alarmist fantasy.

Difficult Choices

These scenarios put Beijing on the horns of a dilemma. Some Chinese strategists see in the current South Asian crisis an opportunity to recover lost ground and thwart India's ambitions to challenge China's future economic and military primacy in Asia. Should another war between India and Pakistan break out, New Delhi's high hopes of an India-US alliance to counter China may never materialize, a welcome development from China's perspective. Some hawks in the PLAsee China even benefiting from an India-Pakistani nuclear war. Hideaki Kase, a former special advisor to Japanese Premiers Takeo Fukuda and Yasuhiro Nakasone, believes that "China wants an Indo-Pakistan war, possibly a nuclear conflict, to weaken India." At the time of the 1999 Kargil War, one Chinese military official had reportedly told a Western diplomat that "should India and Pakistan destroy themselves in a nuclear war, there would be peace along China's southwestern frontiers for at least three decades, and Beijing needs

20 to 30 years to consolidate its hold over restive Tibet and Xinjiang provinces." However, this remains a minority viewpoint, as a nuclear war would have worldwide repercussions in terms of global economic depression, humanitarian crises, WMD proliferation, and China's developmental priorities.

Most Chinese analysts and policymakers believe that Beijing should have absolutely minimum involvement in a situation where there can be no clear winners. Some argue that Beijing should seize the opportunity to coordinate its South Asia policy with Washington as it is in the interests of both countries to avert the world's first nuclear exchange and to use India-Pakistan tensions to strengthen Sino-US ties.

While the Pakistanis are confident that if war comes with India, China will throw its weight behind Pakistan, diplomatically as well as militarily, the Indians remain adamant that the Chinese would not do so for fear of India playing "the Taiwan and Tibet cards." Interestingly, on 31 May 2002, the day Pakistan's new UN Ambassador, Munir Akram, issued an explicit nuclear warning to India, a Chinese Foreign Ministry spokesman denied a *Times of India* report that Chinese President Jiang Zemin had assured a US congressional delegation that China would not favour Pakistan in the existing tensions, and claimed that the report was "not based on facts." A Chinese South Asia analyst at Fudan University in Shanghai, Shen Dingli, told *The Wall Street Journal*: "China needs to send a message: For my own security I will intervene." Though Beijing may not overtly intervene in a limited war, China's geopolitical imperative requires it to come to Pakistan's defence if the latter's existence as a nation-state is threatened by India. Clearly, there is a great deal more to the Chinese role in South Asia than meets the eye. In the final analysis, Beijing's response to the next India-Pakistan war will be shaped by its desire to protect Chinese national interests, no matter what the cost.

THE INDIA-CHINA DIVIDE

The Chinese Communist Party's (CCP) dislike for the 'hardline Hindu nationalist' Bharatiya Janata Party (BJP) is no secret. The shifts in India's China policy since May 1998, as evidenced in the nuclear and missile arena, military spending, and pro-Tibet and pro-Taiwan views expressed by some ministers, are said to have undermined the key assumptions underlying China's India policy. Conversations with officials and strategic analysts reveal that the Chinese are concerned over the rise of BJP as a major political force in Indian politics and its implications for China's strategic objective of supremacy in Asia. Before Pokhran II, China's India-watchers had convinced themselves that there would be 'no significant or fundamental changes' in the BJP-led Government's nuclear policy and that BJP-led India would not take any major strategic initiative (such as overt nuclearisation, strategic alliance with the United States, or support to Tibetan independence).

Although the aspirations for major power status are held by almost all Indian political parties (barring the Communists who fear provoking their Chinese masters), the BJP covets that status most ardently and is the most willing to assert it through military policy. Beijing would prefer a non-BJP weak government like the left-dominated United Front (UF) government before Pokhran II, and the successive Congress governments that preceded it, which had fine-tuned Sino-Indian bilateral relations by playing second fiddle to an assertive China. A policy paper prepared for the Chinese leadership has recommended 'targeting the BJP' as its policies have eroded Beijing's leverage against New Delhi. One analyst compared India with Nazi Germany and Iraq arguing that since the end of the Cold War, India had become too powerful and ambitious (for example, demanding a permanent seat on the UN Security Council) and warned that if India does not wish to suffer the fate of Japan in the 1940s or Iraq in the 1990s, it should give up its ambition for regional hegemony and take concrete steps to improve relations with China.

The main objective of China's Asia policy has always been to prevent the rise of an Asian rival or peer competitor to challenge its status as the Asia-Pacific's sole 'Middle Kingdom'. As an old Chinese saying goes, 'one mountain cannot accommodate two tigers'. That China does not want India to emerge as an equal is evident from its staunch opposition to India's membership of the P-5 (UN Security Council), N-5 (Nuclear Club), ASEM (Asia-

Europe Summit), and APEC (Asia-Pacific Economic Cooperation). (India was made the ARF (ASEAN Regional Forum) member in December 1995 despite Beijing's opposition to it.) Speaking at the Munich Security Conference in February 1999, India's National Security Advisor, Brajesh Mishra, hinted at the BJP government's much broader political ambition by predicting that 'in the 21st century a new security order is likely to arise in the Asia-Pacific region in which India should be granted as much respect and deference by the United States and others as is China today.' Beijing's India-watchers believe that only a firm policy based on absolute strength and proactive containment of India will force the BJP-led government to act soberly towards China. Beijing knows that while China's emergence as a great power has been accepted by Western and Asian nations, India's claim to great power is yet to be accepted. So it is in the CCP's interests to keep the BJP out of power. Beijing has been blamed by India's intelligence agencies, media and some politicians for the overthrow of the BJP-led government in April 1999.

Strange as it may seem, the CCP has more in common with its bete noire, BJP, than its counterpart in India, the Communist Party of India-Marxist (CPM). In the BJP, the CCP has met its match, the latter's 'communist' pretensions notwithstanding. Contrary to the popular conception of the CCP and the BJP occupying opposite ends of the political spectrum, the BJP is the CCP's mirror image. Just as the CCP believes in the superiority of the Han race, Han civilisation and the Han culture while displaying patronising and condescending attitude towards minorities such as Tibetans, Mongols and Muslims and downplaying the repeated colonisation of the Han race first by Inner Asian tribes such as Mongols, Manchus and Hsingnus and then by the Europeans, the BJP believes in the superiority of the Hindu race, Hindu civilisation and Hindu culture while downplaying the repeated colonisation of India by Greek, Muslim and European invaders as a result of Hindu disunity and their contributions to Indian culture. What is more, the CCP's goal of a unified 'Greater China' is not much different from the RSS/BJP's dream of 'Akhand Bharat' (United India). Just as the Chinese

Communists lay claim to territories annexed by non-Chinese Mongol and Manchu empires (such as Tibet, Eastern Turkestan, Mongolia), the 'Akhand Bharat' concept includes territories (such as Burma and Sri Lanka) brought under control by the British. Much like the CCP, the BJP wants India to be an economic and military superpower in order to 'stand up' to great powers' bullying and coercion. Both have long nurtured the belief that as the two oldest civilisations and once great powers which were subjected to centuries of foreign domination, they must acquire the full spectrum of economic, technological and military (conventional, nuclear and information warfare) capabilities in order to be dominant regionally and influential globally.

Furthermore, the BJP's slogan of 'prosperous and powerful country' bears remarkable resemblance to the CCP's national goal: 'rich country, strong military' (fuguo qiangbing). Interestingly, both are courting the United States to help balance their relationships with each other until they are strong enough to do so on their own. Both want a new international status that is commensurate with their size, strength and potential. Historically and civilisationally, while China was the 'Middle Kingdom' of eastern Asia, India was the 'Middle Kingdom' of southern Asia.

The two parties are thus manifestation of the growing nationalism in India and China. Both also share remarkable similarity in economic outlooks and rhetorical excess. The BJP-led government is as aggressive in the pursuit of national interests as the CCP. Nor is it shy of flexing muscles and warning neighbours with 'serious consequences' if they don't behave-just as the Chinese Communists have always done! Although both the CCP and BJP have been labelled 'fascist', 'militarist' and 'ultra-natonalist' parties by their critics, the reality is that both are nationalist parties deeply conscious of their countries' history, culture and civilisational heritage to humankind and committed to restoring their countries' great power status. Both China after a century and India after a millenium of decline are keen to assume the great power roles they believe to be their historical and civilisational right.

Both remain suspicious of each other's long-term agenda and intentions, and are attempting to fill any perceived power vacuum or block the other from doing so. At the heart of Sino-Indian antagonism is the familiar Indian suspicion, which has now matured into a certainty, that China is seeking to deny India its proper stakes in the game of international politics. Both see themselves as newly rising great Asian powers whose time has finally come. This means that BJP's resurgent India will face CCP's rising China which will ensure a conflict of interests between the two giants unless their power competition is managed carefully. Their underlying power rivalry and their self-images as natural great powers and centres of civilisation and culture will continue to drive them to support different countries and causes. India versus China, not India versus Pakistan, has always been the main game in Asia. However, post-colonial Asia has not experienced both a strong China and a strong India at the same time. The BJP-CCP clash is borne not out of conflicting, but complementary, visions for their respective countries.

CHINA'S BORDER SPAT WITH INDIA

The recent meeting between India's National Security Adviser MK Narayanan and China's Vice-Foreign Minister Dai Banggio at Coonoor in Tamil Nadu was the continuation of a series of such meetings in the context of the border dispute between the two countries. While this is a good thing to go by, the main point is: what has been the actual progress in the matter? After every meeting, a standard joint communiqué is issued to the effect that the téte-a-téte was fruitful and the dialogue is being maintained in an atmosphere of friendship and mutual cooperation. Diplomatic jargon cannot be limitless; it must end somewhere. Again, from time to time one hears of Chinese intrusion into Arunachal Pradesh, especially in the area of Sumdorong Chu Valley and the northern range of the Mishmi Hills. There is also the occasional media report that China claims this North-eastern state of ours on the grounds of a combination of history as well as geography.

India's drawback is that our foreign policy has always been linked to the vote bank. In fact it was a vote bank issue that created the border dispute with China in the first place way back in the late '50s and early '60s. The origin of this problem is worth discussing as this itself suggests the solution. Soon after China secured Tibet, Beijing sent a delegation to New Delhi under then Prime Minister Zhou en Lai with a proposal on Aksai Chin in northern Kashmir, adjacent to the Siachen Glacier. The delegation submitted to us that movement from Tibet to Sinkiang province was a huge problem because one had to traverse the inhospitable Kunlun Mountains en route. Hence it was suggested both countries could arrive at an understanding by which India could lease out Aksai Chin to China, as this would enable the latter to build an all-weather highway across this stretch of territory.

Thus movement from Tibet to Sinkiang would not then involve negotiating the Kunluns at all and India, too, could use this highway as a bonus. In any case, Aksai Chin was just an ice desert with an average height of 18,000-19,000 feet and nothing grew there, let alone having any human habitation. New Delhi reacted with its usual brash arrogance, thundering words to the effect that 'not an inch of our sacred motherland' would be given, et al. Zhou en Lai was shown the door gracelessly.

The Chinese delegation went back and decided to implement a tenet in Hindi conveying the meaning that if ghee cannot be taken out by a straight finger then a crooked finger would be used! China militarily attacked India and physically captured Aksai Chin by force in late 1962 and built the desired highway through it. China is still very much in occupation of this area, cocking a snook at India now and then! On our part we bemoaned our fate, blamed Beijing for gerrymandering into our territory and generally made a political nuisance of ourselves. Nothing helped, of course.

During its attack on India, China had also deeply transgressed into what was earlier known as the North East Frontier Agency that later became Arunachal Pradesh. However, after delivering a crushing military-cum-political defeat on India, China moved back to its own side of the border in this area. This apart, China disputes an area along the Uttarkhand-Tibet border named Barahoti. China has a strong army garrison in this area at a place called Taklakot that keeps a watching brief over Barahoti. India, therefore, has been well and truly boxed in by China, courtesy New Delhi's folly of riding the high horse with Zhou en Lai's delegation of yore. Diplomacy has never been a strong point with us and the country has suffered badly as a consequence. The science and art of statecraft continue to be subservient to the omnipotent vote bank as far as our leaders are concerned. New Delhi, for reasons best known to itself, brought out a Lok Sabha resolution in 1994 wherein it was categorically stated that we would retake Aksai Chin by force. Obviously this resolution was nothing but a vote bank gimmick that our näive citizens — including many members of our intelligentsia — swallowed all the way.While firmly occupying Aksai Chin, China periodically needles India over Arunachal Pradesh and Barahoti. Normally, Barahoti remains dormant but Arunachal Pradesh makes news, sometimes with alarm. This has been the state of affairs since 1962. No government at New Delhi since that year has tried to accept the reality and taken any pragmatic steps to reconcile the border situation with China, notwithstanding the fact that currently our relations with China are improving virtually by the day.

The question is, what needs to be done in order to resolve the ongoing impasse? There is only one solution: India must formally accept Zhou en Lai's suggestion of yesteryear but cede Aksai Chin to China. It is doubtful whether China will accept the lease aspect now. The Chinese are a very proud race and will never climb down. In any event, China holds the aces in this matter, never mind the McMahon Line's relevancy to us. Truth to tell, this solution was hinted by China's previous regime under President Jiang Zemin through his then Foreign Minister Tang Jiaxuan during Prime Minister AB Vajpayee's tenure. While the Sikkim issue got reconciled, Aksai Chin could not be followed through due to the change of government in India in 2004.

China is not really interested in Barahoti and Arunachal Pradesh — Beijing uses these two as pressure points on New Delhi to see reason over the border dispute, a dispute that hinges purely on Aksai Chin. The sooner we come to terms with this, the better.

INDIA-CHINA BORDER DISPUTE

On assuming power, the People's Republic of China (PRC) renounced all prior foreign agreements as unequal treaties imposed upon it during the "century of humiliation" and demanded renegotiation of all borders. The Sino-India border remains the only major territorial dispute, other than South China Sea disputes, that China has not resolved. China's growing assertiveness in its territorial claims, especially on Arunachal Pradesh, and its relentless development of infrastructure in Tibet will shape the prospects of Sino-India relations.

The territory stretching from the jungles of northern Myanmar, westward to the Karakoram Range, and northward to the edge of the Tibetan plateau can be seen as a single geopolitical system referred to as the Himalayan-Tibetan massif. The ruggedness of this terrain makes movement of men and materiel extremely difficult, thus preventing Indian and Chinese civilizations from intermingling or projecting military power in these remote areas effectively. Not until 1962 did the Chinese and Indian armies fight each other over these desolate heights, thus altering the geopolitics of the region significantly.

Chinese President Hu Jintao met with Indian Prime Minister Manmohan Singh in Sanya City, south China's Hainan Province, April 13, 2011. Hu said China is willing to further push forward negotiations on border issues on the basis of peace and friendliness, equal consultation, mutual respect and understanding. The two sides should consider setting up a consultation and coordination mechanism on border issues so as to achieve consensus as soon as possible and to better maintain peace and stability at the border regions before the issues are solved.

China wants India to put behind the 1962 war as an "unfortunate" thing of the past and that the two countries should strengthen their military ties including formalising a border management pact under which their troops will not fire at each other. The Chinese assessment was conveyed to the Indian defence ministry team which visited Beijing on 14-15 January 2013 for the third round of the annual defense dialogue between the two countries.

Border tensions between China and India flared after New Delhi claimed a contingent of 30 to 50 PLA soldiers crossed about 12 miles beyond the Line of Actual Control between the two countries on 15 April 2012 and stayed there for three weeks. According to New Delhi, PLA soldiers frequently conduct border incursions (more than 600 times over the last three years) but do not usually cross more than a few miles over the Line of Actual Control nor stay there longer than several hours.

Beijing denied Chinese troops had crossed into Indian territory. A Chinese Ministry of Foreign Affairs spokesperson said, "China has always acted in strict compliance with relevant agreements and protocols between the two countries on maintaining peace and tranquility in the Line of Actual Control area along the border... Chinese patrol troops have never crossed the line." Chinese Premier Li Keqiang attempted to downplay the incident and the risk of conflict. During a state visit to India, he insisted that "a few clouds in the sky cannot shut out the brilliant rays of our friendship." Premier Li did not directly address the alleged Chinese incursion, though he said "both sides believe we need to improve various border-related mechanisms that we have put into place and make them more efficient, and we need to appropriately manage and resolve our differences."

President Xi Jinping met Indian Prime Minister Manmohan Singh at the BRICS Summit in Durban, South Africa, 29 March 2013. Xi urged both sides to use special representatives to strive for a fair, rational framework that can lead to a solution to the border issue as soon as possible. India will abide by political guidelines set by both sides and seek a solution to the border issue with a commitment to safeguarding peace, Singh said. Since 2003, more than a dozen rounds of talks had been launched to resolve the border disputes. But ties have still been occasionally strained by the issue and overshadowed by closer India-US relations amid Washington's accelerating Asia "pivot" policy.

Beijing and New Delhi resolved the April border impasse in May after a series of talks and agreed to pursue a formal agreement to build trust and confidence between the border troops. The two sides signed the agreement during the Indian prime minister's trip to China in October 2013. China and India concluded a border defense cooperation pact 24 October 2013, making it a highlight of Indian Prime Minister Manmohan Singh's visit to the Asian neighbor. The Indian Express newspaper said the pact also puts no restrictions on India developing border infrastructure or enhancing military capabilities along the border. It quoted India's Ambassador to China S. Jai Shanker as saying: "This principle allows both countries to take appropriate measures according to their own security needs."

Nevertheless, the potential for periodic low-level confrontations between border patrols to escalate likely will persist. Indian media have reported several additional albeit briefer incursions by Chinese troops since the April standoff. Furthermore, both China and India continue to boost their militaries' capabilities on the border, adding to mutual suspicion. This has left both sides sensitive to each other's border activities and disposed toward worst-case perceptions of the other sides' intentions and activities. Ely Ratner and Alexander Sullivan of the Center for a New American Security, warn: ''more intense strategic competition between India and China would reverberate throughout the continent, exacerbating tensions in Central Asia, the Indian Ocean, and Southeast Asia. Disruptions to the Asian engine of economic growth caused by these tensions could debilitate the global economy.''

CHINA'S CLAIM TO TIBET IS FACTOR IN BORDER DISPUTE

This is perhaps the most militarized Buddhist enclave in the world. Perched above 10,000 feet in the icy reaches of the eastern Himalayas, the town of Tawang is not only home to one of Tibetan Buddhism's most sacred monasteries but also the site of a massive Indian military buildup. Convoys of army trucks haul howitzers along rutted mountain roads. Soldiers drill in muddy fields. Military bases appear every half-mile in the countryside, with watchtowers rising behind concertina wire.

A road sign on the northern edge of town helps explain the reason for all the fear and the fury: The border with China is just 23 miles away; Lhasa, the Tibetan capital, 316 miles; and Beijing 2,676 miles. "The Chinese army has a big deployment at the border, at Bumla," said Madan Singh, a junior commissioned officer who sat with a half-dozen soldiers one afternoon sipping tea beside a fog-cloaked road. "That's why we're here." Though little known to the outside world, Tawang is a flashpoint in relations between the world's two most populous nations. It is the focus of China's most delicate land-border dispute, a conflict rooted in Chinese claims of sovereignty over all of historical Tibet.

In recent months, both countries have stepped up efforts to secure their rights over this rugged patch of land. China tried to block a $2.9 billion loan to India from the Asian Development Bank on the grounds that part of the loan was slated for water projects in Arunachal Pradesh, the state that includes Tawang. It was the first time China had sought to influence the territorial dispute through a multilateral institution. Then an Indian general announced that the Indian military was deploying extra troops and fighter jets in the area. The growing belligerence has soured relations between the two Asian giants and has prompted one Indian military leader to declare that China has replaced Pakistan as India's biggest threat.

Economic progress might be expected to bring the countries closer. China and India did $52 billion of trade last year, a 34 percent increase over 2007. But businesspeople say that border tensions have infused official deliberations over business deals, dampening the willingness of Chinese and Indian companies to invest in each other's countries. "Officials start taking more time, scrutinizing things more carefully, and all that means more delays and ultimately more denials," said Ravi Bhoothalingam, a former president of the Oberoi Group, the luxury hotel chain, and a member of the Institute of Chinese Studies in New Delhi. "That's not good for business."

The roots of the conflict go back to China's territorial claims to Tibet. Not only does the Dalai Lama, the exiled spiritual leader of the Tibetans, live in the foothills of the western Himalayas with the blessing of the Indian government, but China insists that this swath of northeast India has historically been part of Tibet, and thus should be part of China. Tawang is a thickly forested area of white stupas and steep, terraced hillsides that is home to the ethnic Monpa people, who practice Tibetan Buddhism, speak a language similar to Tibetan and once paid tribute to rulers in Lhasa. The 6th Dalai Lama was born here in the 17th century.

The Chinese army occupied Tawang briefly in 1962, during a war with India fought over this and other territories along the 2,521-mile border. More than 3,100 Indian soldiers and 700 Chinese soldiers were killed and thousands wounded in the border war. War memorials highlighting China's aggressions in Tawang here are big draws for Indian tourists. "The entire border is disputed," said Ma Jiali, an India scholar at the China Institutes of Contemporary International Relations, a government-supported think tank in Beijing. "This problem hasn't been solved, and it's a huge barrier to China-India relations."

In some ways, Tawang has become a proxy battleground, too, between China and the Dalai Lama, who passed through this valley when he fled into exile in 1959. From his home in the distant hill town of Dharamsala, he wields enormous influence over Tawang. He appoints the abbot of the powerful monastery and gives financial support to institutions throughout the area. Last year, the Dalai Lama announced for the first time that Tawang is a part of India, bolstering the Indian government's territorial claims and infuriating China.

Traditional Tibetan culture runs strong in Tawang. At the Tawang monastery, an important centre of Tibetan learning, monks express apprehension about China's rule over Tibet, which the Chinese army seized in 1951. "I hate the Chinese government," said Gombu Tsering, 70, a senior monk who watches over the monastery's museum. "Tibet wasn't even a part of China. Lhasa wasn't a part of China." Few expect China to try to forcefully annex Tawang, but military skirmishes are a real danger, analysts say. The Indian military recorded 270 border violations and nearly 2,300 instances of "aggressive border patrolling" by Chinese soldiers last year, said Brahma Chellaney, a professor of strategic studies at the Centre for Policy Research, a research organization in New Delhi. Mr. Chellaney has advised the Indian government's National Security Council.

"The India-China frontier has become more 'hot' than the India-Pakistan border," he said in an e-mail. China has grown increasingly hostile to the Dalai Lama after a severe outbreak of ethnic unrest in Tibet. This year, it turned its diplomatic guns on India. China moved in March to block a $2.9 billion loan to India from the Asian Development Bank, a multi-nation group based in Manila that has China on its board, because $60 million of the loan had been earmarked for flood-control projects in Arunachal Pradesh, the state that includes Tawang. The loan was approved in mid-June over China's heated objections.

Weeks after China first tried to block the loan, the chief of the Indian air force, now retired, told a prominent Indian newspaper that China posed a greater threat than Pakistan. Another official, J.J. Singh, the governor of Arunachal Pradesh and retired chief of the Indian army, said the next month that the Indian military was adding two divisions of troops, totalling 50,000 to 60,000 soldiers, to the border region over the next several years. Four Sukhoi fighter jets were immediately deployed to a nearby air base. Since 2005, when Chinese Prime Minister Wen Jiabao visited India, the two countries have gone through 13 rounds of bilateral negotiations over the issue. A last round was just held last month, with no results. Though China has actually resolved many of its border disputes in recent years, India remains a glaring exception.

The Government of Tibet in Exile

From July 20 to 23, 1994, Beijing staged the Third Forum on Work in Tibet which recommended the total destruction of an entire civilization flourishing on the Tibetan Plateau for thousands of years. This cultural "empire" once encompassed far-flung areas like Buryatia, Tuva and Kalmykia in Russia; Mongolia; Laddakh, Lahaul-Spiti, Sikkim, and Arunachal Pradesh in India; Mustang, Dolpo and Solo Khumbu in Nepal; Bhutan and parts of western China.

The policy formulated in 1994 in Beijing-and these days pursued with Cultural Revolutionary zeal in Tibet-will mean the annihilation of the spiritual homeland of this shared culture. Implementation of the Third Work Forum is thus having a crippling impact on the traditional culture of millions of non-Tibetans as the well-spring of their cultural inspiration is forcibly drained and there is nothing to replenish the continuous growth and development of this distinct and highly evolved civilization.

Losing Hearts and Minds

The decisions made at the Third Forum rest on two fundamental conclusions which Beijing drew. It realized it was losing out in two vital fields-ideology and propaganda. For a state whose existence is justified by its ideological superiority and the power of its propaganda to shape the thinking of the masses, the implications of this for the future was at best uncertain, at worst dangerous. Beijing concluded it was losing the ideological war because, despite the unrelenting assault on Tibetan Buddhism, Tibetans were as devoted to their traditional beliefs as ever. Beijing has succeeded in physically enslaving the country but it has not won over the hearts, minds and loyalty of the Tibetan populace.

Communist ideology, enforced by the military might of China, had failed to dent the heart of Buddhism. Added to this was the communist authorities' total bafflement at the non-violent policy underpinning the Middle Way Approach advocated by His Holiness the Dalai Lama to resolve the issue of Tibet's future status. For a regime which is based on Mao's dictum that political power grows out of the barrel of a gun, this supposedly eccentric philosophy which says victory lies in capturing the hearts and minds of people by the power of ideas rather than killing by the power of the gun comes as a bolt from the blue. Much of Beijing's knee-jerk reaction to, and its bafflement at, His Holiness the Dalai Lama's new policy of rapprochement lies at the heart of its new hardline policy.

Beijing considered it was losing the propaganda war because, for one reason or the other, the world's media and its pop culture considered-at least for the moment-Tibet and Tibetan Buddhism their very own cuddly pandas. Despite its financial might China found it extremely difficult to exterminate this image of Tibet and get its voice heard on the Tibetan issue in the court of the international media. In order to address these weaknesses the Third Forum concentrated on two issues. One was to focus on Tibet's economic development in the hope that this would keep

Tibetan demonstrations off the streets. This was tantamount to bribing the Tibetans with promises of riches to come if they toed the party line. The other concern was to win the coming and new generations of Tibetans over to the Chinese viewpoint.

Beijing has given up on the present generation of Tibetans as a lost cause. If the coming generations of Tibetans were also lost to the 'Dalai Clique' this, the Chinese concluded, would have dangerous consequences for Chinese rule in Tibet. The 15-year-old Gyalwa Karmapa's dramatic escape from Tibet in January 2000 was a warning to the Beijing authorities of the erosion of loyalty to China. The Karmapa's flight, and the earlier escape of Agya Rinpoche, the abbot of Kumbum Monastery, came as a huge embarrassment for China, because retaining these high lamas gave China a degree of legitimacy for its rule in Tibet. This is the reason why Beijing is enforcing with greater strictness its 1993 instruction of recalling young Tibetans studying in schools and monasteries run by Dharmasala in India. This is also the rationale for Beijing closing down schools in Tibet which are privately run by Tibetans.

For these reasons Tibet today is in the throes of a second Cultural Revolution as the Chinese authorities step up their long-term strategy to exterminate Tibet's distinct cultural and ethnic identity. The authorities are pursuing a four-pronged strategy to achieve their final objective. They have stepped up repression while employing their huge propaganda machine to paint a rosy picture of Tibet. They have quickened the pace of economic development to dampen Tibetan nationalism and are simultaneously moving more Chinese settlers onto the Tibetan Plateau to change Tibet's demographic composition and to ease social unrest because of mounting unemployment back in China.

The Third Work Forum on Tibet was convened by the top Chinese leadership and was presided over by President Jiang Zemin. The authorities have now enshrined this Work Forum as the most "important strategic policy to rejuvenate Tibet" and have hailed its directives as the new manifesto for party work on the plateau. The significance of the Third Work Forum lies in the fact that it overturned the more liberal policies laid out for Tibet's "development" by the First and Second Work Forums held in 1980 and 1984. The first two work forums were initiated by the late Hu Yaobang, then Secretary General of the Chinese Communist Party.

This liberal and somewhat maverick leader is credited with masterminding a series of measures to improve the social, economic and political conditions in Tibet. The brief spell of liberalization markedly improved the living conditions of the majority of Tibetans and contributed to a more relaxed intellectual and social climate.

The Third Work Forum reversed these policies and reinstated hardline measures under which Tibet is still reeling today. The Tibetans in Tibet perceive the current repressive policies as a second Cultural Revolution. The question is why did China choose to jettison its earlier more liberal policies and adopt a manifesto which is leading to the systematic destruction of Tibet's distinct culture. The answer lies in domestic and international events which forced China to formulate a series of hardline policies on Tibet which eventually crystallized into the Third Work Forum for Tibet. The world which confronted China in the late 1980s and early 1990s was a frightening one.

Starting from 1987, Tibet was rocked by a string of protest demonstrations, which called for Tibetan independence. One of the largest demonstrations which erupted on March 5, 1989 in Lhasa, forced the authorities to impose martial law on the city. These demonstrations are now seen to have been an inspiration behind the outburst of Chinese students' pro-democracy uprisings. The authorities saw the series of Tiananmen Square demonstrations as a sign of their Central Government losing control, and in an attempt to regain supremacy, the authorities slaughtered-perhaps hundreds if not thousands of students on June 4, 1989. These demonstrations were a chilling replay to the authorities of the May 4, 1919 student demonstrations in Beijing which signalled a political and cultural awakening across the erstwhile Middle Kingdom.

Bejing's fears of losing control were exacerbated by external events which saw the unraveling of the communist world. The Solidarity Movement in Poland, the fall of the Berlin Wall, and the implosion of the Soviet Union fed Beijing's paranoia over threats to the Chinese Communist Party hold on power. Official China's fears were further inflamed by the rapidly changing attitude of the broad masses as they turned back from communism to traditional beliefs like Confucionism, Buddhism, Islam, Christianity and indigenous folk cults. In the eyes of ordinary citizens communism was becoming totally discredited and this, more than anything else, was the biggest nightmare for China's leadership. The leadership's justification for staying in power was being disavowed by the masses. For a one-party dictatorship this historically indicates the first step along the slippery road to dissolution and removal of power.

For these reasons the Chinese leadership then reverted to its earlier view that traditional beliefs were its real enemy. In competing with Buddhism, Confucionism, Islam, Christianity and other isms, communism was losing out in terms of its ability to retain the loyalty and allegiance of the masses. The leadership revived the old aphorisms once served up to the Tibetan people to justify their policies to destroy Tibetan Buddhism during the Cultural Revolution. Bewildered Tibetans were then told that just as there cannot be two suns in the sky, so there cannot be both Buddhism and socialism in Tibet. Inevitably Buddhism then had to give way to socialism. And again, today, religion is being blatantly sublimated to Chinese state power.

These were the fears of the Chinese leaders when they met in Beijing in 1994 to hammer out their new Tibet initiatives. For the Chinese authorities Tibet is an especially sensitive issue because of their conviction that hostile Western forces are using the issue of Tibet to "westernize" China and to lead to its territorial fragmentation. The third generation Chinese leaders came to the conclusion that stability in Tibet was vital to the stability of China as a whole. Earlier, Tibet was merely of peripheral concern to the vital interests of China's sprawling communist empire. Now, with the Third Work Forum, the authorities were saying, "We must clearly understand that we must do our work in Tibet not only for the sake our of own region's stability and development, not only for the interests of our people, but also for the sake of the whole nation's stability and development."

In Tibet, China faced peculiar problems because of the inherent strength of Tibetan Buddhism and the depth of devotion of the populace to His Holiness the Dalai Lama. The sustained burst of religious revival that followed in the wake of the brief spell of liberalization in Tibet confirmed the leadership's worst fears that decades of concerted assault on Tibetan culture and religion had not extinguished the people's traditional beliefs and values. From merely nuisance value, the Chinese leadership now viewed Tibetan Buddhism as a very real and imminent threat to the stability of Chinese rule in Tibet.

At the same time the Chinese leadership's attitude towards His Holiness the Dalai Lama changed. From being an uncertain ally in the peace process in Tibet, the current Chinese leadership now saw him as a full-blown "enemy". A top-level conclave held in Beijing on March 10, 1993 concluded that, "There are different factions within the Dalai Clique; they are, however, unanimous in their political nature and position. They differ from each other in ideological viewpoints and ways of expressing them. Different strategies must be adopted to use their differences, to deal with them differently in order to divide and destroy them."

Repeated statements by high-level officials describe the struggle against "splittism", the official term for Tibetan independence, as a "life-and-death struggle". At the 1994 annual meeting of the "TAR" Communist Party Committee to brief members on the policy thrust of the Third Work Forum on Tibet, Raidi, deputy Secretary of the Committee said, "Up to now, his (the Dalai Lama's) standpoint on Tibet's independence has never changed, and we must reveal his double-faced true colour. The focal point in our region in the struggle against splittism is to oppose the Dalai Clique. As the saying goes, to kill a serpent, one must first cut off its head."

In short, the Third Work Forum decided that Beijing was in a position to solve the Tibet issue without the Dalai Lama's involvement. It abandoned the earlier liberal policy of including His Holiness the Dalai Lama in any future settlement of Tibet's status. His Holiness the Dalai Lama was clearly singled out as the cause of China's "Tibet problem".

The Third Work Forum also abandoned the policy of granting concessions to Tibet because of the plateau's "special characteristics". This policy had been the cornerstone of recommendations made by the First and Second Tibet Work Forums.

To carry out its new hardline policies in Tibet, Beijing appointed Chen Kuiyuan as the "TAR" Party Secretary in 1992. Chen Kuiyuan's appointment is significant because he had a track record for being a tough and ruthless administrator. He had already served as the First Secretary of the Chinese Communist Party in Inner Mongolia and is credited with repressing the rebellious Mongols, many of whom refer to him as "the butcher". Chen Kuiyuan was especially recommended to the post by Hu Jintao, the current Vice-President of China, who was then the First Secretary of the Chinese Communist Party in Tibet.

Tackling Tibetan Nationalism

The Third Work Forum policies chalked out for Tibet contained four key elements. China stepped up the scale of repression in Tibet. External propaganda work was escalated. The pace of economic development in Tibet-and its corollary of encouraging more Chinese settlers and businessmen to take advantage of the economic boom on the "roof of the world"-was also increased. In short, Beijing had decided to tackle Tibetan nationalism head-on and observers are still assessing the consequences on both Chinese rule in Tibet and on the populace.

Beijing remains convinced that these key components of its current policy will stabilize Chinese rule over Tibet and solve once and for all, the vexed problem of its negative image over the way Tibet has been handled. One main target of the current policy of repression is Tibetan Buddhism. Chinese leaders are increasingly alarmed by the proliferation of monasteries and temples which the period of liberalization spawned throughout Tibet: they are seen as the bastions of Tibetan nationalism. The authorities have set up "Democratic Management Committees" to control monasteries and nunneries and created "Work Inspection Teams" to supervise the "education" of monks and nuns.

A major thrust is underway to break the bond of loyalty between the clergy in Tibet and His Holiness the Dalai Lama in India. Campaigns like "Strike Hard" and "Patriotic Re-education", unleashed in 1996, are aimed at crippling the rise of Tibetan Buddhism which the authorities suspect is weaning the loyalty of the Tibetan people away from the communist party and towards His Holiness the Dalai Lama. One salient feature of the "Strike Hard" campaign is how differently it is interpreted in China and Tibet. China's "Strike Hard" campaign was started to weed out corruption. Tibet's version is used as a political tool to eliminate those whom the authorities label "splittists". In Tibet, rather than striking at corruption, the authorities turn a blind eye to this social disease in the hope that it will erode the traditional morality of Tibetans and undermine Tibetan Buddhism.

In fact, at a secret meeting held in December 1999 in Chengdu, capital of Sichuan province, Chen Kuiyuan, the hardline Party Secretary of "TAR" recommended to the Central Chinese Government that an all-out effort must be made to eradicate Tibetan Buddhism and culture from the face of the earth so that no memory of them will be left in the minds of coming generations of Tibetans-except as museum pieces.

Chen Kuiyuan stated that the main cause of instability is the existence of the Dalai Lama and his Government-in-Exile in Dharamsala and these must be "uprooted". He recommended that Tibet, Tibetan people and Tibetan Buddhism-in other words the very name of Tibet-must be destroyed and the "Tibet Autonomous Region" be merged with provinces like Sichuan. While treating Tibetans to boot-heel subjugation at home, internationally China was on an overdrive propaganda blitz. At a brainstorming conclave held on March 10, 1993, Zeng Jian-hui, Vice-Minister of the Propaganda Ministry, told participants, "The propaganda work on the question of Tibet is one of the focal points of the entire external propaganda work...With regard to attacks by the West and the Dalai Clique and their frequent activities, our external propaganda should launch offensive. We should expand our spheres of influence; in particular, we should infiltrate our propaganda into the mainstream life of the West.

"Firstly we should continue to send Tibetan scholars and Tibetan singing and dancing troupes abroad to lecture and perform. Secondly, relevant embassies and consulates should aim at the public opinion and the activities of the Dalai Clique in the countries where they are stationed and utilize speeches, picture exhibitions, special articles and other forms to carry out propaganda work, so as to win over officials and people of those countries... We should reinforce the work of utilizing the power of foreign propaganda. A few years ago, in the light of the situation of that time, we made arrangements for foreign journalists to visit Tibet."

The September 3, 2000 edition of *People's Daily* carried a story headlined "Tibet Welcomes Foreign Journalists for Objective Reporting". It stated that "A senior Tibetan official said Sunday that Tibet welcomes foreign journalists to come for objective and just reporting, but not those who take distorted views. Raidi, Deputy Secretary of the Tibet Autonomous Regional Committee of the Communist Party of China and Chairman of the Standing Committee of the Tibetan Autonomous Regional People's Congress, made the remarks at a meeting here with a press delegation of Thailand." In this context, it is interesting to note that N. Ram, the editor of India's *Frontline* magazine, devoted 36 pages of the September 15, 2000 issue to promote the Chinese line and recommended that the Indian Government expel the Central Tibetan Administration from Indian soil for being the main stumbling block to normal relations between India and China. It is difficult to assess to what extent the views contained in his stupendous reporting marathon are his own.

These editorial outbursts are in line with policy decisions outlined in the early nineties. During a two-day secret conclave in March 1993 in Chengdu, Vice-Minister Zeng Jian-hui, told participants, "All foreigners that we entertain and send to Tibet must have a relatively objective opinion of Tibet. We should use people from abroad to carry out the propaganda on Tibet for us, which is more powerful than if we do it."

Along with its external public relations strategy, China is presently carrying out a potentially much more dangerous policy of speeding up the pace of Tibet's economic development and its related drive to bring more Chinese settlers onto the Tibetan Plateau. Beijing's Western China Development Programme, which incorporates Tibet in its ambit, is devised to shift the focus of China's economic activities from Coastal China to the interior-both to narrow the imbalance in the level of economic development between the two regions and to ease population pressure on the coastal areas which attract millions of migrant workers. The focus of Beijing's Western China Economic Development Programme in Tibet is to exploit the plateau's still untapped minerals and other natural resources and to upgrade Tibet's infrastructure-like roads and telecommunications-to facilitate transportation of these resources to China. The other purpose of the heightened level of economic activity is to divert the Tibetans' attention from their political fate to focus on their livelihood-thus undermining Tibetan nationalism. The Chinese authorities aim to manipulate the situation in Tibet still further by bringing in more Chinese settlers who would then demographically cement Chinese rule once and for all. These current hardline policies and their implementation in Tibet are impacting the stalled Sino-Tibetan Dialogue and will vitally affect the ability of Tibetans to survive as a distinct people and culture.

Beijing's Flawed Perceptions

The basic flaws in China's new policy in its search to resolve the problem of Tibet is thinking the solution can exclude the involvement of His Holiness the Dalai Lama. The other is in attempting to solve the problem over the heads of Tibet's citizens.

These two fundamental mistakes will exacerbate China's Tibet problem, not solve it. The reason lies in the history of Tibet and in the sentiments of the people. The institution of the Dalai Lamas of Tibet is more than 600 years old, if we start from the birth of the first Dalai Lama in 1391. In the course of its growth and development, the very institution itself came to symbolize fundamental beliefs and the political destiny of the nation. The bond between the Dalai Lamas and the Tibetan people is fundamental and unbreakable; any attempt, however sustained, will never succeed in driving a wedge between the two.

Consequently, China's current policy of forcing Tibetans-especially monks and nuns-to denounce His Holiness the Dalai Lama and pledge loyalty to the Chinese Communist Party will prove counterproductive. In view of this the Third Work Forum's basic assumption that in the case of Tibet time is on the side of China, and that Beijing can stall the problem of Tibet till the demise of the present Dalai Lama whereupon the issue of Tibet will solve itself, is fatally flawed-based as it is on a mistaken perception of the role played by the institution of the Dalai Lamas in the development of Tibetan history.

This assumption, if not reviewed, revised and abandoned, will prove catastrophic for the Chinese leadership and for those who chose to turn their whimsical personal analysis into state policy. The reason is simple. The Chinese Communist Party was founded in the 1920s and came to power in 1949. Within this short span of time the masses have lost faith in communist ideology, and members of the party these days pay mere lip service to the ideological justifications of the party. Conversely, the institution of the Dalai Lamas as a political force is more than 300 years old. These days the Dalai Lama is recognized by Tibetans throughout the world as the heart of Tibetan nationalism. How can a party which has lost its soul outlast an institution which symbolizes the very soul of a people? For these reasons it is imperative for China to review and re-assess its current hardline stance towards Tibet. China must re-start its stalled peace process over Tibet and consider His Holiness the Dalai Lama as a vital and active partner in the procedures. If China does this it will have won a powerful ally and companion along the road to peace, stability and continued prosperity.

4

Border Conflict an Obstacle to Building Trust between China and India

The then Indian chargé d'affaires Brajesh Mishra couldn't believe his ears at Chairman Mao Zedong's cue as they shook hands at a May Day parade on the Tiananmen rostrum in 1970. The wounds of the 1962 border war, in which India suffered a humiliating defeat, were still raw. Pointedly, Mishra was placed at the end of the line-up of diplomats arranged in order of precedence to meet Mao - after the British chargé d'affaires - making the gesture all the more dramatic.

Mishra immediately saw the opening Mao was creating for ties to resume, and was relieved it meshed with his own brief. Before he left for Beijing, then prime minister Indira Gandhi had laid it out for him in one sentence: "I am in a box so far as relations with China are concerned, and I want us to get out of that box." Despite this common yearning for détente, China and India would soon drift further apart - this time over the Bangladesh liberation war in 1971. While India backed the Bengali freedom fighters, Beijing threw its lot behind its "all-weather friend" Islamabad - a relationship that would dog Sino-Indian relations for decades. It wasn't until the 1990s that China and India would finally start a structured process of normalising ties. Economic relations have since gone from strength to strength, with China now India's largest trading partner. But as the recent three-week Himalayan stand-off brought home, the undercurrent of animosity still runs deep, and the possibility of unfriending each other all over again is never far away.

Arcing a curious trajectory, India and China's modern history would easily qualify for an "it's complicated" relationship status: active courting, followed by demonstrative friendship, violent break-up and now cautious reconciliation. It is this pull of a volatile past and the prospect of profitable cohabitation that Premier Li Keqiang will negotiate as he starts his India visit on Sunday. Li has already had a foretaste of the job at hand. His goodwill gesture of picking India as his first foreign destination on assuming power almost came undone with last month's border crisis. Even though both sides agreed to stand down, the episode will continue to hang heavy when Li lands in New Delhi.

According to Neville Maxwell, author of the seminal *India's China War*, such run-ins are natural as history shows an undefined border acts as a running sore between even the least bellicose of neighbours and can quickly turn malignant. "However much the neighbours may try to develop cordial relations in other aspects, the territorial dispute lurks in the background, making full trust unattainable," he says. Not that the "other aspects", notably economic engagement, are insignificant. Chinese goods have flooded Indian markets and Indian companies routinely raise yuan debt from Chinese banks. As the two sides have set a goal of US$100 billion trade by 2015, Li's visit is likely to see a raft of billion-dollar deals, with the attendant fanfare and boilerplate diplomatese on "strategic partnership".

But Professor Ma Jiali, executive deputy director of the Strategy Study Centre at the Beijing think tank China Reform Forum, points out: "The border dispute is the biggest obstacle to building strategic trust between China and India. It is directly related to the territorial sovereignty, core interests and national sentiment of the people of both countries." The dispute is over two separate territories, one in the western sector of the border and the other in the east. In the west, both China and India lay claim to 38,000 square kilometres of snowy wastelands known as Aksai Chin.

There is no demarcated border there, only a Line of Actual Control that fuzzily separates the territories controlled by them. And, each side has its own perception of where that line lies. It was in these icy heights that the recent stand-off took place. In the eastern sector, China claims some 90,000 square kilometres to the south of the McMahon Line, which was agreed to by Britain and Tibet in a secret deal in 1914 and not recognised by China. While China calls the region South Tibet, for India it is its Arunachal Pradesh state. The McMahon Line is the de facto border in this sector. Although China never accepted the McMahon Line, it was open to a land swap, under which India could keep what it claims on the eastern border while China would keep Aksai Chin in the west. Providing the best route into Tibet from the rest of China, Aksai Chin was non-negotiable for Beijing. For Delhi, both territories were off the table as inviolable flanks of national identity.

India and China have held 15 rounds of border talks at the special representative level since the mid-1990s but the gains have been limited. The border is remarkably well managed, with not a shot fired across it in over 20 years, but it's far from being settled, meaning the pre-1962 claims still hold for both sides. Half a century later, the border war today is seen largely as a dispute over land in the high mountains. But for a long time, India's first prime minister, Jawaharlal Nehru, who invested, and lost, substantial political capital in a policy of friendship with China (embodied in the early 1950s Indian slogan of *Hindi-Chini bhai bhai,* or India and China are brothers), would describe Aksai Chin as a place "where not a blade of grass grows".

And, in the course of the 1962 war, Chinese troops swept towards the plains as Indian forces retreated. Rather than holding on to their gains, China called a ceasefire and the troops returned to their old positions. Land was not the only thing the war was about. Far deeper factors were at play. The war coincided with the Sino-Soviet split. Declassified documents show Soviet leader Nikita Krushchev's irritation with China's handling of the border tension, and the Chinese leadership's anger at the Soviet backing of Nehru. For China, showing India its place was also a loaded message for the Soviet Union.

In India, Nehru was being squeezed between a rising left movement and the ascent of the right. In China, Mao was trying to reassert power within the party as the voices against the Great Leap Forward grew louder. And then there was Tibet. Nehru, while accepting China's sovereignty over Tibet, sought greater autonomy for it to act as a buffer between the two Asian giants. For him, Sino-Indian friendship was the cornerstone of Asia's rise, and for the relationship to work, China and India needed some space. Tibet would give them that space and guarantee the two armies would never come face to face. But for China, as Ma puts it, Tibet is a "core national interest". It is just as central to China's national pride as the border lands are for India's, with or without grass.

Dibyesh Anand, an associate professor at London's Westminster University, says: "There is a nationalist-security dissonance at the heart of how China and India approach Tibet and the border dispute. For China, Tibet is a nationalist issue and the border is a strategic issue, while for India, Tibet is a strategic issue and the border is a nationalist issue. The difference is, you can bargain over a strategic issue but not over a nationalist one." In *Protracted Contest: Sino-Indian Rivalry in the Twentieth Century*, sinologist John Garver notes the "brief period of Sino-India friendship from 1954 to 1958 coincided with a limited but genuine degree of Tibetan autonomy". India interpreted a 1954 pact signed with China on Tibetan border trade as an implicit guarantee of Tibet's relative autonomy while China read it as India's promise to keep its hands off Tibet. The honeymoon ended when they started blaming each other for breaking the deal.

Things came to a head when the Dalai Lama fled to India following the Lhasa revolt of March 1959. China was furious that India provided him refuge and allowed him to set up a government-in-exile. Nehru was peeved that China wasn't cutting him any slack on Tibet, weakening his position at home. Mao was convinced India was colluding with the Americans to incite Tibetan refugees and India started patrolling the far-flung borders more aggressively under a "forward policy". From there on, war was but a matter of time. Many of the anxieties of 1962 linger. China still feels encircled by hostile powers and is as insecure over Tibet. "India uses the special status of Dalai to allow Tibetan refugees to launch separatist activities for creating trouble to resolve the border problem in the future. Indian politicians also interact with officials of the government-in-exile and Dalai," complains Ma. But Professor Susan Shirk, author of *China: Fragile Superpower*, believes that for the Chinese, it should be possible to shelve the territorial dispute. "This is because the media and the nationalist public don't pay much attention to it," says Shirk.

China sees India as one of the possible sources of trouble. For India, China*is* the trouble. India's sense of betrayal, at what it sees as a sudden and unwarranted land grab by a trusted friend, has festered with time, with China's rise and its proximity to Pakistan only fuelling its own fears of encirclement. "Tibet and the border dispute can take them back to a 1962-like situation. Economic interdependence should not be seen as replacing political negotiation," warns Anand. Unless, of course, they find a way to live with their differences and yet profit from each other.

Mishra, the chargé d'affaires in Beijing who went on to become India's national security adviser, would later recall in *Across the Himalayan Gap* that during his stint in China, he would attend the regulation diplomatic banquets but never actually got to eat anything. This was because the speeches would start during the second course and since the Chinese hosts would invariably lay into India and praise Pakistan, Mishra and his wife would have to walk out in protest. This went on for a while until Mishra noticed the speeches weren't starting until after the cakes and ice cream came out. A Pakistani diplomat told him the Chinese had noticed the Mishras were missing out on the food and decided to hold the speeches until after dessert.

CURRENT SCENARIO: BORDER DEFENCE

With unity of command having been compromised, our border defence has been woefully inadequate. Reportedly, some 400 sq.km. of territory has been lost in Ladakh over and above the Aksai Chin. Responsibility of border defence is divided between the Ministry of Defence (MoD) and the Ministry of Home Affairs (MHA), with the Central Armed Police Force (CAPF) deployed in sensitive areas without placing them under the command of the Army. This facilitates smuggling of narcotics, fake currency, goods and even illegal immigration with indicators that some of these activities are institutionalised. Chinese goods are being smuggled into India also through the India-Myanmar border. Not only is the ULFA hierarchy located at Ruli on Chinese soil but China is also pumping in weapons and communication equipment through the Kachen rebels in Myanmar to the PLA in Manipur and onwards to the Maoists in India. Deployment of the Indo-Tibetan Border Police (ITBP) in sensitive areas of Ladakh without placing them under the command of the local Army formation is a folly that has been capitalised by the Chinese who have made deep intrusions without qualms.

Border Infrastructure

Despite the Border Road Organisation (BRO) being directly under the MoD, border infrastructure has been severely neglected. In February 2014, NDTV reported that out of the 26 border roads sanctioned in recent years, only one has been completed. China, on the other hand, has developed excellent infrastructure that permits quick mobilisation and vehicular movement. This includes construction of a ten-kilometre road in Pangong Tso area. In 1970, at Nathu La, the Chinese could ply a five-tonne vehicle vis-à-vis a one-tonne vehicle of ours. Today, over four decades later, the status remains the same. Lack of development of border infrastructure on the Indian side is the main reason why the Chinese could intrude freely and our security forces are unable to react effectively and in time.

Intrusions

Similar is the story with our poor response to Chinese intrusions. Criticism and shame had to be faced in wake of deep intrusions such as the one at Raki Nala in Depsang during April 2013 when even the MEA admitted that the intrusion was five to seven kilometres beyond the line of Chinese claim. It is a wonder how a 1.2 million strong army could permit 20 Chinese soldiers to sit 19 km deep inside Indian territory for 25 days. Ironically,

Chinese troops had reportedly intruded into the same area on earlier occasions albeit this time the media got wise.

Such intrusions have been occurring at many places along the LAC despite the 1993 India-China Agreement on Maintenance of Peace and Tranquility Along the Line of Actual Control in the India-China Border Areas, Agreement on Confidence Building Measures in the Military Field Along the Line of Actual Control in the India-China Border Areas, 2005 Protocol on Modalities for the Implementation of Confidence Building Measures in the Military Field Along the Line of Actual Control in India-China Border Areas, and the 2012 Agreement on Establishment of a Working Mechanism for Consultation and Coordination on India-China Border Affairs.

Now, even after signing the China-drafted Border Defence Cooperation Agreement (BDCA) in 2013, the Chinese intruded into Depsang and Chumar on December 19 and 20. Then, in the first week of January 2014, intrusions took place in the Takdip area where incursions had been spotted in December 2013 as well. Now, China has proposed a Code of Conduct to be introduced along the border. Obviously China wants to play at signing agreement after agreement without changing her aggressive stance. Chinese occupation of the Depsang plains in conjunction with her presence in Gilgit-Baltisatn would threaten India's deployments in Siachen and sever the approach to Karakoram Pass. India has also lost substantial territory in the India-China-Myanmar tri-juncture area; China is also staking claims to the Tatu Bowl, loss of which would enable the Chinese to easily roll down the plains. POK is already a strategic objective of China that provides her access to the warm waters of the Indian Ocean, to Afghanistan and the CARs.

Prospects of Conflict

Much has been talked of about the possibilities of future Sino-Indian conflict from the Chinese gameplan to place India in the vice-like grip of a python to gobble up what the former wants, active defence to short swift offensive even using tactical nuclear weapons to force India to surrender territory, acupuncture warfare and the like. China's 'active defence' doctrine is a transformation from Mao's large scale people's land-centric war to high intensity, short duration localised war under informationised conditions. In this context, the chances of conflict remain.

Despite the progressing economic relations, China's focus in the Indian Ocean Region (IOR) remains a cause for concern. China has been making every possible effort to find her way to the Indian Ocean through Myanmar and Pakistan along the land routes. Her strategic interests clash with the US and her allies in the Asia-Pacific; China desperately needs another oceanic front and a strong India is hardly to her liking. Besides, for Chinese Carrier Battle Groups (CBGs) to operate effectively in the IOR, China needs land-based air and missile support. This is one reason why China is deploying missiles in the Gilgit-Baltistan area of Pakistan and developing or planning to develop ports in countries such as Myanmar, Thailand, Bangladesh, Pakistan, Maldives, Sri Lanka and Seychelles in the IOR. Not only has China colluded with Pakistan on a conventional and nuclear front but also in the sub-conventional field by waging a collusive asymmetric war against India including through irregular forces and proxies. With China's aggression on the rise, the collusive China-Pakistan threat has multiplied exponentially with both countries following a policy of ambiguity, denial and deceit, what with repeated Chinese intrusions, claim to entire Arunachal Pradesh as "South Tibet" and now demanding a Code of Conduct for forward troops, indicating the futility of the recently signed Border Defence Cooperation Agreement (BDCA).

On balance, the prospects of Sino-Indian conflict remain. What appears certain is that China's aggressive stance and the initiation of conflict will be aimed at undermining India's status as a regional power. If India fails to respond adequately, she will be projected as a 'Soft State' susceptible to coercion. Simultaneously, the Chinese aim would be to keep India embroiled in fighting internal/regional conflicts. In doing so, China maybe expected to virtually abrogate any agreements such as Border Peace and Tranquility Agreement and Confidence Building Measures and BDCA leading to incremental build up and conflict.

Should the US get more involved in the Middle East or in new and likely hotspots such as Ukraine and the CAR, Chinese adventurism in India can be expected to escalate. The US may have announced the Asia Pivot in recent months but China already has in place a globally deployable military force with nuclear/non-nuclear allies/proxies in North Korea, Pakistan, Iran, Libya, Sudan and Syria as a countermeasure even if one discounts China not resorting to the employment of large scale nuclear force.

GLOBAL VARIABLES LEADING TO CONFLICT: CHINA

The systemic level variables motivating China towards conflict, like in India, revolved around Chinese national interests, the system's influence on Chinese behaviour through structural constraints, and the role of anarchy in the system. Because of the anarchic structure of the international system, China is no different than India and state security must be its prime end. China's membership in the communist bloc does not grant it any guarantee of protection, and therefore its national interests are calculated in ways of maximizing national security. As such we shall discuss the three main interests affected by the border dispute with India.

As in India's case, the delineation of official borders for the PRC was a prime interest in order to gain legitimacy in the international system. This legitimacy is rooted within the conventions of the Westphalian system, where borders are paramount as they define the extent of sovereignty and political self-determination. The PRC's inheritance of territory which was divided by Western imperialists had a strong legal and pragmatic interest in negotiating legitimate borders with its neighbours. The basis of Chinese territorial definition was on the extent of historical holdings, but the PRC had determined in 1950 to negotiate borders based off the alignments they had inherited. This meant that China would not bog itself down in unreasonable claims in Indochina or other areas of traditional imperial suzerainty. This mentality guided border settlement by peaceful means with Burma, Nepal, Pakistan, Afghanistan, Mongolia, Cambodia, and Laos. Peaceful settlement of the Sino-Indian border however, was not possible due to Indian unwillingness to negotiate based on the perceived legitimacy of the McMahon Line.

A second national interest challenged by the border dispute with India was the Chinese right to non-intervention of foreigners in their domestic affairs. This principle of domestic sanctity from outside interference is also one of the rights of states in the Westphalian system. Chinese security was undermined by India's role in manipulating domestic events in both Tibet and in Ladakh. The Indian military's establishment of forward posts and patrols of the Ladakh region, beginning in 1960, was direct interference in Chinese domestic areas. While it was true China did not have legal sovereignty over the Ladakh area due to its position south of the McMahon Line, that argument remains moot as international boundaries must be agreed upon at least bilaterally, and the PRC gave it no such recognition. Furthermore, Ladakh, and more importantly the Aksai-Chin plain was a strategically important tract of land connecting Xinjiang and Tibet.

Indian interference in Tibet after the 1959 uprising was also taken as a direct violation of domestic sanctity, and a challenge to Chinese security and interests. The PRC became aware of Indian efforts to covertly aid the Dalai Lama and Tibetan separatists shortly after the PLA moved in to suppress the uprising. In fact, India had gone so far as to allow the CIA bases of operation along the border for a covert campaign in Tibet from 1957 to 1961. Furthermore, a series of four Indian military bases were constructed and manned in Tibet north of the McMahon Line. These actions illustrated India's desire to keep Tibet as a buffer state, and recognize Chinese suzerainty instead of sovereignty in the region, thus directly challenging China's security.

The Chinese interest of maintaining a secure, border with India was also threatened by the border dispute. Reinforcement of Tibet after 1959, the Aksai-Chin road way, and Chinese military patrols of the border were an attempt to maintain their territorial integrity. This added military presence created a security dilemma for India, and they began building up and strengthening their own military capacity near contested areas. The adoption of a forward Indian military policy in 1960, coupled with Indian scouting patrols across the border and the construction of military posts around Ladakh and Tibet severely undermined Chinese border security.

This led to the PLA "digging in" around contested border areas and effectively militarizing the border.

China's response to the Indian military buildup as well as their covert programs in contested border areas was constrained by the structure of the international environment. A major constraining force on Chinese action was the geostrategic situation in Asia during the late 1950's. Beginning in 1950 with the Korean War, the major battles of the Cold War were fought in Asia in the West's effort to contain the communist bloc. The PRC had to contend with anti-Chinese forces in South Korea, a U.S. backed ROC in Taiwan, a U.S.-fortified Japan, and increasing U.S. involvement in Indochina by 1960. These numerous threats on China's Western front were significant, and severely limited their maneuverability in other areas of concern. Unbeknownst to the West, the PRC was increasingly unable to depend on the support of the communist bloc due to increasing belligerence from the U.S.S.R. on various diplomatic and territorial issues. The Soviets pressured the PRC to acknowledge Indian border claims, and Sino-Soviet relations strained under their own border issues.

Acknowledging the limiting effects of these security threats on Chinese military power, the PRC advocated a policy of peaceful border settlement. China used this policy to its advantage and scored a critical victory in neutralizing a potential Pakistani threat to their security interests by a warming of relations. The geostrategic environment in which the PRC found itself was one of being surrounded by a ring of hostile states. Indian diplomatic intransigence on border issues and known subversion in Tibet added another threat in that ring. Thus, the structure of the international environment drove the PRC to rely on diplomacy to achieve its interests against minor powers in order to preserve its military power for guarding its borders against larger threats. This situation explains a seemingly coincidental rapprochement in relations with Pakistan, India's arch-rival, while Sino-Indian relations simultaneously deteriorated in 1959.

This hostile geostrategic environment ruled out the option of using military force to settle the border dispute with India because of the potential pitfall of starting a two front war. Thus PRC actions along the Indian border were limited by the international structure to defensive posturing, deterrence, and entrenchment. This is illustrated by the numerous Chinese overtures to Indian representatives to keep patrols 20km behind each border. Rapprochement with Pakistan was pragmatic in the freedom of action the PRC gained by not needing to guard the Sino-Pakistani border heavily. Therefore, Chinese policy was constrained by the system to not initiate force against India in order to settle the border dispute, but instead to bolster its defenses. However, the PRC declared that "force would be met with force" on the border issue, and this is evidenced by the PLA counter offensives launched on October 20 and November 16, 1962.

Finally, the anarchy present in the international system played a significant role in the actions of the PRC on the border issue. Unlike their Indian counterparts, China properly assessed the international situation and never lost sight of the fact that only China could assure Chinese security. The emerging Sino-Soviet split was a key element in the PRC's unwillingness to rely on outside support for their interests. Not only did the Soviets urge China to a settlement counter to their interests, but they openly aided India in both the construction of a domestic MIG program and a pledge to help them develop nuclear energy. Simultaneously, Soviet aid to China was severely cut including assistance in developing a nuclear program. Clearly a common Soviet-Sino communist ideology was unimportant to their "allies," as they even ventured to grant India great power status through nuclear development.

In addition to the Soviet military aid was U.S. support of India in the form of agricultural assistance and millions in financial aid packages. Although India pledged neutrality, the PRC clearly believed that they were in the West's bloc. Indian based CIA operations into Tibet and India's role in the Korean War helped bolster this perception. Unable to rely on either superpower for protection or intervention on their behalf, the PRC assessed that any military movements in securing the border would have to be proportional, decisive, and most importantly retaliatory. This assessment was gained from a rational calculation of the potential geostrategic and political consequences of a PLA initiation of force. While neither the PRC nor India possessed nuclear weapons, they feared a PLA offensive into India would be interpreted by the West as communist advance and therefore provoke a nuclear response. In the wake of the Taiwan Straits Crisis, and keeping in mind Sino-Soviet agitation, China was unwilling to risk a potential nuclear strike from the West, especially without full Soviet support. This being the case, China resolved that its armed response to Indian aggression would be purely political. The PRC would paint itself as the victim of aggression, but would then unleash a massive but calculated counterattack to force diplomatic concessions by India on the border issue, thereby resolving the issue once and for all. While the systems level of analysis plainly explains both the motives and limitations of India and China leading to the Sino-Indian War, it is contended that the model overlooks key motivations of either state leading to conflict.

GLOBAL VARIABLES LEADING TO CONFLICT: INDIA

The three main variables motivating Indian behaviour towards conflict with China on the systemic level are: Indian national interests, the system's influence on Indian behaviour through structural constraints, and the relationship between Indian perception of the international structure and reality. To begin a systemic explanation of India's actions we must first identify its national interests, as it is what drives Indian action throughout the international structure. According to neorealist thought the primary end of all states is security. This being the case, not only is security the primary Indian national interest, but any issue relating to national security becomes a primary interest.

Official borders, and their enforcement is a primary interest of each state for obvious reasons. However, in the Indian case this issue takes on greater importance than it otherwise would for other nations. This can be attributed to two factors. The most prevalent factor was that India bordered a nation which not only questioned the legitimacy of the established border, but also violated it. The second factor is the modern international system is formed by the interaction of nation-states, which as defined by the Westphalian system are the only entities capable of legitimately exercising sovereignty.

A key component of nation-state status under the Westphalian system is the existence of demarcated and respected borders. These borders represent the extent of national sovereignty and define where each nation's authority begins and ends. The questioning of India's established border by China undermines both Indian sovereignty and security. Security is undermined first by the direct military and administrative challenge to Indian territory, and second by delegitimizing India's position as a nation-state. If India can neither defend nor define borders respected by other nations, other states may begin to question their position as a nation-state in the system and then their sovereignty. This was a chief concern for India as they regarded the Chinese threat to their border as one compromising their "independence, self-determination, and position as a great power in Asia".

Another issue of national security relating to Indian interests was defense of the McMahon Line. Two key issues aided the creation of security dilemma situation along the McMahon Line. The first was the discovery of the Chinese road connecting Xinjiang and Tibet through the Aksai-Chin area in 1957. The second was the imposition of martial law on Tibet in 1959 by the PLA. China argued that completion of the road southeast of the McMahon Line in Aksai-Chin was simply the reestablishment of a historical commerce route from Xinjiang to Tibet. This road not only represented a blatant Chinese violation of India's McMahon Line border, but it also caused armed tension in the region. Shortly after the roads discovery, PLA frontier guards began patrolling the Aksai-Chin region, but never more than 20km away from the road's location. The issue of the road in Aksai-Chin and the PLA's role in Tibet in 1959 became linked since the majority of Chinese troops entered Tibet via the road from Xinjiang. The surge of PLA soldiers into Tibet aroused suspicions of a forcible border assertion by the PRC. These tensions were heightened by the flight of the Dalai Lama from Lhasa, and the closure of Tibet to commercial and cultural access by India, guaranteed in the 1951 treaty. Defensive maneuvers or not, these activities created a security dilemma along the border as India felt that Tibet was "essential for mastery over South Asia, and the most economical method for guaranteeing India's security". Forced to account for increasing Chinese military power near or past the McMahon Line, India responded by deploying their military in forward positions along the border with China as early as 1960. Accounting for India's national interest with force posturing, they attempted to both affirm the legitimacy of the McMahon Line as a border and to account for the security dilemma created by the hardening of PLA positions in Tibet and Aksai-Chin.

The second way a systemic level analysis accounts for the 1962 war is the manner in which India's policy was defined by the structure of the international system. In looking at the geostrategic positioning of India within the system, it is immediately apparent that they attempted to remain neutral or unaligned in the bipolar structure. India remained a powerful enough state to deter the third world adventurism of either bloc within its territory, but weak enough to be challenged by hostile neighbours. An excellent example of this was the persistent threat of Pakistan on their Northwestern border. The poor relationship of Pakistan and India is rooted in domestic level variables, but a systemic level cause was a disputed claim over the sovereignty of Kashmir. Both sides claim the right to sovereignty over Kashmir, and this has resulted in a heavily armed border. Additionally, appearances of a Sino-Pakistani agreement to hem in India developed with Chinese diplomatic overtures to Pakistan for peaceful border settlement beginning in 1961. This forced India to take a hard-line stance in their border dispute with China out of fear that concessions would show weakness, and endanger their control of Kashmir in a Domino-Theory type logic train.

Another structural element of the international system was the existence of nuclear weapons. Nuclear weapons invalidated traditional calculations of deterrence, and thus the great powers were those whom possessed them. In India's regional calculations neither themselves, nor did any other surrounding nations possess nuclear weapons keeping intact the use of deterrence as a method of securing or defending interests. This being the case, the option of engaging in armed conflict with surrounding nations remained possible as long as in India's force calculations they were superior to their target. A prime example of India's employment of force to further interests was their invasion of Portuguese controlled Goa on December 17, 1961. This use of force to assert sovereignty over perceived territory is an excellent precedent for the October 9, 1962 offensive against the PLA in Ladakh. Force against PLA incursions remained off the table as long as the Indian military believed their strategic position and capabilities to be inferior to the Chinese. Returning from a 1960 diplomatic tour of the U.S., Nehru expressed the idea that due to Soviet and Western military aid, "the military balance had changed in favour of India". Thus in the absence of nuclear weapons, India disregarded the Chinese effort at deterrence and employed the use of force to settle their territorial claims.

Finally, it is necessary to point out how India's perception of the international system, which differed from reality, influenced their decision to employ force against the PRC. India perceived the international system as open to change from a bipolar to a multi-polar structure. This was based in their success of remaining unaligned to either bloc, while still receiving significant military and economic aid from both camps. Given India's strategic geographic position in the system, both superpowers sought to gain the allegiance of India to their side through the use of aid. Understanding this, India played both sides against each other, and assumed that either superpower would be willing to intervene on their behalf in the event of Sino-Indian hostilities for pragmatic and alliance building reasons. Thus, India viewed its use of force as a no lose situation. Either the force would succeed in attaining their national interests, or if Indian power proved to be inadequate, "the superpowers would intervene to prevent any large-scale war between India and China;" therefore, bailing out India from a potential catastrophe. This perception of Indian value to either superpower and the general misperception of the international system would cost them.

Ultimately the Indians failed to acknowledge that while the interests of the superpowers may partially depend on India's well being, the system is ultimately in anarchy and each nation is responsible for assuring their own security. Additionally, India had miscalculated both the willingness and ability of the superpowers to intervene on their behalf.

In reality the Soviet Union could not exercise restraint on Chinese actions or compel them to drop the border issue. The Sino-Soviet split had not yet occurred, but its origin is in the late 1950's, and the attempt to restrain PRC actions towards India was a contributing factor in the decline of Soviet influence.

Indian belief in U.S. intervention was based on a miscalculation of U.S. interests in Asia, as well as willingness to repel PRC advance based on the Domino Theory. While the U.S. intervened in Korea, Taiwan, and Indochina, India overlooked the essential element common to each.

This element was the inability of each nation to resist communist advance on its own. In this case, the projected image of Indian power was a liability. The realities of the international system and its anarchic nature would ensure that their decision to use force would not be consequence free. Now the Chinese causes for war will be evaluated at the systemic level.

ALTERNATIVE EXPLANATIONS OF CONFLICT: DOMESTIC LEVEL ANALYSIS

A valid criticism of a systemic level approach to explaining conflict is that it overlooks key variables and differences between states in the assumption that all states are equal due to constraints that the structure of the international system places upon them.

Singer argues that at this level of analysis "actors are characterized and their behaviour predicted in relatively gross and general terms".

To account for the generalization of state behaviour inherent in a systemic level analysis a brief domestic level analysis explaining the Sino-Indian war will be attempted. Based on Vertberger's literature review on the subject, my domestic level analysis will be limited to the most influential domestic variable driving China and India to war; ideological and political considerations.

Indian ideological and political causes for war centered on the belief in non-alignment as a viable alternative to the bipolar system. The source of Indian non-aligned thought was that the Cold War was a conflict between the imperialist Western nations, and therefore newly independent former colonies had no reason or interest in siding with their former masters.

The Indians by remaining non-aligned, hoped to establish a third pole of power in the international system organized by the nations of the Third World. This third bloc of nations would fight for issues that really mattered to them such as ending colonialism, racial discrimination, and raising living standards in the developing world. Nehru envisioned that this Third World bloc would act as an arbiter in the West's conflict, thereby gaining both moral authority and legitimacy.

In concert with the Bandung Conference in 1955 and the Sino-Indian Panchsheel Agreement, Nehru hoped to expand his concept of non-alignment into a full-blown pan-Asianism movement. This pan-Asianism was based in the common historical experience of colonialism that these nations shared, but Nehru failed to account for historical differences and regional rivalries.

Nehru asserted that, "the basic challenge in Southeast Asia is between India and China," but he forgot this reality in supporting an Asian solidarity bloc. Nehru, and India's conception of a non-aligned third world was based on not only its viability, but that India would be both the natural and unchallenged leader of such a group. Traditional Sino-Indian rivalry for influence in Asia challenged Indian thinking as China asserted its right to be the leader of such a group. The need to exert its regional great power status over China led to diplomatic intransigence on the issue of border negotiations. Thus, India saw Chinese dispute of border areas to be a political challenge to their right to lead Asia, and in turn pushed backed in order to show strength.

Chinese ideological and political causes for war centered on the belief that its Maoist interpretation of communist revolution was not only correct, but purer than the Soviet model. This dispute on the merits of Maoism over Leninism was focused squarely on the Soviet Union's insistence on backing the Indian position in the border dispute through political and military aid. The PRC challenged Soviet actions on three points; that their diplomatic position showed a lack of solidarity with a fellow communist nation, that Soviet support of a bourgeoisie regime in India would not forward the goal of communist revolution, and that India wasn't truly non-aligned but in fact in league with the imperialists.

Soviet military aid inflamed the PRC, especially in light of Soviet cuts to Chinese aid, because it appeared as if the Soviets were turning their backs on a Marxist brother.

Furthermore, the PRC believed that only through struggle and challenge, not foreign aid, could they achieve the end of global Marxist revolution.

Finally, Indian overtures to the West for aid, and their assistance to the West in fomenting problems on China's border led the PRC on a quest to convince the Soviets that they were being used. The PRC concluded that superior PLA military forces and position in the region would force the Indians to rely on Western intervention to bail them out in the event of hostilities. This would both expose the Indians as true imperialists, and score an ideological victory against the Soviet Union in the enlarging diplomatic split.

The domestic level analysis contends that it is domestic differences between states that drive them towards conflict. Examining the most influential domestic factors (according to scholars on the subject) on Chinese and Indian decision making leading to the 1962 war, it seems as if ideology had differing levels of importance for each nation.

Indian ideology and their belief in leading a pan-Asian bloc nationalized tensions with China, creating a zero-sum game. If the Indian's backed down they would seem weak, and to avoid this they took a non-compromising stand on border issues.

In China, Maoist ideology was more so an issue with hierarchy within the Soviet bloc than with Indian recalcitrance on border issues. The PRC actively believed the Indians not to be non-aligned, but this was not important as ideologically they did not pose a threat to the Chinese communist system. As such, Chinese ideology was not as important in crafting policy, and Zhou Enlai was able to take a pragmatic stand. As Singer points out the overgeneralization of a systemic analysis, he also points out that a domestic analysis suffers from the same weakness but instead an undue focus on state differences.

The domestic analysis helps us better understand the importance of the border issue in each nation's context, but in this case it does not adequately explain the actions undertaken by either regime.

Furthermore, only with a systemic level analysis can we explore the limitation on action caused by the international structure on each state. Ultimately, Chinese ideology does not explain why they did not take the offensive to oust India as imperialists, or why India decided to change its military policy towards an aggressive forward base strategy. Therefore, a systemic level analysis is more suited to explaining the actions leading to the Sino-Indian War.

While valid alternative theoretical models explaining the causes for war exist, a neorealist systems-level analysis best explains the factors leading India and China to war in 1962.

Keeping in mind the historical context of generally cordial Sino-Indian relations prior to 1959 it seems unlikely that solely ideological differences drove the two nations to war. If ideology was such an important motivator behind the militarization of the Sino-Indian border dispute, then it is unlikely conflict would have waited to develop until 1962.

Additionally, if Sino-Indian rivalry for dominance in Asia was so virulent why did India recognize PRC sovereignty in Tibet in 1951, and later agree to a mutual treaty of peaceful coexistence in 1954? A domestic level analysis cannot account for these otherwise amicable diplomatic relations.

What a systemic level analysis reveals is certain changes in national interests, geostrategic positions, and the anarchy of the international system brought both nations closer to the precipice of conflict. Various actions and reactions by both nations along the border created a security dilemma for each, and this brought the border dispute to the forefront of Sino-Indian relations. Furthermore, India believed they had the power to reshape the international system from a bipolar to multi-polar world. Their lack of either nuclear capability or significant conventional power exposed their status as simply a minor power of strategic importance in the international system. Thus either superpower was only motivated to preserve their security so long as it was in their interests to do so, and not as an ultimate necessity contrary to Indian belief.

The ultimate cause for war in 1962 was India's assertion that it was a major power in world affairs. China's incentive in limiting their defeat of the Indian military was motivated by their interest in de-legitimizing the McMahon Line and consolidating their sovereignty in Tibet. The systems level analysis reveals not only what urged each nation to war, but also explains how the anarchy of the system limited the extent of the fighting.

5

Sino-Indian Border Dispute and their Competitive Symbiotic Relationship

Recently, the Sino-Indian border dispute once again became a focus of for the world's mass media. A "tent confrontation" between the Chinese and Indian armies took place and continued near the Line of Actual Control (LAC) for several days. From the Indian point of view, the Chinese army invaded Indian territory, and this incident was "the most serious one in the past 25 years". Level-headed analysis will indicate, however, that China would not wish to provoke simultaneous conflicts with Japan and India, two major Asian powers. In fact, the Indian mass media's reports about Chinese incursions have been heard continually in recent years. Some reports that the Chinese have invaded India for more than 600 times in the past three years are ridiculous.

The Sino-Indian border issue is very complicated. It was left over from the time of British rule in India and has never been resolved. In the 1960s, a military conflict broke out between China and India over territorial boundaries. That conflict became the excuse for India to develop its armed forces vigorously, to get ready for battle, and to make nuclear weapons. The root reason cause of many of the "incursion" incidents reported by India is that the two sides have never reached a consensus on the position of the LAC since the boundary conflict in 1962. They have never delimited the LAC, let alone a formal border. It is therefore debatable to say the Chinese army invaded Indian territory.

Since 1993, however, China and India have signed two agreements and one protocol on the maintenance of peace and tranquillity and the establishment of confidence-building measures in the border areas. They have set up a working mechanism for consultation and coordination on border affairs. These efforts have helped ensure a durable peace and stability in the border areas. The possibility that China and India will come to serious conflict is very small.

Bilateral relations between China and India are very subtle; apart from the boundary problem, the issues of China-Pakistan relations, the Dalai Lama and water resources also hinder the promotion of China-India relations. These problems have given India a deep-seated distrust of China. Some Indians are gradually losing self-confidence as they observe the growing economic gap between China and India. The Indian mass media and some Indian strategic scholars frequently refer to a "Chinese incursion" and the "China threat" and propagate an attitude of no confidence in China's intentions. This situation provides opportunities for some Western countries to undermine Sino-India relations. With the US "rebalancing" toward the Asia-Pacific, the Sino-Indian relationship is undergoing subtle changes these days. Some Indian scholars promote an alliance under the US leadership to counterbalance China. For example, Harsh V. Pant, a professor of defence studies at King's College London, argues that India's strategic interests can only be realised by an Asia-Pacific arrangement in which the US retains its predominant status. The Indian Express columnist C. Raja Mohan similarly urges India to shift its policy of strategic autonomy and strategically cooperate with the US.

So far, India has concentrated on strengthening its "Look East" Policy to enhance strategic and security cooperation with countries such as Japan, South Korea, Malaysia and Vietnam. It has also taken a high profile in the South China Sea disputes. In December 2011, the first trilateral dialogue between the US, Japan and India was presided over by the US. One of the discussion topics was China's growing military and political global position. It is no wonder that many think that India may abandon strategic autonomy to ally itself with the US and contain China.

Currently, Indian policymakers have a relatively clear view of Sino-Indian and India-US relations. India doesn't yet have the ability to directly confront China, and, as a country prioritising economic development, it is in need of a peaceful neighbouring environment. History shows that the US is not a reliable ally for India. Because of the effect of the economic crisis, the US is heavily burdened by its domestic economic problems, and there are doubts about how much money can be invested in counterbalancing China. The US anchors its hope on the strategy of "offshore balancing" to achieve balance with, or even contain, China by stirring up tensions between it and its Asian strategic partners. It is just taking advantage of India's strength to balance China, which, in effect, should kill two birds with one stone.

So, at present, we have the ironic spectacle of articles in both the US and Indian media trying to provoke each other into tensions with China. The Indian media highlights the idea that Uncle Sam is well-prepared to battle China, while the US media points out that India is engaging in military expansion in preparation for possible Sino-Indian boundary conflicts. India still maintains its status as a "swing state" in the international system. Although it has recently become more pro-US, since the US recognised India as a nuclear power despite it not being a signatory to the Nuclear Non-Proliferation Treaty (NPT), India will not abandon its strategic autonomy to ally with the US. Sino-Indian relationship is, in essence, a competitive symbiotic relationship. I say that for the following reasons: First of all, there really are some areas of competitions between China and India, mainly in geopolitics, trade and energy, etc. But that competition is not necessarily cutthroat and zero sum. China and India can cooperate if they have mutual trust. In fact, they do cooperate in fields such as energy and anti-terrorism.

In addition to the aspect of competition, the Sino-Indian symbiotic relationship can be divided into four areas: First, as two big powers that are rising simultaneously, China and India are in similar positions in the current international system. They are beneficiaries of that system, but at the same time, they are constrained by it and also suppressed by the dominant power in the system. They want to gradually advance the reform of this system. So, China and India have common interests on many global issues, such as the reform of the international financial system, climate change, and the WTO negotiations. China, India, Brazil and South Africa have organised the BRICS and BASIC groups, which promote the reform of the international order. If China, India and other countries cannot consolidate their views on these global issues, they could be crushed one by one by the dominant power in the system and lose forever the chance to rise again.

Secondly, in the trilateral relations between China, India and the United States, India's status will benefit from China's rise. China's growth is a prerequisite for India's rise. If India really becomes embroiled in conflicts with China, it's hard to say whether the US will stretch out a hand to help it. But if India surpasses China, it will definitely replace its neighbour as the target of the US.

Thirdly, as two neighbouring powers in Asia, both China and India need a peaceful and stable periphery to develop their economies. Statesmen in both countries know clearly that development is their primary task, and that development needs stable circumstances. So, China and India have a common task to maintain the stability of the region. This is the determining factor that encourages China and India to keep their border areas stable for at least 10 years.

At least, the Chinese and Indian economies are complementary. Since they are in symbiosis, they could, theoretically, nourish and assist each other's survival and development. Sino-Indian bilateral trade has developed quickly in the past ten years, and the trade volume has risen 20 fold. Although India complains that there are some problems in the bilateral trade structure, and the Indian trade deficit is too large, it is evident that Chinese goods, which are of good quality and cheap, raise Indian people's living standards. China and India have ample room to cooperate, especially in infrastructure construction. China has large amounts of capital and extensive experience in the construction of infrastructure; India on the other hand needs to improve its infrastructure facilities, but lacks finance. Sino-Indian cooperation in this field will benefit both sides.

Within India, the so-called "China threat" is a trick of Indian political figures to pull the wool over the eyes of their people and Western countries. From the aspect of domestic politics, by making waves in relations with China, Indian politicians can obscure domestic contradictions, bolster up national morale, pull votes, and the military can get an increasing budget. From the aspect of international politics, India can obtain advanced weaponry and technologies from Western countries. In fact, the major direction of Indian military expansion is the Indian Ocean - the Navy received the largest part of India's rapidly growing defence budget. India's military strategy on land is defensive in nature but in the Indian Ocean, India has another competitor that is much stronger than China. The so-called "China threat" is just a cover.

The direction of Sino-Indian relations is determined for the medium-term at least, but the border issue is still a hindrance to bilateral relations. India did undertake some domestic reflection on the Sino-Indian conflict of 1962 and Nehru's policy towards China at that time, but no consensus was achieved. The Indian government never released publicly the Henderson-Brooks report that summarised the reasons why India was defeated. Taking a coherent view of this history will play a decisive role in the peaceful resolution of the Sino-Indian border problem. We should not neglect the negative role of the Indian multiparty system, in which foreign policy is often hijacked by domestic affairs. The role of the opposition parties and mass media in the Sino-Indian border conflict of 1962 is a case in point. It is necessary for the Indian government to reveal the truth about the Sino-Indian boundary conflict to the Indian people, and for Chinese and Indian scholars to conduct joint research projects on some historical problems, to alter the longstanding misconceptions held by both sides.

LOOK BEYOND THE SINO-INDIAN BORDER DISPUTE

The Sino-Indian border dispute originated from the British and Russian expansion in Central Asia in the early 20th century. Since the 1950s, the border dispute has always shadowed the ebb and flow of the Sino-Indian relations. The simmering border dispute erupted after the revolt the Dalai Lama clique engineered in 1959. The CIA-supported revolt in Tibet, India-embraced the Dalai Lama, and India-hosted Tibetan Government-in-exile turned out to be one of the causes of the border war in 1962. Nehru's policy of no-dispute and no-negotiation and his forward policy became a direct cause of the border war. Then the China-India relationship dramatically moved toward hostility and confrontation from brotherhood and friendship and entered an era of cold war which lasted nearly two decades.

The Chinese and Indian governments have attempted to resolve the border dispute through diplomatic negotiations since the1980s. The border negotiations have been institutionalized and generated several meaningful documents. However, each other's position on the border disputes themselves has never been changed.

To accelerate and intensify the boundary negotiations, the two governments have agreed to appoint the two Special Representatives. They have periodically met and conducted an in-depth exchange of views on resolving the boundary question. Both sides have agreed to press ahead with the framework negotiations in accordance with the agreed political parameters and guiding principles so as to seek for a fair and reasonable solution acceptable to both. Prior to that, both sides should work together to maintain peace and tranquility in the border areas. Although the border dispute remains unresolved in all the sectors, peace, stability, and tranquility have been maintained by the joint efforts of the two governments.

While we are cautiously optimistic about the steady improvement of the bilateral relations between the two rising Asian giants, we are increasingly concerned about the consequences of their geopolitical rhetoric and strategic suspicion originated primarily from the unresolved border dispute.

ACHIEVEMENTS IN THE BORDER NEGOTIATIONS

Since the 1980s, the China-India border talks have experienced three stages, with each stage covering roughly one decade. The first stage covered the 1980s culminated in Indian Prime Minister

Rajiv Gandhi's visit toChina in December 1988. The second stage covered the 1990s ended with India's nuclear tests in 1998; and the third stage covered the past 10 years marked with Indian President Patil's China trip during the celebration of the 60th anniversary of the establishment of China-India diplomatic relations in May 2010.

The Eight-Round Border Talks in the 1980s

The eight-round border talks took place in the period from hostility to detente in the China-India-relations. The talks obviously eased the tensions in their bilateral relations and resulted in agreement on the disagreements. These talks relieved both governments of pressing too hard on matters of substance while procedural disagreement seemed to be employed as excuse for no-progress. This suggests that neither government found it urgent to resolve the border dispute in the 1980s. Both sides hoped to reduce tensions and stabilize and improve bilateral relations, but they realized it premature to proceed to resolve their border disputes.

The 1988 China-India summit was the first meeting of he top leaders of the two countries in the 28 years since premier Zhou Enlai's visit to India in 1960.

Rajiv gandi's Beijing trip in December 1988 ushered in a new era of China-India relationship. With the detente prevailed in the world during the last years of the Cold War, India's diplomacy has lost the fulcrum of Indo-Soviet strategic partnership while China's diplomacy has lost the pillar of Sino-US cooperation. China andIndia suddenly found that they needed to re-orient their foreign policies within the context of the changed world power structure. The five principles of peaceful co-existence again became the common basis of their foreign policy reorientation.

In his inaugural address on December 31, 1984, Rajiv Gandhi stressed the continuation of a non-alignment policy and expressed his desire to improve relations with neighboring countries.

Huang Hua's India's trip was marked by the agreement to open negotiations on the border dispute and the development of China-India relations. There followed eight rounds of China-India talks as an official channel of the China-India dialogue on the border dispute.

China's strategy on the eight-round border talks comprised two main aspects. One was to insist on a package deal, and the other was to develop their bilateral relations in other fields with the border dispute shelved. During his interview with Krishna Kumar, the editor of *Vikrant*, on June 21, 1980, Deng Xiaoping renewed the "package" approach on the border issue. He stated that China would be willing to accept the watershed principle in the eastern sector in exchange for India's renunciation of claims to Aksai Chin. In other words, both sides should agree to accept the present line of actual control as their boundary. During his meeting with Indian Prime Minister Atal Vajpayee in February 1979, Deng stated that " We shall seek common ground while reserving our differences. We can solve the boundary question through peaceful consultation. This question should not prevent us from improving our relations in other field.

India insisted on sector-by-sector negotiations and refused China's package deal and both sides failed to narrow their differences during the eight rounds of talks. However, all the principles and concerns put on the table by both sides constituted sme mutually acceptable principles for substantive discussions on the border question. Both sides cautiously inched forward without getting bogged down in differing interpretations.

At the eighth round held in New Delhi, on November 14-17, 1986, India gave up its position of "boundary settlement or nothing." China had accepted the approach of the sector-by-sector review within the framework of comprehensive settlement in 1984.

Both agreed that pending a settlement of the border issue, the two governments should develop friendly relations and strengthen cooperation in other fields. Both sides agreed that peace and tranquility should be maintained all along the border. Both sides are prepared for Rajiv Gandhi's Visit to China. Apparently, the stage as set for raising the border dialogue to the political level.

The eight rounds of the border talks in the 1980s showed that India's policy on the border talks changed first from non-negotiation to negotiation, and then from "boundary settlement or nothing" to overall development in all fields. China-India dialogue of the 1980s substituted China-India Detente for their enmity.

Rajiv's visited symbolized the general trend of transition from hostility and confrontation to detente and dialogue. The 1988 summit also marked a departure from the previous approach, political settlement approach substituted for the legalistic approach. Both sides reduced their stress on historical documents and focused instead on their respective security interests by attaching inpotance to mutual bargaining and mutual understanding.

Line of Actual Control Clarification and CBMs Implementation

The eight rounds of border talks demonstrated that their conflicting border versions, based on historical-legalistic arguments, could not find common ground because no mutually acceptable border treaties or agreements existed. The eight rounds of border talks raised the hope for a political solution to the border dispute.

In 1991, Premier Li peng visited India and signed the Sino-Indian Joint Communique on December 16, 1991. In the joint communiqué, they reaffirmed their independent foreign policy and the five principles of peaceful co-existence. The two sides appealed for the joint efforts for the establishment of a new international political and economic order. India reiterated its position that Tibet is an autonomous region of China and it does not allow Tibetans to engage in anti-china political activities in India.

After the two summit meetings in 1988 and 1991, China-India interactions shifted from the border dispute to the identification of a mutually acceptable lie of actual control along the China-India border. In 1993, Indian Prime Minister Rao visited China and signed an agreement on maintaining peace and tranquility along the line of actual control and reduced military forces in the border areas. This peace pact, under which both sides agreed to respect and observe the LAC, is a big step forward in exploring a lasting border solution, eliminating concerns about events such as the Sumdurong Chu incident which nearly sparked another border war in 1987. Under the LAC agreement in 1993, the two sides agreed that the boundary question shall be resolved through peaceful and friendly consultations. Neither side shall use or threaten to use force against the other by any means. Pending an ultimate solution to the boundary question, the two sides shall strictly respect and observe the LAC.

Each side will keep its military forces in the areas along the LAC to a minimum level compatible with the friendly and good-neighborly relations between the two countries. Both sides shall work out effective confidence-building measures (CBMs) in the areas along the LAC.

However, the two sides agreed that references to the LAC in this agreement do not prejudice their respective positions on the boundary question. Under this agreement, both sides agreed that each side of the China-India Joint Working Group on the boundary question shall appoint diplomatic and military experts, advising the Joint Working Group on resolution of differences on the alignment of the LAC and address issues relating to military redeployment in the border areas along the LAC.

In 1996, the Chinese president Jiang Zemin visited India and both sides decided to develop a cooperative and constructive partnership, further raising political level of bilateral cooperation between the two countries. However, the Indian nuclear tests in 1998 and its leaders indicated India's nuclear tests for counter-China's nuclear threat dashed the healthy momentum of China-India relations in the late 1990s.

Apparently, China-India interactions in the 1990s focused on political and security fields. The line of actual control, the CBMs in the areas along the China-India border, and emphasis on the establishment of an international political and economic order and even India's nuclear tests are all pointed to political and security dimension of the China-India relations.

Shift Back to the Settlement of the Border Dispute in the New Century

Ushering in the new 21st century, China and India, the two Asian giants, are rising at the same time. Their bilateral relationship has its regional and global significance. As the two largest emerging powers in Asia and the world, their roles have been played far beyond the bilateral context. Certainly, their bilateral dispute, particularly the border dispute, has constrained each other's capability to play their responsible role in the regional and global affairs.

If they focused on stabilizing their relations and securing their border areas in the 1990s, they have shifted their attention to the settlement of their border dispute by developing their political and economic relations while taking concrete and substantive measures to resolve the border dispute. They understand that their bilateral problems have complicated their policy coordination and cooperation in the regional and global issues. Their bilateral differences have tended to be manipulated by other powers to serve their geostrategic interest.

For the past decade, in terms of the border dispute, they have taken three substantive steps to intensify their efforts to resolve it.

The first step is that India has accepted Tibet is an autonomous region of China, implying that India has given up the intention to use Tibet as a buffer zone between China and India and recognizes China's sovereignty overTibet. However, although India does not allow the Tibetans in India to engage in Anti-China political activities, it still hosts the Dalai Lama's government-in-exile. China has recognized Sikkim's status as a state of India's federation by signing the agreement on the cross-border trade with India.

The second step is that China and India signed an agreement on political parameters and guiding principles on the settlement of the China-India border dispute. This document is regarded as a big breakthrough in the joint efforts for resolving the border dispute. The third step is that the two governments have appointed their special representatives to promote the negotiations on a framework of the border settlement. The two governments have paid importance to the annual meetings of the two special representatives. The Chinese special representative is State Councilor Dai Bingguo and The Indian special representative is India's National Security adviser M. K. Narayanan.

After the two special representatives were appointed, they started to work together for a framework settlement of the border dispute according to the agreed political parameters and guiding principles. Under the current circumstances, although the two governments continue to work on the settlement of the border dispute, peace, stability, and tranquility in the border areas have remained. No armed conflicts or even skirmishes happened although some media has played up such noises of China's invasions into India's territory dozens or hundreds of times.

THE CHINA-INDIA BORDER DISPUTE

The entire China-India boundary has never been formally delimited by any mutually-accepted treaty. There has existed a boundary line of actual control between the two countries. It took shape on the basis of the extent of each other's administrative jurisdiction over a long course of time. The entire boundary has been traditionally divided into three sectors—the eastern sector, the middle sector, and the western sector with all in dispute. The western sector involves the dispute over the Aksai Chin area India claims as part of Latah andChina claims as part of Xinjiang. The middle sector involves a dispute over various points between the Tibet-Kashmir- Punjab border junction and the Nepal-Tibet-Uttar Pradesh border junction. The eastern sector involves a dispute over the area between the pre-1914 Outer Line and the McMahon Line.

In the eastern sector, the British–Indian government had observed the foothills of the Himalayas as the "Outer Line" of its administrative jurisdiction by 1914. Although the Chinese-Tibetan authorities had claimed the tribal areas beyond the British Outer Line within the Tibetan jurisdiction, their administrative jurisdiction actually covered only Tawang tract, the Walong area along the Lohit valley, and some other scattered enclaves in the tribal areas.

Today the line of actual control observed by both sides conforms to the McMahon Line. The disputed area between the pre-1914 Outer Line and the McMahon Line covers a total area of 90,000 square kilometers. According to China, this area is composed of

Tibet's three districts of Monyul, Loyul and lower Zayul. According to India, this area is its Arunachal Pradesh, formerly the North-East Frontier Agency of Assam State.

In the western sector, the line of actual control runs roughly along the Karakoram range, conforming to the Chinese claim. The Indian government claims that the boundary runs along the Kunlun range from theKarakoram Pass. The disputed Area is the Aksai Chin region between the two ranges, covering a total area of about 33,000 square kilometers. This area falls mainly in China's Xinjiang and part of it belongs to the Ari District of Tibet. India claims that it is part of its Ladakh area of the State of Jammu and Kashmir. This area, sparsely inhabited, serves as the traffic artery linking Xinjiang and Tibet.

Therefore, in terms of the general China-India border dispute, the McMahon Line in the eastern sector and Aksai Chin in the western sector have been central to the negotiations on the settlement of the border dispute.

The Mystery of the McMahan Line

After Russia successfully divided Mongolia into Outer and Inner Mogolia with the Outer Mongolia as a buffer zone between China and Russia, the British- Indian authorities dreamed the same dream and tried to divideTibet into Outer Tibet and Inner Tibet and made the Outer Tibet as a buffer zone between British India andChina. To achieve such a objective, the Simla conference was held in 1914,with British Henry McMahon, Chinese Chen Ivan, and Tibetan Lonchen shatra as representatives.

There were actually two parallel conferences at Simla, the tripartite conference focusing on the division ofTibet, and the other was the secret one, keeping Chen Ivan out of their negotiations on the Indian-Tibetan boundary. In early 1914, Henry McMahon and Lonchen Shatra secretly negotiated on the division of Tibet and the boundary between Assam and Tibet as a package deal. An agreement was reached through a secret exchange of notes in Delhi on March 24 and 25, 1914. This boundary line, later known as the McMahon line, was shown on a map in two sheets.

The tripartite conference focused on McMahon's proposal referring to China's suzerainty over Tibet and the outer-inner division of Tibet. On the map attached to the draft convention of the conference, two lines were drawn, one red and the other blue. The red line showed Tibet as a geographical and political unit, and the blue line divided Inner from Outer Tibet. In its southern extension, the red line curves around along the crest of theHimalayas, roughly conforming to the McMahon Line except in the Tawang tract where the McMahon Line reached short of the Tawang tract, implying that the Tawang tract remained part of Tibetan territory. On this map, the Tawang tract was not put within the British-Indian territory.

Without the consent of the Chinese government, Chen Ivan, under McMahon's threat and pressure, initiated the draft convention on April 27, 1914, but with the clear understanding that "to initial and to sign are two different actions," and that his initials would not bind his government, whose views he would immediately seek. The next day, the Chinese government instructed Chen Ivan that "The Chinese representative was forced to initial the draft convention. The Chinese government cannot accept it. You should declare it invalid." Since Chen Ivan refused to sign the draft convention, it was then amended and initialed by McMahon and Lonchen Shatra on July 3, 1914. On the map attached to the draft convention, the McMahon Line was marked just across the town of Tawang, indicating that the area to the north of Tawang would fall within the Tibetan territory.

The British-Indian government did not accept the Simla convention. Viceroy Hardinge forwarded McMahon's report on the Simla conference to London on July 23, 1914, stating that the Indian government recognized that a consideration of the northeastern frontier did not form part of the functions of the conference, and the views and proposal put forward might be regarded as personal to Henry McMahon, not carrying the endorsement of the Government of India. Chen was also instructed to declare that the Chinese government "would not recognize any treaty or similar document that might now or hereafter be signed between Great Britain and Tibet." The Tibetan authorities understood that without securing the Sino-Tibetan boundary, they could not accept the Indo-Tibetan boundary.

The Dalai Lama even recognized the logic relationship between the status of Tibet and the legality of the McMahon Line. In his 1959 address to the Indian Council of World Affairs, he contended that if Tibet had no sovereignty when the Simla convention laid down the McMahon Line, that line was invalid. He challenged Nehru that if you deny the sovereign status to Tibet, you deny the validity of the McMahon Line."

Three maps are related to the Simla conference. One is attached to the March 24 notes; one to the April 27 convention, and the third to the July 3 convention. As far as the Tawang Tract is concerned, the three maps show the McMahon line quite differently. On the first map, the McMahon Line was shown running alng south of the Thagla range far north of Tawang; on the second map, it is not shown in the Tawang tract; and on the third one, it is superimposed on the word " Tawang".

In 1936, Basil Gould, Political Officer in Sikkim, was dispatched to Lhasa and discussed the Tawang issue with the Tibetan government. The Tibetan attitude was Tawang had been Tibetan up to 1914 and they regarded the adjustment of the Tibet-Indian boundary as part and parcel of the general adjustment and determination of boundaries contemplated in the 1914 convention. If they could, with British help, secure a definite Sino-Tibetan boundary, they would observe the Indo-Tibetan border as defined in 1914.

In 1944, just before the British quit from India, basil Gould informed the Tibetan authorities that the Bitish-Indian government was willing to modify the McMahon Line soas to exclude Tawang from the territory it claimed.

He also proposed that the Se La range should be a new boundary line. However, The Tibetan authorities did not accepted it and continued to collect revenues in the Tawang tract and remained administrative control over the Tawang tract. It was in February1951 that the Indian government took over the Tawang tract by force before the PLA entered and liberated Tibet. The

Tibetan authorities organized protest demonstrations in Tawang and Lhasaagainst India's occupation of the Tawang tract, but no avail.

As far as the objective of the Simla conference was concerned, it certainly aborted. The McMahon Line was not even accepted by the British-Indian government. After the Simla conference, from 1914 to 1935, on the official maps published by the Survey of India, the McMahon Line was not shown, but instead the Outer Line along the foothills of the Himalayas was shown.

The Tibetan authorities continued to exercise administrative jurisdiction in the tribal areas as they did before.

The Simla conference went down in history as an unaccomplished cause. As to the Simla conference, the first official record appeared in Volume XIV of the 1929 edition of Aichison's Treaties. It did not refer to the McMahon Line, but to the discussion on the Sino-Tibetan frontier. It was stated that a tripartite convention was drawn up and initialed in 1914, but the Chinese government refused to permit its representative to proceed to full signature.

In 1935, Olaf Caroe, deputy secretary of the Foreign and Political Department of the British-Indian Government discovered the secret documents of the Simla conference in dealing with a case involving the illegal entry into Tibet through the Tawang tract. He realized that the northeastern frontier might be a matter of dispute with the Chinese in the future. He proposed to revise the official record of the Simla conference in the Aichison's Treaties and show the McMahon Line on the official maps. The British government approved his proposal.

This original 1929 edition was soon withdrawn from circulation and replaced by a spurious edition, actually printed in 1938, but with an imprint of 1929. However, at least three copies of the original 1929 edition survived, one in Peking Library, one in Harvard University library, and one in the India Office. In the revised edition, it was stated that the Simla conference negotiated an agreement on the status of Tibet and the boundary of Tibet with both China and India. Such a revision was nothing but scandalous diplomatic forgery. Then the McMahon Line began to appear of the Indian official maps. However, it was still marked as "Undemarcated Boundary."

The Puzzle of Aksai Chin

In the western sector of the China-India border, the dispute has centred on the Aksai Chin area. The British left Aksai Chin area as "undefined" at the time of their transfer of power in 1947.nehru himself once stated that " it is a matter of argument as to what art of it (Aksai Chin) belongs to us and what part of it belongs to somebody else.... The point is, there has never been any delimitation there in that area and it has been a challenged area." Before the British left India, the British-Indian government had shown no boundary at all in that area on its official maps. In Volume XII of Aichison'd Treaties published in 1931, it was stated that"The northern as well as the eastern boundary of the Kashmir state is still undefined." The Survey of India maps published in the 1900s and 1930s did not indicate any boundary alignment or show any colour difference in this are, and wide spaces between Kashmir and Xinjiang and between Kashmir and Tibet were shown blank. Louis Dane, Indian Foreign Secretary, stated clearly in a letter to the Indian office that Aksai Chin was I Chinese Xinjiag. The neighbourhood of the Lanak Pass at the head of the Changchenmo valley was supposed to be the most northerly boundary point on the Kashmir-Tibet border.

In 1945, guided by Olaf Caroe, then foreign secretary of India, on new Survey of India maps the Aksai Chin area began to be shown by a colour-wash with the words "Boundary Undefined" marked on it. In 1947, the Indian Army in its "top secret" m submitted to the British Cabinet Mission accepted the Karakoram range as the northern boundary of India in the western sector.

However, after the signing of the trade agreement concerning Tibet in 1954, following Nehru's instructions, new Survey of India maps began to show an international boundary in the western sector running along the crest of the Kunlun range, which for the first time placed the whole Aksai Chin area within the Indian territory. According to Sir H.A.F. Rumbold, an official in the Indian Office, the Simon Commission wished to include a map of India in Volume I of their report in 1929. Rumbold found nothing in the India office to justify the line on the Kunlun range shown on some maps. The Commission accordingly adopted a line roughly along the crest of the Karakoram range, excluding the Aksai Chin area. Nehru, even on August 28, 1959, stated in the Lok Sabha that "This was the boundary of the old Kashmir state with Tibet and Chinese Turkestan. Nobody had marked it."

On the other hand, Chinese maps have shown the Karakoram range as its boundary in the western sector at least since the 1920s. There was no evidence that the British-Indian authorities ever disputed this with the Chinese government before they left India in 1947. The widely accepted modern concept of boundary marking involes three steps: delimitation, delineation and demarcation. Delimitation involves defining the boundary in written terms through treaties and agreements. Delineation involves sketching the boundary in maps through joint boundary surveys. Demarcation involves marking the boundary line on the ground through pillars, chains and other markers.

Reviewing the historic facts for the entire China-India border, such a China-India boundary has never existed, though each side has made its own territorial claims. Historical facts have also showed that, in the old days, wide desolate tracts in the remote high mountains between the two countries were physically inaccessible. Therefore, the China-India border dispute has been the dispute on the "zone" rather than the " line" in the eastern and western sectors. Mutual understanding and recognition of such historical evolution of the China-India border should become the starting point for the future border deliberations.

The Sino/Indian Dispute

Ever since its establishment in 1949, the attitude of the Communist Chinese Government towards India has been bound up with the Tibetan issue. India had, on gaining independence in 1947, inherited the British "special position" in Tibet, along with the Mission in Lhasa and trade agencies in larger towns. It had retained the services of British officials stationed in Tibet. When, in 1949, Tibetan leaders made their bid to contact foreign

Governments, they first contacted these officials, and it was only a short step for the suspicious minded Chinese to regard this as evidence of Indian collusion with the British.

The Communist Chinese also had ideological reasons for believing that such collusion existed. At the time of their coming to power, Moscow was propagating the line of a world divided into two camps, with the Indian Government depicted as a tool of British imperialism and firmly situated in the opposing camp. The Communist Chinese leaders, who previously had little contact with the outside world, faithfully repeated these accusations against Nehru and his Government. The Chinese occupation of Tibet in late 1950, Peking's suspicions of the Indians were further aroused when Nehru, in notes to the Chinese Government, expressed the "surprise and regret" of his Government at the Chinese action. He described as "deplorable" the Chinese use of force in Tibet.

Standard diplomatic practice stipulates that a state does not criticise the behaviour of another state acting within its own territorial boundaries unless there are special reasons for so doing. The Indians justified their criticism of the Chinese on the ground of their special interest in Tibet, from which the Chinese inferred that the Indians were implying some restriction on Chinese sovereignty. A sharp reply was received from the Chinese accusing the Indians of unwarranted interference and claiming that the policy of the Indian Government was "affected by foreign influences hostile to China in Tibet".

Nevertheless, whatever suspicions the Chinese may have felt about the Indians in 1949-50 must to some extent have been allayed by subsequent developments. India opposed the 1950 Tibetan appeal to the United Nations; it was one of the few non-communist countries not to condemn China's intervention in the Korean War; it sought to have China seated an the United Nations. The culmination of these moves to improve relations with China was the signing, in April 1954, of an agreement by which India recognised without qualification China's sovereignty over Tibet and conceded many of India's former rights there. A few months later the Chinese Premier, Chou En-lai, paid a successful visit to India, and in October of the same year Nehru visited Peking.

The very considerable improvement in Sino/Indian relations from 1950 to 1954 was on the Indian side almost entirely the result of efforts by Nehru, who saw friendship between China and India as the starting point of a new order in world affairs. It must have been obvious to the Chinese that considerable opposition to Nehru's pro-China policies, at least as far as Tibet was concerned, existed both within and outside the Indian Government. It should also have been clear that problems were going to arise over wide discrepancies in the claimed Sino/Indian border, as shown in maps published by both sides.

However, as long as Nehru's China policy appeared to produce results, his opposition in India remained silent. It was important for both Nehru and the Chinese that this policy continued to appear to give results, and hence the efforts made by both sides to keep intact the edifice of good relations. The Chinese, under the 1954 agreement, allowed India to maintain certain trade and pilgrimage rights in Tibet. They sought to play down the significance of border differences, stating that they had simply inherited their claimed Sino/Indian frontier from the pre-1949 Nationalist Government and that it would be "revised" in due course. Nehru, for his part, avoided public mention of the reality and extent of border differences, and it seemed that both sides were moving towards a compromise settlement of the question.

What were these differences, and what evidence was there that both sides were in fact prepared to compromise? The Sino/Indian border can be divided into three sectors: (i) an eastern sector where 99,000 square kilometres of territory described by the Indians as the Northeast Frontier Agency, or N.E.F.A is in dispute: (ii) a middle sector where some 2.000 square kilometres of territory on either side of the main Himalayan passes is disputed: and (iii) a western sector where the Indian province of Ladakh borders on Tibet and Sinkiang and where both the Indian/Tibet and Indian/Sinkiang borders are disputed, in particular the ownership of some 30,000 square kilometres of high plateau country known as the Aksai Chin.

To an outside observer looking at the frontier as it stands, an apparent basis for a compromise settlement would be for China to drop its claim to the N.E.F.A. in exchange for India dropping its claim to the Aksai Chin, with both sides making concessions over the middle sector and the Ladakh/Tibetan border. Such a settlement accords with the realities of both geography and administrative control two important criteria in the settlement of border disputes. The N.E.F.A. lies to the south of the Himalayan watershed and is controlled by India. The Aksai Chin, for the most part, lies to the north of the main range, and the Chinese claim to have controlled the area since 1950. In 1956-7, they built a strategic road across the Aksai Chin, linking Sinkiang with Tibet. That the Indians learnt about the road only from a map published by the Chinese in 1958 is substantial evidence that India was not in control of the area.

The historical basis of the border is more confused. The Indian claim to the N.E.F.A. rests almost entirely on acceptance of the McMahon Line, a line agreed to by the Tibetans and British in 1914 as the border in this area. In the Aksai Chin area no agreement has ever been reached on the alignment of the border. Nevertheless, if both sides were to take a generous view of the historical data, a basis for a N.E.F.A./Aksai Chin exchange could be found. During the post-1954 honeymoon period of Sino/Indian relations, both sides did in fact seem prepared to take a generous view of the situation and to move towards a compromise settlement. In 1956, Chou En-lai admitted privately to Nehru that, although lie thought the McMahon line "was not fair", nevertheless China would accept the line as the border with India after they had "consulted with the Tibetan authorities". Chinese recognition of the McMahon Line was also implied when its eastern extension was accepted as a basis for border negotiations with Burma, and by Chinese de facto acceptance of the line as the dividing line between Chinese and Indian forces in the area.

Nehru, for his part, appeared willing to play down the Indian claims to the Aksai Chin. He tried to delay disclosure if the news that the Chinese had built a road in the area. After the news had been revealed, he sought to play down the economic significance of the area, describing it as a "barren tundra". He even went so far as to cast doubt on the validity of the Indian claim to the area.

In statements to the Indian Parliament during early 1959, Nehru pointed out that "during British rule, this area was neither inhabited: nor were there any outposts", adding that "this place, Aksai Chin area, is distinguish completely from other areas. It is a matter for argument which part belongs to us and which part belongs to somebody else. It is not clear".

Nehru's efforts to take the heat out of the Aksai Chin question were not entirely successful. (One of his critics even suggested building an atomic reactor in the area to promote its economic development.) News of the Chinese road in the area appeared to trigger off long-suppressed Indian sensitivity over the border issue, and, in August 1958, the Indian Government made a formal claim to the disputed territory in all three sectors.

In a letter to Nehru of January 1959, Chou En-lai claimed that the Aksai Chin was Chinese territory and added that the McMahon Line was a "product of British aggression", illegal, and had "never been recognised by the Chinese Central Government". He proposed that the existing status quo he maintained, however, pending a negotiated settlement of the dispute, and added that China would take a "realistic attitude" over the McMahon Line.*

The Tibetan uprising of March 1959 upset the delicate balance of Sino/Indian relations. Reports of Chinese military action to suppress the uprising, together with the sight of thousands of Tibetan refugees crossing into Indian territory, quickly aroused feelings of alarm and anger in India, particularly among those who believed their country had an historic interest in Tibet.

Nehru's Right-Wing critics charged that India should never have allowed the Chinese into Tibet in the first place. Nehru, influenced possibly both by Indian public opinion and his own feelings on the question, came out in open condemnation of Chinese behaviour in Tibet.

The Chinese reacted even more strongly than they had in 1950. Nehru, in addition to condemning the Chinese, had spoken of his sympathy with "the aspirations of the Tibetans for autonomy". He had given asylum to the Dalai Lama, who was also allowed facilities to make his 1959 appeal for U. N. action over Tibet. And finally, the Chinese had reason to believe that the

Tibetan guerrillas were receiving arms from across the Indian border.

In May 1959 the Chinese published a long article urging, almost begging, Nehru not to be swayed by his reactionary Right-Wing critics and to return to the path of Sino/Indian friendship. With a frankness and detail probably unmatched by any other Chinese statement on foreign policy, the article set out the Chinese case over Tibet, and accused the Indians of unjustified interference. Indian trade with Tibet was greatly restricted. Clashes involving casualties occurred at several points along the disputed border as the Chinese Army extended its control over border areas in an effort to restrict the move- court of Tibetans across the frontier.

These border clashes, following in the wake of the Tibetan uprising, appeared to put an end to Nehru's willingness to compromise over the border dispute. Having earlier in 1959 cast doubt on the Indian claim to the Aksai Chin, in September he stated before the Indian Parliament that the Chinese claims were "absurd" and would mean "handing over the Himalayas to them as a gift". A Chinese call in November 1959 for negotiations and a twenty-kilometre military withdrawal from the McMahon Line in the east and the "line of actual control" in the west to prevent a recurrence of border clashes was met with an Indian demand for a prior Chinese withdrawal from the Aksai Chin. A Chinese reply pointing out that this should also be paralleled by an Indian withdrawal from the NE.F.A. was ignored. In the end the Chinese appeared to settle for a freezing of the existing status quo - without negotiations or a twenty-kilometre withdrawal.

However, if the Chinese were happy to keep things as they were (keeping also their road across the Aksai Chin), Nehru and his Government were not. Throughout 1960-61 Indian opinion progressively hardened, and demands for the Government to do something about Tibet and the disputed border increased. The army was given full control over the frontier districts and it proceeded to build up its strength in these areas. During the summer (northern) of 1962, Indian military patrols repeatedly crossed the Chinese-claimed line of actual control in the western sector of the frontier. Posts were established well behind the Chinese forward positions in territory claimed and occupied by the Chinese. Frequent and insistent Chinese protests were met with the bald statement that the Indians were merely operating in Indian territory. By August 14, Nehru was able to announce that India had three times as many posts in the western sector as the Chinese. He asked for a free hand to continue the build-up of Indian strength in the area.

The Chinese had repeatedly warned that a continuation of such activity would end in hostilities. On July 9, they had warned the Indians "to rein in on the brink of the precipice". On August 4, they called for immediate negotiations on the border. The Indians replied that negotiations could not be held until the Chinese had ceased their occupation of "every square inch of sacred Indian territory", and that the Chinese must first "vacate their aggression" in the Aksai Chin. The Chinese replied on September 13 proposing talks to begin on October 15 "without preconditions", that is, without a Chinese withdrawal from the Aksai Chin. The Indians refused the offer.

While Indian military pressure was building up along the Chinese-claimed border in the western sector, a curious situation was developing along the McMahon Line in the eastern sector. The Indians claim that at its western end the McMahon Line was not accurately drawn: that it was meant to have followed the crest of a line of hills known as the Thag La ridge. The Chinese claim, and have produced the original McMahon Line from the Tibetan archives to prove their point, that the line as originally drawn lies approximately twelve miles south of this ridge along the southern side of a small river valley. (Western maps show the McMahon Line in conformity with the Chinese claim.) The area between the Indian and Chinese versions of the McMahon Line is described by the Indians as the Dho La strip. This was not the only unilateral revision of the McMahon Line carried out by the Indians. In his letter to Chou En-lai of September 29, 1959, Nehru admitted that in the Migyitun area (to the east of the Dho La strip) the border shown on Indian maps "differs slightly from the boundary shown in the Treaty map". He claimed that when the McMahon line was drawn, "the exact topographical features in this area were not known". The Indians have also now come to admit that "blind adherence" to the original McMahon Line would leave the Dho La strip on the Chinese side at the border.

It is not clear who first occupied the Dho La strip. The Chinese claim that the area had always been under their control and that Indian troops moved in during 1962. The Indians claim they had long occupied the area and that the Chinese began a to establish posts in the area after September 8, 1962. What is clear is that on October 12, 1962, Nehru announced in the Indian Parliament that he had given the order to drive the Chinese out of the Dho La strip.

Eight days later, on October 20, the Chinese attacked in force across the Thagla La ridge and into the disputed strip, while advancing their troops into the Chinese-claimed territory in the western sector where the Indians had earlier established posts. Four days later, the Chinese called for a ceasefire to be followed by a withdrawal of both sides from the line that separated them at that moment (the so-called October 24 line of actual control). Failing to get a satisfactory response from the Indians, they advanced troops south of the Dho La strip into the N.E.F.A., defeating Indian military forces in the area. Two weeks later, they withdrew to the positions occupied on October 24. The main point of contention between the Chinese and Indians ever since has been whether the Chinese should maintain their October 24 positions or withdraw further to the positions they occupied before fighting broke out.

The Chinese attack of October 1962 has led to an almost complete breakdown in relations between China and India. The level of each country's diplomatic representation in the other has been greatly reduced. Many thousands of Chinese nationals have been expelled from India. The few Indian nationals living in China have, in one way or another, been forced to leave. Border incidents have continued. Both sides have launched extreme propaganda campaigns against each other, the Chinese denouncing Nehru as a representative of the "big bourgeoisie" and a tool for U. S. aggressive designs against Tibet, while the Indians denounce the Chinese for having aggressive, imperialist designs against Indian territory. Both sides have gone to great lengths to discredit each other inter- nationally. Both sides have increased their military preparedness along the Himalayan frontier, particularly India, which has doubled its military budget to a level it cannot afford.

The question thus arises: Who is primarily to blame for the hostility in Sino/Indian relations? From the account already given, the primary cause of the hostility was the post-1959 dispute over the Sino/Indian border leading to the Chinese attack of October 20. But why the sudden emergence of such a dispute between two countries previously enjoying good relations? Reverting to the terminology of our previous discussion on hostility between states, both sides see the breakdown in relations as being caused by the active hostility of the other side. This hostility, they claim, is both ideologically and national- interest based. The Chinese are accused of having acted in a hostile manner out of a desire to acquire territory and out of strong ideological dislike for the Indian Government. The Chinese claim the Indians have designs against Chinese territory and that their Government is under the influence of anti-Chinese and pro-U. S. reactionary elements.

Both sides realise that they have somehow or other to explain why the other side suddenly, in 1959, decided that its interests were no longer served by the maintenance of normal relations. The Indian explanation is that Chinese pre-1959 policy was designed to lull India into a false sense of security and so facilitate Chinese ambitions. The Chinese explanation was that reactionary elements began to gain the upper hand in the Indian Government in 1959, and point to the post-1959 increase in U. S. aid to India as evidence.

In fact there is good reason to believe that the hostility shown by each side towards the other was reactive rather than active: that each side was reacting to the believed hostility of the other. To take the Chinese side of things first.

In terms of the account already given, it seems likely that the Chinese attack of October 20, 1962, was primarily a reaction to Indian military pressure along the disputed frontier during preceding months. It could be argued, however. that the behaviour of the Chinese before October 20, and in particular their propaganda attacks against the Indians from 1960 onwards, cannot be explained simply as a reaction to previous events: that overall Chinese behaviour must therefore include some aggressive component.

The Chinese had in fact made their first hostile move against the Indians back in 1959 when they restricted Indian trading and other rights in Tibet. The Chinese had also, according to the Indians, extended somewhat the area they claimed in the western sector. And they had, according to the Indians, been responsible for the 1959 border clashes already mentioned. The Indian charge is based on alleged differences between the frontier claimed by the Chinese to 1956 and that shown on a map of the claimed Sino/Indian frontier handed to the Indians by the Chinese in 1960. The Chinese deny any difference between the two lines.

Unless these apparently hostile acts of the Chinese can be explained in reactive terms., in terms of their reacting to previous Indian actions, then it would seem that the Chinese had taken the initiative in hostility towards India and were largely responsible for the eventual breakdown in relations.

The hardening of the Chinese attitude towards India in 1959 was clearly related to Tibetan developments in that year. In judging the behaviour of the Chinese, we need, in effect, to ask whether their sensitivity over Tibet was sufficient to explain this hardening of attitude.

To accept that the Communist Chinese are, in fact extremely sensitive toward Tibet does not necessarily imply a simple acceptance of Chinese propaganda. What we know of Chinese thinking and behaviour, strongly suggests that this sensitivity does exist. If all non-communist Chinese believe that China has the right to consider Tibet as an integral part of her territory, we should accept that Communist Chinese are equally convinced. If many non-communist Chinese believe (as they do) that Britain had designs against Tibet, we should accept that Communist Chinese, educated to believe in the evils of US Western imperialism, will be at least equally fearful. We do not need accept that these views are correct; we may even consider they are absurd. But if we are going to get anywhere in trying to understand China's behaviour, we should start from the assumption that these views may be sincerely hold in Peking.

Nor may it be so absurd for the Communist Chinese to think along these lines. The Chinese legal claim to Tibet, it has been argued, appears difficult to refute. As for fears of foreign designs, if the British had earlier convinced themselves that the activities of one Russian agent in Lhasa could lead the politically unstable Tibetans to ally themselves with Tsarist Russia, the Chinese could be excused for thinking that the presence of a British Mission in Lhasa dealing directly with the independent-minded Tibetans and arranging on occasion for the supply of arms from India was evidence of British ambitions eventually to detach Tibet from China, and that India may have inherited these ambitions. Similarly, it would not be entirely surprising if the Chinese viewed the supply of foreign arms to Tibetan guerrillas from northern India in 1959 as confirmation that such ambitions existed. Finally, the Chinese were hound to be impressed by the demands of the Indian Right Wing for action against the Chinese in Tibet.

For example: some weight could be attached to the fact that the then Chief of the Indian Army Staff wrote a not unenthusiastic foreword for a book published in 1961 entitled The Chinese Aggression. The author of the hook, a Dr. Satyanarayan Sinha, predicted that the "clash of the Indochinese weapons for the possession of the Himalayas will lead to making Tibet an independent country again", and suggested ways in which this could be done.

These, then, are the reasons for believing the Chinese may he sensitive about Tibet. Chinese behaviour provides further confirmation. British officials captured in Tibet in 1950 were subjected to long imprisonment and continual interrogation - treatment far more severe than that meted out to British nationals who fell into communist hands elsewhere in China. And there was Nehru's sad admission to the Indian Parliament in 1959 after talks with Chou En-Iai, of the Chinese having "some sort of kink in their minds... of foreign countries, United Kingdom or America, somehow making incursions into Tibet".

In sum, therefore, it does not seem unreasonable to conclude that the Communist Chinese sincerely believed they had a right to Tibet and that their position in the area was threatened from the direction of India. In which case they would have interpreted Indian behaviour in 1959 as an indication of hostility to which they felt compelled, or entitled, to react.

However, if Chinese behaviour in 1959 can be explained in reactive terms, can the same be said about the Chinese attack of October 1962? Even if the Indian claim to the Dho La strip was doubtful, does not the violence and intensity of the 1962 attack suggest that China was doing more than retaliate for any wrongs she may have believed the Indians to base committed?

By 1962, the Chinese were confronted not only by Indian agitation over Tibet, but also by two further aspects of Indian behaviour which would even more easily have been misunderstood. They were: (i) the Indian military build-up along the Sino/Indian border in 1961-2 and (ii) rigid Indian insistence that, as a precondition to border negotiations, the Chinese must first evacuate the whole of the Aksai Chin.

At the time, the Indians justified their position on negotiations and their military build up in terms of the correctness of their border claims. Indeed, the official Indian position was that the line claimed by India as a border had already been defined historically, and that the only purpose of negotiations was to demarcate on the ground the exact alignment of this border. From this it followed that they were justified (a) in regarding rival Chinese claims, and the occupation of the Aksai Chin, as evidence of Chinese hostility, and (b) in insisting that occupied territory had to be vacated before there could be negotiations. In the meantime the Indians had no alternative but to use military means to counter the Chinese "aggression".

If India was in fact the injured party in the territorial dispute, the Indian attitude over the disputed border would have been explicable at least to an impartial observer, and possibly even to the less impartial Chinese. There would be less justification for the Chinese reacting in the way they did. But was this the case? To answer this question we need to take a closer look at the historical background to the Sino /Indian frontier, and shall begin with the eastern sector, or N.E.F.A.

Until the 1920's, the region now known as the N.E.F.A. was largely unexplored. It was, and still is, inhabited by tribes of Tibeto-Burmese origin, some of which enjoyed trade and tributary relations with Tibet. Certain areas in the north of the region, the Tawang district for example, were inhabited by Tibetans and were under administrative control from Tibet.

The McMahon Line was negotiated with the Tibetans in 1914 at the time of the Simla Conference. It was drawn as far to the north as possible, since the British at the time sought to forestall a feared Chinese expansion into the foothills bordering the Assam plains. The McMahon Line as part of a bargain whereby the British would press the Chinese to concede territory elsewhere to Tibet.

Even so, the Tibetans were not entirely happy about losing territory south of the McMahon Line, the Tawang district in particular. Their acceptance of the line was conditional on possible future adjustments in their favour. No such adjustments, were ever made. The British also failed to extract the promised concessions from the Chinese, since the latter refused to accept the Convention produced at the Simla Conference. Thus, even as a Tibetan/British frontier, the McMahon Line does not have full validity, particularly as the Tibetans subsequently, in 1936, made a formal request to the British for revision of the line in their favour a request which the British ignored. As late as 1946, the Tibetans were still collecting taxes in the Tawang area. And, in 1947, the Tibetans approached the newly established Indian Government, seeking the "return" of "Tibetan territories" from Assam to Ladakh.

The Indian reply to this approach may be of interest in the light of complaints to be voiced later by the Indians over the manner in which the Chinese spoke of their border claims being inherited from previous Chinese Governments "The Government of India should be glad to have an assurance that it is the intention of the Tibetan Government to continue relations an the existing basis until new Agreements are any reached... This is the procedure adopted by all other countries with which India has inherited Treaty relations from His Majesty's Government".

The validity of the McMahon Line as a Chinese/Indian frontier is considerably more doubtful. True, in rejecting the draft Simla Contention, the Chinese did not specifically object to the McMahon Line as drawn on the map of Tibet attached to the Convention. But, as the Chinese point out, the then Chinese Government had no way of knowing what this line was supposed to represent, since the terms of the McMahon Line agreement were for some reason kept secret by the British and Tibetans until 1929. It could, in theory, have been a border between Tibet and a Chinese-owned N.E.F.A. Moreover, Chiang Kaishek's Government was later to make it clear to the British (and the Indians after 1947) that it did not accept the McMahon Line. The Chinese have also pointed out that, since neither the British nor the Chinese regarded Tibet as a sovereign entity, the Tibetans were obliged to obtain Chinese approval for any frontier negotiated with a foreign power. * Failure to obtain this approval, both at the Simla Conference and later, meant that the McMahon Line never at any stage enjoyed international legality. And finally, as the Chinese never tire of pointing out, many Western and Indian maps, including one reproduced in a book by Nehru himself, Discovery of India, have, even in recent years., shown the Sino/Indian border as running along the edge of the Assam plain in conformity with the traditional Chinese claim.

The 1906 Convention between Britain and China had required China to accept responsibility for Tibet's foreign relations. "The 1907 Anglo/Russian Convention required Britain 'not to enter into negotiations with Tibet except through the intermediary of the Chinese Government". Negotiations with the Tibetans over the McMahon Line were thus a breach of both conventions - a possible reason why the terms of the McMahon Line agreement were kept secret.

For the Communist Chinese to appear to be willing to drop their N.E.F.A. claim is no small concession in view of the very considerable doubts as to the validity of the McMahon Line. Indeed, the Nationalist Government in Taiwan feels so strongly shout the justice of the Chinese clams that its official newspapers have accused Peking of being willing to abandon "sacred" Chinese territory. They have predicted that the present Communist Chinese leaders will be condemned by future generations of Chinese for their betrayal of China's interests. Nevertheless, the Indian position was that the Chinese should not only drop their claim to the N.E.F.A. but to the Aksai Chin also. How strong is the Indian claim in the western sector of the disputed frontier?

The province of Ladakh, which lies on the Indian side of the disputed western sector, was originally a semi-independent state with a complex tributary relationship with Tibet. It was far from being clearly defined Indian territory. These links with Tibet were severed as a result of the 1841 invasion of Tibet from Kashmir, and Ladakh was incorporated into India. In the agreement which followed the invasion, the Ladakh/Tibet border was defined simply as following "the old established frontier", and it was only subsequently that British cartographers decided where this frontier should lie. A small area lying between the Chinese-claimed and Indian-claimed frontiers is in dispute.

By far the larger area in dispute, the Aksai Chin, lies for the most part north of the Ladakh/Tibet frontier, and its ownership depends on a definition of the Ladakh/Sinkiang border. At the end of the nineteenth century, the British decided an effort should be made to define this border, and in 1899 a note was delivered to the Chinese suggesting a possible alignment.

This alignment is shown on the map above, and it will be seen that it leaves with China much of the territory at present in dispute. The Chinese never replied to the note. Shortly afterwards, the British attitude changed.

Alarmed by growing Chinese weakness in Central Asia, and fearing Russian expansion into the area (fears similar to those being entertained in connection with Tibet), the British felt they should establish the border as far north as possible to forestall any southward advance by the Russians. British maps began to show the border as lying far to the north along the Kun Lun mountains. Chinese agreement was never sought for this claimed border (despite the fact that the British recognised Chinese sovereignty in Sinkiang) ; presumably it was only being put forward as an emergency measure in case the Russians attempted to seize

Sinkiang. By the 1920's the Russian threat had disappeared, and it was deemed safe to drop this particular claim.

In subsequent years, British and Indian maps showed a variety of claim lines some coinciding with the present Chinese claim line, some the claim line along the Kun Lun mountains, and some an in-between claim line which ran south of the Kun Lun mountains but which included the Aksai Chin as Indian territory.

Maps showing this last claim line were in general use at the time of the 1947 transfer of power, and appear to constitute the basis of the present Indian claim to the Aksai Chin. However, the only border to have ever been officially proposed to the Chinese by the British in this area was that of 1899, and, as already mentioned, this border left most of the Aksai Chin with China.

Whatever the merits of rival Chinese and Indian claims to the Aksai Chin area, it does seem clear that the Indians can hardly speak of the frontier they claim in this area as being already defined by history and therefore subject only to demarcation.

In this connection a rather curious aspect of the Indian position should be mentioned - an aspect which has been overlooked by most students of the Sino/Indian dispute.

Numerous Indian authorities, including Nehru himself, have claimed historical validity for their version of the Indian! Sinkiang frontier on the ground that the line proposed by the British in 1899 "ran along the Kun Lun range to a point east of 80° longitude, where it met the eastern boundary of Ladakh". In fact, the 1899 line ran well to the south of the Kun Lun mountains, and the text of the proposal speaks only of the tine meeting "the spur running south from the Kun Lun range, which [the spur] has hitherto been shown on our maps as the eastern boundary of Ladakh. This is a little east of 80° east longitude".* A misquotation of these dimensions is rather serious, particularly when it is used to justify an official claim to some 30,000 square kilometres of territory, and when, on the basis of this claim, negotiations are refused in favour of a military solution of a complex border dispute.

The only observer who appears to have noted this misquotation is Alastair Lamb. In his book, *The China-India Border,* he gives the full text of the British note of 1899 and lists some of the Indian authorities who have misquoted the 1899 proposal. Distribution of his book within India has been banned.

It would seem, therefore, that an impartial observer who takes into account not only the historical background of the border dispute, but also the equally relevant criteria of geography and administrative control, would agree that the Chinese are not being unreasonable when they call for border negotiations on the basis of the present status quo.

If, as seems to be the case, the Chinese are prepared to do a N.E.F.A./Aksai Chin exchange leaving India in control of far the largest and most valuable of the territories in dispute, he may even feel that the Chinese are being quite generous. And if our impartial observer were to reach such a conclusion, it seems highly likely that the Chinese would be convinced of the reasonableness of their position and the unreasonableness of the Indian demand for a unilateral Chinese withdrawal from the Aksai Chin.

If the Chinese were in fact convinced that they were in the right over the border dispute, they would in all probability have interpreted the Indian military build-up along the disputed border in 1961-2 as evidence of active hostility.

Striking confirmation that this was the case is contained in the "Tibetan Documents" - official Chinese documents which were captured by Tibetan rebels in 1961 and which subsequently found their way to the U.S., where they have been translated and published.

These documents were intended as background briefing to senior Chinese military commanders stationed along the Sino/ Indian border. As such, their contents cannot be dismissed simply as propaganda. The documents warned of U.S./Indian collusion to build up pressure along the Tibetan frontier as a prelude to a joint attack against Tibet. Military commanders were instructed to observe strictly the twenty-kilometre troop withdrawal from the line of actual control and to avoid clashes with advancing Indian patrols since this would provide the "imperialists" with the pretext they needed to justify their planned attack.*

SECTORS OF SINO-INDIAN BORDER: WESTERN SECTOR, MIDDLE SECTOR AND EASTERN SECTOR

The Sino-Indian border is generally divided into three sectors namely: (i) the Western sector, (ii) the Middle sector, and (iii) the Eastern sector.

The Western Sector

This 2,152 km long sector of the Sino-Indian border separates Jammu and Kashmir State of India from the Sinkiang province of China. The frontier between Sinkiang and Pakistan occupied Kashmir (PoK) is about 480 km long. The rest is boundary between Ladakh and Tibet.

The boundary in the western sector runs along the Muztagh Ata Range and the Aghil Mountain across the Karakoram Pass via Quara Tagh pass and along the main Kunlun Range to a point east of 80°E longitude and 40 km north of Hajit Langer. It forms a physical boundary between Gilgit area and Sinkiang following the main Karakoram watershed separating the streams flowing into the Indus basin from those flowing into the Tarin basin.

Farther south-east the boundary runs along the watershed across Lanak La, Kone La and Kepsang La, then follows the Chemesang River across Pergyon Lake and the Kailash Range. Here the boundary constitutes the watershed between the Indus system in India and the Khotan system in China. The western sector boundary is the outcome of the British policy towards the state of Jammu and Kashmir. These boundaries were defined by the treaties of 1665 and 1686 (known as Ladakh-Tibet agreements) and were confirmed by 1842 Dogra-Ladakh agreement among Kashmir, Tibet and China.

However, this boundary was never delimited precisely on maps and has led to several boundary disputes between China and India. The Chinese claim rests mainly on ethnic grounds, and on the assertion that the wastelands of the Aksai Chin in disputed territory were always linked more with Tibet and Sinkiang. The Chinese claim that Aksai Chin is just an extension of Tibet with regard to language, religion and culture. But in Chinese documentation regarding the actual occupation of the area by Tibet in inconclusive.

The Indians, on the other hand, claim that the area has been historically administered by the state of Jammu and Kashmir since 1849, and that the Indo-Tibet Treaties of 1665, 1684 and 1842 confirmed the boundary between Tibet and Ladakh. China claims the Aksai Chin district, the Changmo valley, Pangong Tso and the Sponggar Tso area of north-east Ladakh as well as a strip of about 5,000 sq km down the entire length of eastern Ladakh. China also claims a part of Huza-Gilgit area in North Kashmir (ceded to it in 1963 by Pakistan), although the whole territory has been effectively under the British sovereignty since 1895.

Since 1954, the Chinese have repeatedly violated the international border between India and China and penetrated deep into the Indian Territory in the western sector. China renewed aggression in 1959 and the Line of Actual Control (LoAC) become of series of positions occupied by the Chinese forces rather than a well defined border between the two countries. In 1962, China waged a full scale war and its forces intruded far deeper into the Indian Territory. Currently the Chinese occupation line runs 16 to 240 km west of traditional line. China is in actual possession of about 54,000 sq km of the Indian Territory of which 37,555 sq km is in Ladakh area alone.

The Middle Sector

The middle sector boundary between China and India is 625 km long and runs along the watershed from Ladakh to Nepal. Two Indian states of Himachal Pradesh and Uttaranchal touch this border. The boundary of Himachal Pradesh follows the water parting between the Spiti and Para Chu rivers and continues along the watershed between the eastern and western tributaries of the Satluj. The Uttaranchal boundary is demarcated by the watershed between the Satluj on one hand and the Kali, the Alaknanda, and the Bhagirathi on the other. This boundary crosses the Satluj near the Shipki La on the Himachal-Tibet border.

Thereafter, it runs along the watershed passes of Mana, Niti, Kungri-Bingri, Dharma and Lipu Ladakh. It finally joins trijunction of China, India and Nepal. This part of the border was approved by the Tibetan and the British governments under the 1890 and 1919 treaties. Although there are not much seriòus territorial problems between the two countries, the Chinese lay claim on nearly 2,000 sq km area in this sector.

The Eastern Sector

The 1,140 km long boundary between India and China runs from the eastern limit of Bhutan to a point near Talu-Pass at the trijunction of India, Tibet and Myanmar. This line is usually referred to as the Me Mahon Line after Henry Me Mahon, a British representative who signed the 1913-14 Shimla Convention. This line normally runs along the crest of the Himalayas between Bhutan and Myanmar. India has stressed that the Me Mahon Line is the international boundary between Tibet and India as was agreed to between the governments of India, China and Tibet. On the other hand China considers the Me Mahon line as illegal and unacceptable, claiming that Tibet had no right to sign the 1913-14 convention held in Shimla which delineated the Me Mahon Line on the map.

India challenges such a position, maintaining that Tibet was independent and in fact concluded several independent treaties which were considered valid by all parties, and were in operation for decades. China declined the validity of the Me Mahon Line as an international boundary and laid claims to areas south of this line up to the foot of the Himalayan range in the Brahmaputra valley. The whole of Arunachal Pradesh, measuring over 88 thousand sq km has been claimed by China as the Chinese territory. This area has been administered by India since 1947.

Chinese government never formally questioned the validity of 1913-14 Shimla convention until 1959. India has been striking at the two crucial points. First, Britain and India had been exercising jurisdiction over the area since 1914 and 1947 respectively and second China never disputed the Indian control over the area until 1959. Even in 1956 when the Chinese attention was drawn to certain maps drawn by China which showed these areas to be parts of China, the Chinese government promised to look into the 'cartographic errors' in their maps.

China's relations with India started taking a bad turn in 1950s when China started consolidating its position in Tibet and then in Ladakh. By 1956, China started intensifying its intrusions into the Indian Territory. India wishfully hoped that the insurmountable barrier of the Himalayas would prevent Chinese to attack Indian Territory. Indian apprehensions grew in 1956 when China built a road through Ladakh linking West Tibet with Sinkiang and quickly moved into Aksai Chin and eastern Ladakh. China also moved its forces into the North-East Frontier Agency (NEFA), the present Arunachal Pradesh. Reported small-scale armed clashes between 1959 and 1962 escalated into a full-scale war in October, 1962 when China launched a major offensive in Ladakh in the western sector and NEFA in the eastern sector. Indian armed forces were not well trained to fight a modern war in a rough and rugged mountainous terrain. They were outnumbered and outgunned by the Chinese forces.

Following lessons have been learnt from Chinese aggression over India:

(i) The myth that the Himalayas were an effective defense barrier was exploded.

(ii) India's naive confidence in China's friendliness had dulled its perception regarding effective security measures in the Indo-China borderlands.

(iii) The prompt and positive response of western countries in rushing military supplies to the war zone helped improve the image of the West in Indian eyes.

(iv) India realised that posture of "non-alignment" was no substitute for defense preparedness.

Surprisingly, Chinese forces pulled back without annexing the disputed territory in the eastern sector. In the western sector, however, they did not pull out of most of Aksai Chin. Perhaps they did so due to the fear that their advance troops would have been cut off from supply bases in Tibet in winter of 1962 when the high passes in the Himalayas would have been closed by snow. The Chinese justified their withdrawal by stating that they had no further territorial ambitions.

The primary aim of Chinese invasion was to deprive India of its moral leadership in the world especially among the Afro-Asian countries, and to put pressure on it to join the socialist camp. China's collusion with Pakistan is a clear indication of this political ambition. Perhaps China miscalculated its political power strategy. The support of the Western countries to India compelled China to rethink its strategy. India's unity in the face of Chinese aggression was another deterrent for China to achieve political mileage.

An uneasy truce had been prevailing for a long time since the October, 1962 war. Neither side made a serious effort to normalise the situation on the border. The Colombo powers, spearheaded by Ceylon (now Sri Lanka) and the erstwhile Soviet Union failed to bring about a respectable agreement between the two countries. Several countries condemned China as an aggressor. However, Cuba, Albania and Portugal supported the Chinese. Of late, leaders of both the countries have engaged themselves in improving the bilateral relations. Several meetings have been held to resolve the problem of border issues. A major development took place in October, 2003 when China made a significant change in its official website. It removed the mention of Sikkim from its list of nations.

In May, 2004, China recognised Sikkim as a part of India for the first time. The world map in World Affairs Year Book 2003/2004 does not show Sikkim as separate country in Asia. It also does not mention Sikkim in its index of countries.

The move was significant since it involves recognition of Sikkim-China border which is a part of the Me Mahon Line. If things go as planned, the two nations should be able to work out the guide lines for transforming the Line of Actual Control (LoAC) into a mutually acceptable and internationally recognised boundary. However, China still insists that Arunachal Pradesh is a disputed territory. China has also suggested a 'package deal'. It asked India to accept Chinese domination over Aksai Chin in return of China's acceptance of Me Mahon Line as the international boundary.

India, however, has advocated 'sector-by-sector' approach. Indian side is hopeful because China has settled border disputes with Russia and Vietnam.

6

The Collision of the Sino-Indian War

In many ways, how China and India relate to each other indicates where they see themselves in the international system. Firstly, however, it is necessary to have an understanding of the events leading up to and following the 1962 Sino-Indian War, as this continues to affect the contemporary Sino-Indian relationship. The major causes of conflict between China and India – namely, the disputed border and the issue of Tibet, including the fourteenth Dalai Lama's ongoing residency in India – have their roots in the political dealings that went on in the late 1800s and early 1900s between British India, pre-Communist China and feudal Tibet. The major question was whether treaties signed by British India and Tibet demarcating the border – known as the McMahon Line – were valid, given that, according to the Chinese, Tibet was part of China and had no authority to act unilaterally. Disagreements of this nature and the exact location of the border persisted throughout the early twentieth century, further complicated by Indian independence in 1947 (which removed British backing and so altered the balance of power in the region in favour of China) and the Chinese 'liberation' of Tibet in 1950.

1954, marked with a visit to India Chinese by Premier Zhou Enlai in June, and a reciprocal visit by Indian Prime Minister Jawaharlal Nehru to China in October, was a high point in the relationship; it was during the latter visit that the term 'Hindi-Chini bhai-bhai' (Indians and Chinese are brothers) was coined, and denoted a period of rapprochement after decades of strife over the disputed India-Tibet border.

This new-found friendship in theory forged a renewed basis for discussions over the disputed border, though this was tested only two years later. There were (and still are) two contested areas: the north-eastern stretch, which was known under the British as the North-East Frontier Agency (NEFA) and since 1986 has been the Indian state of Arunachal Pradesh (claimed by the Chinese as Southern Tibet), and the western region of Aksai Chin (claimed by the Indians and currently administered by the Chinese), which borders the Indian state of Jammu and Kashmir. Although up until the mid-50s most of the border tensions had existed over the eastern stretch – and specifically the disputed border known as the McMahon Line – the western region became the focus when in 1956 the Chinese constructed a highway from Xinjiang province to Tibet through the Aksai Chin to allow the rapid movement of troops between the two restive provinces. In spite of disputing the occupation of the territory, India did not actually administer the Aksai Chin in any way, and consequently after the building of the road the region effectively passed into Chinese hands. Nevertheless, the Aksai Chin continued to be a volatile area – not helped by the fact that the rest of Jammu and Kashmir was the subject of an ongoing and often violent dispute between India and Pakistan – and subsequently provided one of the flashpoints for the 1962 Sino-Indian war.

Matters were further complicated with the Lhasa Revolt of March 1959, an uprising of Tibetans which culminated in the fleeing of the fourteenth Dalai Lama (and subsequently thousands of Tibetan refugees) to India and the systematic crushing of the resistance by Chinese forces. In the northern autumn Chinese and Indian troops clashed along the McMahon Line border.

An attempt at resolving the border issue was made during a visit by Premier Zhou Enlai to Delhi from19-25 April 1960, but "the talks…did not resolve the differences that had arisen and the two Prime Ministers decided that officials of the two Governments should examine the factual material in the possession of the two Governments in support of their stands" (Ministry of External

Affairs, 1961:1). The committee met three times throughout 1960, with both sides producing reports of the discussions for their respective governments.

The contents of these reports illustrate how intractable the border problem was and indeed still is, with the two sides unable to agree even on the basic tenor of the talks, such as whether the border had ever been officially delimited (no, according to China; yes, according to India). Consequently no resolution was reached at the 1960 talks which, with hindsight, were really the last opportunity to effect an agreement before relations broke down completely.

The Sino-Indian War began on 8 September 1962 when the Chinese crossed into NEFA (now Arunachal Pradesh) and attacked an Indian border post, alleging that the Indians had already violated the McMahon Line. This was the first time the conflict flared along the McMahon Line, though there had been some fighting around the Aksai Chin region, inflamed by Sino-Pakistani border talks which the Indians alleged were aimed at undermining their position in Kashmir. These skirmishes continued throughout September and into October.

On 20 October the Chinese launched a full-scale offensive all along the frontier, from Ladakh to NEFA, arguing that it was a pre-emptive strike against Indian aggression. This was significant because it moved the conflict beyond the disputed areas and into Indian territory, essentially becoming an invasion of India. The Indian force was fatally under-prepared and crumbled before the Chinese onslaught.

The fighting lasted for just over a month, with the Chinese declaring a unilateral ceasefire on 21 November. Statistics released by the Indian government on 29 October had between 2000 and 2500 Indian soldiers killed during the first week of fighting, with 1102 held prisoner, 291 wounded and 5174 missing and presumed dead.

On 8 November the Chinese proposed a ceasefire agreement whereby both parties would withdraw twenty kilometres behind the positions held on 7 November, 1959. This meant that the Chinese would withdraw back behind the McMahon Line, but they would maintain control of Indian-claimed territory in Ladakh, including the strategically important Aksai Chin road linking Xinjiang and Tibet.

This was initially rejected by the Indians, but after another fortnight of fierce fighting the Chinese surprised everyone by announcing a unilateral ceasefire and the withdrawal of troops from 1 December to the 7 November 1959 positions. The Chinese also added that, provided the Indian government took corresponding measures, the two parties could meet to discuss troop withdrawal and an end to hostilities. Militarily weakened, and with the rest of the world supporting all measures to solve the conflict, India was in no position to argue.

In December 1962 six non-aligned nations (Ceylon, Burma, Cambodia, Indonesia, the United Arab Republic and Ghana) met in Colombo to try to broker a formal peace deal, but their lack of condemnation of the Chinese invasion incensed India. India nevertheless accepted the Colombo proposals, but China rejected them, insisting on a "unilateral implementation" of its 21 November 1962 statement; consequently the talks broke down and nothing was resolved, even in subsequent bilateral meetings.

Sino-Indian relations did not begin to normalise until the mid-1970s; a turning point was the resumption of ambassadorial relations in 1976. Although the two countries retained non-official diplomatic relations throughout the 1960s (with missions headed by a *charge d'affairs* rather than an ambassador), interaction was minimal. In fact, Gautam Das describes the period between 1962-76 as a period of "cold peace" rather than cold war, and notes that " Sino-Indian relations after 1962 are, in substance if not chronology, Sino-Indian relations after 1976 [because very little of note happened in the intervening period]".

Rapprochement continued after the resumption of diplomatic relations, albeit with a few hiccups, but it wasn't until 1988 that the turning point came with Indian Prime Minister Rajiv Gandhi's visit to Beijing. This made him the first Indian Prime Minister to visit China since Nehru in 1954 and marked the end of the impasse on the border issue which had lasted for most of the 1980s; the two sides agreed to maintain peace and stability along the Line of Actual Control (LAC) in Arunachal Pradesh (roughly equivalent to the McMahon Line), and they also agreed to set up a Joint Working Group (JWG) to help defuse the border issue. In addition, India agreed to curtail the anti-China actions of Tibetans in India. According to Das, "the decade that followed the Rajiv Gandhi visit up to the 1998 Indian nuclear explosions (Pokhran-II) has been the most cordial phase of Sino-Indian relations after 1962".

These warm relations continued during the mid-1990s, and were further consolidated by Chinese President Jiang Zemin's visit to India in 1996, where four mutual cooperation agreements were signed, and it appeared that a breakthrough in the tensions had finally occurred.

Unfortunately, this series of small steps forward was followed by a giant leap backwards in 1998. During a visit of the People's Liberation Army (PLA) Senior General Fu Quanyou to New Delhi, the Indian Defence Minister, George Fernandes, publicly stated that he believed China was continuing to carry out border incursions into Indian territory, and later accused China of being India's number one security threat, greater even than Pakistan. This was immediately followed by India's second ever nuclear tests, known as Pokhran II (ibid). The fact that the tests occurred before Fu had even arrived back in Beijing caused a huge loss of face for the Chinese, because they felt that after a decade of overtures to the Indians they had been callously rebuffed and humiliated.

Nevertheless, the overall Chinese reaction to the tests was initially quite controlled, and might have remained so, had India not justified the tests by claiming they were in response to the 'China threat'. This was articulated in a letter from Indian Prime Minister Vajpayee to US President Bill Clinton, which was printed in the *New York Times* on 13 May (ibid). This was seen as "unwarranted and provocative", and the fact that the issue was given such a public airing caused another immense loss of face for the Chinese; consequently they reacted angrily, cancelling the next meeting of the Joint Working Group on the border issue. This issue of the 'China threat' still permeates relations today, with more than one Chinese interviewee claiming that the Indian military deliberately promotes China as a threat in order to get increased defence spending, and that 1998 was one of the clearest examples of this (Author interviews with Wang Dehua and anonymous interviewee, 2010).

After the low point of the 1998 tests, relations began once again to normalise, in spite of a brief hiccup over Tibet when 14-year-old Ugyen Thinley Dorje, the 17th Karmapa Lama of the Kagyupa sect of Tibetan Buddhism, fled China for Dharamsala in January 2000.

Nevertheless, in February 2000 India and China concluded an agreement for China's accession to the World Trade Organisation ; in March India participated in the first ever Sino-Indian security dialogue in Beijing, and the Joint Working Group sessions resumed in April of the same year.

In 2003 an incursion by Chinese troops into Indian territory occurred in Arunachal Pradesh, shortly after Indian Prime Minister Vajpayee's visit to Beijing; Vajpayee put this down to "differences in perceptions" regarding the Line of Actual Control, but some politicians and analysts took it much more seriously. This incident shows that in spite of another gradual thawing of relations, the border question still remains a highly contentious issue in the Sino-Indian relationship.

Furthermore, in addition to ongoing Indian concerns about the Sino-Pakistani relationship, China is also disturbed about the growing relationship between India and the USA, fearing that such an alliance will upset the balance of power in the region.

Seen in the light of history, the most recent incidents to affect the Sino-Indian relationship – the 2008 Tibet protests and the subsequent disruption of the Olympic torch relay (including in Delhi); and the border skirmishes and associated negative media coverage throughout 2009 – are unlikely to cause permanent damage to the relationship.

They do, however, highlight the fact that the border issue is still unresolved, and most analysts agree that the Sino-Indian relationship will not be able to move forward in any meaningful way until this question is answered. As well as being rooted in political reality, however, a large element of the Sino-Indian conflict also stems from misplaced perceptions, both of each other's motives and of their own place in the world order.

The concept of 'Chindia' is popular at present but it is based on flawed logic. Although the geo-civilisational aspects, where cultural practices flowed freely across what is now Central Asia to India and China and back again, cannot be denied, China and India are also distinct civilisations with their own histories and cultures and to conflate them is to understate the importance of this in shaping their distinctive governments and policies. It also minimises the very real animosity which remains between them and deeply influences not only the Sino-Indian relationship but also how they see themselves and how they relate to the wider international community.

On a political and strategic front, India and China have followed extremely different developmental trajectories with different outcomes and they also have different aims for their status in the international system. These differences in aims, policy and strategic thought can be seen to be playing out in Central Asia at present.

The 'Chindia' concept is for the most part a Western construct developed as a response to the 'China threat' perception and tied into the former US and ASEAN policy of containment, in which India would play an important role. This idea of a mutual rise or equating China and India was seized upon by some in India who were attracted by the idea that India has or will soon have the same type of international economic and political clout as China, even when the present reality suggests otherwise.

In fact, India should not seek to emulate China because it is unlikely that such a course of action would succeed; in any case the two countries' systems are extremely different. Rather, India must forge its own path and decide what kind of a role it wants to play internationally, and how it will achieve this.

It must also in the immediate-term concentrate on domestic development and remember that 'national security' cannot just be about the military but must also include human, food, environmental and other types of security as well as poverty reduction.

This seems to be the path which the Indian government is beginning to take and it is likely to be far more successful than any which frames the question of India's development in relation to China. Regarding China, we need to rethink the way we examine it in terms of international relations theory in order to avoid overlooking the real issues in Chinese strategic thought because of a desire to fit Chinese development into an established international relations model.

Finally, scholarship – both in China and India and further afield – needs to be developed so that more scholars are educated in the practices and policies of both countries, and communication is facilitated between China and India scholars the world over, rather than operating simply in closed 'China studies' or 'India studies' spheres. This would not only prove beneficial to promoting stability in the Sino-Indian relationship, but would also go some way to ensuring that the two countries can be viewed as separate but parallel entities rather than as 'Chindia'.

LOCATION

China and India shared a long border, sectioned into three stretches by Nepal, Sikkim (then an independent kingdom), and Bhutan, which follows the Himalayas between Burma and what was then West Pakistan. A number of disputed regions lie along this border. At its western end is the Aksai Chin region, an area the size of Switzerland, that sits between the Chinese autonomous region of Xinjiang and Tibet (which China declared as an autonomous region in 1965). The eastern border, between Burma and Bhutan, comprises the present Indian state of Arunachal Pradesh (formerly the North East Frontier Agency). Both of these regions were overrun by China in the 1962 conflict.

Most combat took place at high altitudes. The Aksai Chin region is a desert of salt flats around 5,000 metres above sea level, and Arunachal Pradesh is mountainous with a number of peaks exceeding 7000 metres. According to military doctrine, to be successful an attacker generally requires a 3:1 ratio of numerical superiority over the defender for foot soldiers ; in mountain warfare this ratio should be considerably higher as the terrain favours defence. The Chinese Army had possession of one of the highest ridges in the regions. The high altitude and freezing conditions also cause logistical and welfare difficulties; in past similar conflicts (such as the Italian Campaign of World War I) more casualties have been caused by the harsh conditions than enemy action. The Sino-Indian War was no different, with many troops on both sides dying in the freezing cold.

Background

The cause of the war was a dispute over the sovereignty of the widely separated Aksai Chin and Arunachal Pradesh border regions. Aksai Chin, claimed by India to belong to Kashmir and by China to be part of Xinjiang, contains an important road link that connects the Chinese regions of Tibet and Xinjiang. China's construction of this road was one of the triggers of the conflict.

The Johnson Line

The western portion of the Sino-Indian boundary originated in 1834, with the Sikh Confederation's conquest of Ladakh. In 1842, the Sikh Confederacy, which at the time ruled over much of Northern India (including the frontier regions of Jammu and Kashmir), signed a treaty which guaranteed the integrity of its existing borders with its neighbours. The British defeat of the Sikhs in 1846 resulted in transfer of sovereignty over Ladakh, part of the Jammu and Kashmir region, to the British, and British commissioners contacted Chinese officials to negotiate the border. The boundaries at its two extremities, Pangong Lake and Karakoram Pass, were well defined, but the Aksai Chin area in between lay undefined.

W. H. Johnson, a civil servant with the Survey of India proposed the "Johnson Line" in 1865, which put Aksai Chin in Kashmir. Johnson presented this line to the Maharaja of Kashmir, who then claimed the 18,000 square kilometres contained within. Johnson's work was severely criticized for gross inaccuracies, with description of his boundary as "patently absurd" who even extended his claim 80 miles further into China when India and China went into conflict over the border. Johnson was reprimanded by the British

Government for crossing into Khotan without permission and resigned from the Survey. According to Francis Young husband, who explored the region in the late 1880s, there was only an abandoned fort and not one inhabited house at Shahidulla when he was there - it was just a convenient staging post and a convenient headquarters for the nomadic Kirghiz. The abandoned fort had apparently been built a few years earlier by the Kashmiris. In 1878 the Chinese had reconquered Xinjiang, and by 1890 they already had Shahidulla before the issue was decided. By 1892, China had erected boundary markers at Karakoram Pass.

Throughout most of the 19th century the expanding British and Russian empires were jockeying for influence in Central Asia, and Britain decided to hand over Aksai Chin to the Chinese administration as a buffer against a Russian invasion. The newly created border was known as the MacCartney-MacDonald Line, and both British-controlled India and China now began to show Aksai Chin as Chinese. In 1911 the Xinhai Revolution resulted in power shifts in China, and by 1918 (in the wake of the Russian Bolshevik Revolution) the British no longer saw merit in China's continuing possession of the region. On British maps, the border was redrawn as the original Johnson Line, but despite this reversion, the new border was left unmanned and undemarcated. According toNeville Maxwell, the British had used as many as 11 different boundary lines in the region, as their claims shifted with the political situation. By the time of Indian independence in 1947, the Johnson Line had become India's official western boundary. On 1 July 1954, India's first Prime Minister Jawaharlal Nehru definitively stated the Indian position. claimed that Aksai Chin had been part of the Indian Ladakh region for centuries, and that the border (as defined by the Johnson Line) was non-negotiable. According to George N. Patterson, when the Indian government finally produced a report detailing the alleged proof of India's claims to the disputed area, "the quality of the Indian evidence was very poor, including some very dubious sources indeed".

In 1956–57, China constructed a road through Aksai Chin, connecting Xinjiang and Tibet, which ran south of the Johnson Line in many places. Aksai Chin was easily accessible to the

Chinese, but access from India, which meant negotiating the Karakoram mountains, was more problematic. The road came on Chinese maps published in 1958. The McMahon Line

In 1826, British India gained a common border with China after the British wrested control of Manipur and Assam from the Burmese, following the First Anglo-Burmese War of 1824–1826. In 1847, Major J. Jenkins, agent for the North East Frontier, reported that the Tawang was part of Tibet.

In 1872, four monastic officials from Tibet arrived in Tawang and supervised a boundary settlement with Major R. Graham, NEFA official, which included the Tawang Tract as part of Tibet.

Thus, in the last half of the 19th century, it was clear that the British treated the Tawang Tract as part of Tibet. This boundary was confirmed in a 1 June 1912 note from the British General Staff in India, stating that the "present boundary is south of Tawang, running westwards along the foothills from near Ugalguri to the southern Bhutanese border."

A 1908 map of The Province of Eastern Bengal and Assam prepared for the Foreign Department of the Government of India, showed the international boundary from Bhutan continuing to the Baroi River, following the Himalayas foothill alignment. In 1913, representatives of Great Britain, China and Tibet attended a conference in Simla regarding the borders between Tibet, China and British India.

Whilst all three representatives initialed the agreement, Beijinglater objected to the proposed boundary between the regions of Outer Tibet and Inner Tibet, and did not ratify it. The details of the Indo-Tibetan boundary was not revealed to China at the time.

The foreign secretary of the British Indian government, Henry McMahon, who had drawn up the proposal, decided to bypass the Chinese (although instructed not to by his superiors) and settle the border bilaterally by negotiating directly with Tibet. According to later Indian claims, this border was intended to run through the highest ridges of the Himalayas, as the areas south of the Himalayas were traditionally Indian. However, the McMahon Line lay south of the boundary India claims. India's government held the view that the Himalayas were the ancient boundaries of theIndian subcontinent, and thus should be the modern boundaries of India, while it is the position of the Chinese government that the disputed area in the Himalayas have been geographically and culturally part of Tibet since ancient times.

Months after the Simla agreement, China set up boundary markers south of the McMahon Line. T. O'Callaghan, an official in the Eastern Sector of the North East Frontier, relocated all these markers to a location slightly south of the McMahon Line, and then visited Rima to confirm with Tibetan officials that there was no Chinese influence in the area. The British-run Government of India initially rejected the Simla Agreement as incompatible with the Anglo-Russian Convention of 1907, which stipulated that neither party was to negotiate with Tibet "except through the intermediary of the Chinese government". The British and Russians cancelled the 1907 agreement by joint consent in 1921. It was not until the late 1930s that the British started to use the McMahon Line on official maps of the region.

China took the position that the Tibetan government should not have been allowed to make a such a treaty, rejecting Tibet's claims of independent rule. For its part, Tibet did not object to any section of the McMahon Line excepting the demarcation of the trading town of Tawang, which the Line placed under British-Indian jurisdiction. However, up until World War II, Tibetan officials were allowed to administer Tawang with complete authority. Due to the increased threat of Japanese and Chinese expansion during this period, British Indian troops secured the town as part of the defence of India's eastern border.

In the 1950s, India began actively patrolling the region. It found that, at multiple locations, the highest ridges actually fell north of the McMahon Line. Given India's historic position that the original intent of the line was to separate the two nations by the highest mountains in the world, in these locations India extended its forward posts northward to the ridges, regarding this move as compliant with the original border proposal, although the Simla Convention did not explicitly state this intention.

FACTORS RESPONSIBLE FOR WAR

Tibet Controversy

The 1940s saw huge change in South Asia with the Partition of India in 1947 (resulting in the establishment of the two new states of India and Pakistan), and the establishment of the People's Republic of China in 1949. One of the most basic policies for the new Indian government was that of maintaining cordial relations with China, reviving its ancient friendly ties. India was among the first nations to grant diplomatic recognition to the newly-created PRC. At the time, Chinese officials issued no condemnation of Nehru's claims or made any opposition to Nehru's open declarations of control over Aksai Chin.

In 1956, Chinese Premier Zhou Enlai stated that he had no claims over Indian controlled territory. He later argued that Aksai Chin was already under Chinese jurisdiction, implying that there was therefore no contradiction with his earlier statement since China did not regard the region as "Indian controlled", and that since the British hand-over China had regarded the McCartney MacDonald Line as the relevant border. Zhou later argued that as the boundary was undemarcated and had never been defined by treaty between any Chinese or Indian government, the Indian government could not unilaterally define Aksai Chin's borders. However, within a short time the PRC announced its intention to reclaim Tibet from the British, and later extended its influence by placing border posts within the Indian-claimed territory of Aksai Chin. India protested against these moves and decided to look for a diplomatic solution to ensure a stable Sino-Indian border.

To resolve any doubts about the Indian position, Prime Minister Jawaharlal Nehru declared in parliament that India regarded the McMahon Line as its official border. The Chinese expressed no concern at this statement, and in 1951 and 52, the government of China asserted that there were no frontier issues to be taken up with India. In 1954, Prime Minister Nehru wrote a memo calling for India's borders to be clearly defined and demarcated: in line with previous Indian philosophy, Indian maps showed a border that, in some places, lay north of the McMahon Line. Chinese

Premier Zhou Enlai, in November 1956, again repeated Chinese assurances that the People's Republic had no claims on Indian territory, although official Chinese maps showed 120,000 square kilometres of territory claimed by India as Chinese.

CIA documents created at the time revealed that Nehru had ignored Burmese premier Ba Swe when he warned Nehru to be cautious when dealing with Zhou. They also allege that Zhou purposefully told Nehru that there were no border issues with India. In 1950 the Chinese People's Liberation Army invaded Tibet. Four years later, in 1954, China and India negotiated the Five Principles of Peaceful Coexistence by which the two nations agreed to abide in settling their disputes. India presented a frontier map which was accepted by China, and the Indian government under Prime Minister Nehru promoted the slogan *Hindi-Chini bhai-bhai* (Indians and Chinese are brothers). According to Georgia Tech political analyst John W Garver, Nehru's policy on Tibet was to create a strong Sino-Indian partnership which would be catalyzed through agreement and compromise on Tibet. Garver believes that Nehru's previous actions had given him confidence that China would be ready to form an "Asian Axis" with India. This apparent progress in relations suffered a major setback when, in 1959, Nehru accommodated the Tibetan religious leader, the Dalai Lama, who was fleeing Lhasa after a failed Tibetan uprising against Chinese rule.

The Chairman of the Chinese Communist Party, Mao Zedong, was enraged and asked the Xinhua News Agency to produce reports on Indian expansionists operating in Tibet. Border incidents continued through this period. In August 1959, the PLA took an Indian prisoner at Longju, which had an ambiguous position in the McMahon Line, and two months later in Aksai Chin a clash led to the death of nine Indian frontier policemen. On 2 October, Soviet Premier Nikita Khrushchev defended Nehru in a meeting with Mao.

This action reinforced China's impression that the Soviet Union, the United States and India all had expansionist designs over China. The PLA (People's Liberation Army) went so far as to prepare a self-defensive counterattack plan. Negotiations were restarted between the nations, but no progress was made. As a consequence of their non-recognition of the McMahon Line, China's maps showed both the North East Frontier Area (NEFA) and Aksai Chin to be Chinese territory.

In 1960, Zhou Enlai unofficially suggested that India drop its claims to Aksai Chin in return for a Chinese withdrawal of claims over NEFA. Adhering to his stated position, Nehru believed that China did not have a legitimate claim over either of these territories, and thus was not ready to concede them. This adamance was perceived in China as Indian opposition to Chinese rule in Tibet. Nehru declined to conduct any negotiations on the boundary until Chinese troops withdrew from Aksai Chin; a position supported by the international community. India produced numerous reports on the negotiations, and translated Chinese reports into English to help inform the international debate.

China believed that India was simply securing its claim lines in order to continue its "grand plans in Tibet". India's stance that China withdraw from Aksai Chin caused continual deterioration of the diplomatic situation to the point at which internal forces were pressurizing Nehru to take a military stance against China.

The Forward Policy

At the beginning of 1961, Nehru appointed General B M Kaul as army Chief of General Staff, but he refused to increase military spending and prepare for a possible war. That summer, China's continuing patrols south of the McMahon Line provoked an Indian response known as the "Forward Policy". According to James Barnard Calvin of the U.S. Navy, in 1959, India started sending Indian troops and border patrols into disputed areas. This program created both skirmishes and deteriorating relations between India and China. The aim of this policy was to create outposts behind advancing Chinese troops to interdict their supplies, forcing their return to China. There were eventually 60 such outposts, including 43 north of the McMahon Line. China viewed this as further confirmation of Indian expansionist plans directed towards Tibet. According to the Indian official history, implementation of the Forward Policy was intended to provide evidence of Indian occupation in the previously unoccupied region through which

Chinese troops had been patrolling. Kaul was confident, through contact with Indian Intelligence and CIA information, that China would not react with force. Indeed at first the PLA simply withdrew, but eventually Chinese forces began to counter-encircle the Indian positions. This led to a tit-for-tat Indian reaction, with both forces attempting to outmanoeuver each other. However, despite the escalating nature of the dispute, the two forces withheld from engaging each other directly.

Chinese attention was diverted for a time by the military activity of the Nationalists on Taiwan, but on 23 June the U.S. assured China that a Nationalist invasion would not be permitted. China's heavy artillery facing Taiwan could then be moved to Tibet. It took China six to eight months to gather the resources needed for the war, according to Anil Athale, author of the official Indian history. The Chinese sent a large quantity of non-military supplies to Tibet through the Indian port of Calcutta.

Early Incidents

Various border conflicts and "military incidents" between India and China flared up throughout the summer and autumn of 1962. In May, the Indian Air Force was told not to plan for close air support, although it was assessed as being a feasible way to repel the unbalanced ratio of Chinese to Indian troops. In June, a skirmish caused the deaths of dozens of Chinese troops. The Indian Intelligence Bureau received information about a Chinese buildup along the border which could be a precursor to war.

During the period of June–July 1962, the Indian military planners began advocating "probing actions" against the Chinese, and accordingly, moved mountain troops forward to cut off Chinese supply lines. According to Patterson, the Indian motives were threefold:

1. Test Chinese resolve and intentions regarding India.
2. Test whether India would enjoy Soviet backing in the event of a Sino-Indian war.
3. Create sympathy for India within the US, with whom relations had deteriorated after the Indian annexation of Goa.

On 10 July 1962, 350 Chinese troops surrounded an Indian post in Chushul but withdrew after a heated argument via loudspeaker. On 22 July, the Forward Policy was extended to allow Indian troops to push back Chinese troops already established in disputed territory. Whereas Indian troops were previously ordered to fire only in self-defence, all post commanders were now given discretion to open fire upon Chinese forces if threatened. In August, the Chinese military improved its combat readiness along the McMahon Line and began stockpiling ammunition, weapons and gasoline.

Confrontation at Thag La

In June 1962, Indian forces established an outpost at Dhola, on the southern slopes of the Thag La Ridge. Dhola lay north of the McMahon Line but south of the ridges India maintains the McMahon Line was supposed to represent. In August, China issued diplomatic protests and began occupying positions at the top of Thag La. On 8 September, a 60-strong PLA unit descended to the south side of the ridge and occupied positions that dominated one of the Indian posts at Dhola. Fire was not exchanged but Nehru said to the media that the Indian Army had instructions to "free our territory" and the troops had been given discretion to use force. On 11 September, it was decided that "all forward posts and patrols were given permission to fire on any armed Chinese who entered Indian territory".

However, the operation to occupy Thagla was flawed in that Nehru's directives were unclear and it got underway very slowly because of this. In addition to this, each man had to carry 35 kg of luggage over the long trek and this severely slowed down the reaction. By the time the Indian battalion reached the point of conflict, Chinese units controlled both banks of the Namka Chu River. On 20 September, Chinese troops threw grenades at Indian troops and a firefight developed, triggering a long series of skirmishes for the rest of September.

Some Indian troops, including Brigadier Dalvi who commanded the forces at Thag La, were also concerned that the territory they were fighting for was not strictly territory that "we should have been convinced was ours". According to Neville Maxwell, even members of the Indian defence ministry were categorically concerned with the validity of the fighting in Thag La.

On 3 October, a week before the triggering of the war, Zhou Enlai visited Nehru in New Delhi promising there would be no war. On 4 October, Kaul assigned some troops with securing regions south of the Thagla Ridge. Kaul decided to first secure Yumtso La, a strategically important position, before re-entering the lost Dhola post. Kaul had then realised that the attack would be desperate and the Indian government tried to stop escalation into an all-out war. Indian troops travelling to Thagla had suffered in the previously unexperienced conditions, two Gurkha troops died of pulmonary edema.

On 10 October, an Indian Punjabi patrol of 50 troops to Yumtso La were met by an emplaced Chinese position of some 1,000 soldiers. Indian troops were in no position for battle, as Yumtso La was 16,000 feet (4,900 m) above sea level and Kaul did not plan on having artillery support for the troops. The Chinese troops opened fire on the Indians under their belief that they were north of the McMahon Line. The Indians were surrounded by Chinese positions which used mortar fire. However, they managed to hold off the first Chinese assault, inflicting heavy casualties.

At this point, the Indian troops were in a position to push the Chinese back with mortar and machine gun fire. However, Brigadier Dalvi opted not to fire, as it would mean decimating the Rajput who were still in the area of the Chinese regrouping. They helplessly watched the Chinese ready themselves for a second assault. In the second Chinese assault, the Indians began their retreat, realising the situation was hopeless. The Indian patrol suffered 25 casualties, with the Chinese suffering 33. The Chinese troops held their fire as the Indians retreated, and then buried the Indian dead with military honours, as witnessed by the retreating soldiers. This was the first occurrence of heavy fighting in the war.

This attack had grave implications for India and Nehru tried to solve the issue, but by 18 October it was clear that the Chinese were preparing for an attack on India, with massive troop buildups on the border. A long line of mules and porters had also been observed supporting the buildup and reinforcement of positions south of the Thagla ridge.

POSTWAR PERIOD

China

According to the China's official (communist) military history, the war achieved China's policy objectives of securing borders in the western sector, as China retained de facto control of the Aksai Chin. After the war, India abandoned the Forward Policy, and the de facto borders stabilized along the Line of Actual Control. However according to James Calvin even though China had won a military victory it may have lost in terms of its international image. Western nations, especially the United States, were already suspicious of Chinese attitudes, motives and actions. These nations saw China's goals as world conquest, and clearly viewed China as the aggressor in the Border War. China's first nuclear weapon test in October 1964, and her support of Pakistan in the 1965 India-Pakistan Border War tended to confirm the American view of communist world objectives, including Chinese influence over Pakistan.

India

The aftermath of the war saw sweeping changes in the Indian military to prepare it for similar conflicts in the future, and placed pressure on Indian prime minister Jawaharlal Nehru, who was seen as responsible for failing to anticipate the Chinese attack on India. Indians reacted with a surge in patriotism and memorials were erected for many of the Indian troops who died in the war. Arguably, the main lesson India learned from the war was the need to strengthen its own defences and a shift from Nehru's foreign policy with China based on his stated concept of "brotherhood". Because of India's inability to anticipate Chinese aggression, Prime Minister Nehru faced harsh criticism from government officials, for having promoted pacifist relations with China. Indians in general became highly skeptical of China and its military. Many Indians view the war as a betrayal of India's attempts at establishing a long-standing peace with China and started to question Nehru's usage of the term "Hindi-Chini bhai-bhai" (meaning "Indians and Chinese are brothers"). The war also put an end to Nehru's earlier hopes that India and China would form a strong Asian Axis to counteract the increasing influence of the Cold War bloc superpowers. The Indian role in international affairs after the border war was also greatly reduced after the war and India's standing in the non-aligned movement suffered.

The unpreparedness of the army was blamed on Defence Minister Menon, who resigned his government post to allow for someone who might modernize India's military further. India's policy of weaponisation via indigenous sources and self-sufficiency was thus cemented. Sensing a weakened army, Pakistan, a close ally of China, initiated the Second Kashmir War with India in 1965, however, India had set up the Henderson-Brooks-Bhagat Report to determine what the reason was behind India's unpreparedness in the war, and, when Pakistan attacked, India was prepared. The result was inconclusive, since sources were divided on what decides victory. Some sources argued that since India had captured more territory than Pakistan, India had clearly won. However, others argued that India had taken significant losses considering the country's larger military and hence, the outcome of the war was inconclusive. Two years later, in 1967, there was a short border skirmish known as the Chola Incident between Chinese and Indian soldiers. In this incident 8 Chinese soldiers and 4 Indian soldiers were killed.

British journalist Neville Maxwell writes that the "hopelessly ill-prepared Indian Army that provoked China on orders emanating from Delhi, and paid the price for its misadventure in men, money and national humiliation". As a result of the war, the Indian government commissioned an investigation, resulting in the classified Henderson-Brooks-Bhagat Report on the causes of the war and the reasons for failure. India's performance in high-altitude combat in 1962 led to an overhaul of the Indian Army in terms of doctrine, training, organization and equipment. According to James Calvin, an analyst from U.S. Navy India gained many benefits from the 1962 conflict. This war united the country as never before. India got 32,000 square miles of disputed territory even if she felt that NEFA was hers all along. The new Indian republic had avoided international alignments; by asking for during the war, India demonstrated her willingness to accept military aid from several sectors.

And, finally, India recognized the serious weaknesses in her Army. She would more than double her military manpower in the next two years; and she would work hard to resolve the military's training and logistic problems. India's efforts to improve her military posture significantly enhanced her army's capabilities and preparedness.

Series of Skirmishes

India also reported a series of skirmishes after the 1962 war, which were never confirmed by China. One report provided by India shows that in late 1967, there were two skirmishes between Indian and Chinese forces in Sikkim. The first one was dubbed the "Nathu La incident", and the other the "Chola incident". Prior to these incidents had been the Naxalbari uprising in India by the Communist Naxalites and Maoists.

Bilateral Peace

In 1993 and 1996, the two sides signed the Sino-Indian Bilateral Peace and Tranquility Accords, an agreement to maintain peace and tranquility along the Line of Actual Control (LoAC). Ten meetings of a Sino-Indian Joint Working Group (SIJWG) and five of an expert group have taken place to determine where the LoAC lies, but little progress has occurred. India is concerned about China's military modernisation.

On 20 November 2006 Indian politicians from Arunachal Pradesh appealed to parliament to take a harder stance on the PRC following a military buildup on the border similar to that in 1962. Additionally, China's military aid to Pakistan as well is a matter of concern to the Indian public, which fought another war with Pakistan in 1999. On 6 July 2006, the historic Silk Road passing through this territory was reopened. Both sides have agreed to resolve the issues by peaceful means.

7

India's China Policy since the End of the Cold War

Certain scholars believe that India's China policy has undergone three major phases of adjustment since the end of the Cold War: the pre-1998 phase policy of reconciliation; the 1998–2000 phase policy of hostility; and the 2000 to present phase policy of engagement. The second phase around the time of the 1998 nuclear tests featured harangues from the Indian government regarding the 'China threat' and a brief deadlock in Sino–Indian relations. The author, however, believes that two, rather than three, phases of adjustment are applicable to an explanation of the state of bilateral relations between China and India in the post-Cold War era.

When considering India's overall strategic aims at the time of the 1998 nuclear tests and the implications and specific actions of its subsequent China policy, it is difficult to pinpoint two 180 degree-policy shifts in the course of just two years. Facts demonstrate that India named China as a threat at the time of the 1998 tests as a matter of expedience to acquiesce in the anti-China stance of certain parties in the United States and other Western nations; it was a ploy whose purpose was to divert attention from and rationalize the nuclear tests, thereby dispelling any notion of sanctions.

It should be borne in mind, however, that India's understanding of comprehensive national strength deepened after the Cold War, as did its leaders' belief that nuclear arms and credible nuclear deterrence were hallmarks of a superpower. Entering the nuclear club was consequently a stride towards achieving one of the sub-continent's greatest national aspirations. The Rao government, which pursued a China policy of reconciliation and engagement, had made preparations for nuclear tests but stopped short of carrying them out for fear of the potential burden on the newly recovered economy of international sanctions.

Prime Minister Vajpayee and other political leaders repeatedly and publicly expressed soon after the 1998 tests that India had no wish to hold China as an enemy or a threat, stating, to the contrary, their desire for reinforced friendly relations.

At no point during this period did diplomatic engagement between India and China cease. Indian External Affairs Minister Jaswant Singh's visit to China in June 1999 demonstrated that the Sino–Indian relationship had recovered in the space of a year from any damage that the nuclear tests had inflicted upon it.

That becoming a nuclear power while maintaining stable relations with China were post-Cold War India's strategic goals was also implied by the sub-continent's explicit moves towards repairing its relationship with China. The 1998 nuclear tests constituted no fundamental change to India's China policy and should, within the scope of Sino–Indian relations, be regarded as a minor episode.

Moreover, the shift of India's China policy in 1988 was not prompted by any change of security concept; Prime Minister Rajiv Gandhi's trip to China that year was motivated by the fact of Sino–Soviet reconciliation. Changes in security concept explicitly propelled India's; post-Cold War China policy adjustments. This book, therefore, primarily examines developments and changes in India's China policy after the Cold War. It holds that a substantive change indeed occurred; specifically from one of hostility and antagonism during the Cold War (especially 1962–1988) to reconciliation and engagement thereafter. This policy change, however, was by no means instantaneous but characterized by gradual, phased development. Two, rather than three, phases of adjustment tally with changes in India's post-Cold War security concept.

India's China Policy from the End of the Cold War to 1998

Indian leaders believed after 1962 that hostilities between China and India were inevitable, and viewed China as a major enemy. Prime Minister Indira Gandhi considered Sino–Indian antagonism as going far beyond border disputes, and that China was pursuing the more 'complex' policy of pressing India on all fronts and, moreover, displacing the sub-continent by establishing its own dominant position in the Asian power hierarchy.

The goal of India's China policy during this period, therefore, was to ensure its supremacy over China in Asia and, in the event of armed conflict, to avoid repeating mistakes that had led to its defeat in the 1962 Sino–Indian conflict. India's policy at the time can be so summarized: strengthen military capability and deployment; seek aid from major powers, respectively, the United States, United Kingdom and USSR; and support Chinese separatist forces. After the Cold War ended, however, changes in India's domestic and international situation brought tremendous challenges, and its position as regards China and its related policy goals showed clear adjustments. India considered China as a nation going through a reflective, 'inward looking' period and, as such, had no intention of attacking the sub-continent. In the short-term, therefore, it constituted no threat. The goal of India's new China policy was to maintain stability in Sino–Indian relations, ensure peaceful borders and create conditions suitable for India to gather its resources and restore economic and military strength. The specific policy adjustments were as follows.

Achieve Simultaneous Progress in Solving Border Disputes

For almost two decades after 1962, India made resolution of border disputes a pre-condition for normalizing relations with China. Its insistence in this regard was the main reason for the longstanding chill in Sino–Indian relations. Although the two nations restored ambassadorial-level diplomatic relations in 1976, and in 1981 agreed to begin talks on the border issue, this principled standpoint did not change. Upon meeting with visiting then-External Affairs Minister Vajpayee early in 1979, Comrade Deng Xiaoping proposed an agreement that would provide 'a package solution' for relevant border disputes. He said that if it were not possible completely to resolve border disputes at an early date, he would consider cooperation in other areas. But it was not until 1988 during Rajiv Gandhi's trip to China that the Indian government accepted this suggestion and formally initiated the process of normalizing bilateral relations which the successive Indian governments pursued and implemented after the Cold War ended. It is notable that during the time the two sides promoted negotiations on border issues they also exchanged high-level visits in which the two nations signed cooperative agreements in such areas as trade, technology, education and culture, and that cooperation between them grew ever greater in depth and breadth.

Shift Strategies on Border Talks

As India needed a peaceful, stable environment in which to concentrate on economic recovery, securing Sino–Indian borders was its primary goal in the early 1990s. Because of India's; pre-1988 insistence on not normalizing Sino–Indian relations until the border issues were settled, there were suspicions that the sub-continent was 'taking improvements in bilateral relations as a bargaining chip through which to force China to yield in border disputes'. India consequently insisted in the talks that began in 1981 on its own position as regards a segmented solution to the issue. India's objective understanding of the complexity of the Sino–Indian border dispute after the Cold War and of realistic strategic considerations and needs prompted an adjusted strategy for these talks. This was manifest in its suggestion of a gradual solution to border disputes: the first step would be to stabilize the Line of Actual Control (LAC) situation and eliminate disagreements over its demarcation; the second to reach agreement on preserving peace and tranquillity along the LAC; and the third to take measures to establish mutual trust along the LAC.

This accomplished, the two nations could then address substantive problems in their border dispute. This tentative plan enabled India and China to approach a consistent position whereby the two sides worked to achieve a solution to Sino–Indian border disputes and create an atmosphere of reasonableness and peace. The two nations made progress, signing in 1993 the Agreement on Maintenance of Peace and Tranquillity along the Line of Actual Control in the Sino– Indian Border Areas, and in 1996 the Agreement Between the Government of the Republic of India and the Government of the People's Republic of China on Confidence-Building Measures in the Military Field Along the Line of Actual Control in the India–China Border Areas. India saw these two agreements as on the one hand ensuring the two sides could resolve border disputes peacefully without resorting to violence, and on the other that border disputes would not inhibit the development of their bilateral relations.

Tibetan Issue and do not Provoke China

Leaders of India's independence movement had at the time of the British Raj followed the British colonialist concept of Tibet as a 'buffer region' between India and China. After winning independence, therefore, the Indian government supported from the very beginning the so-called 'Tibetan independence movement'. At around the time of the founding of the People's Republic of China, India seized the opportunity offered by China's political upheaval to promote the international standing of the local Tibetan government and thwart China's liberation of Tibet. New Delhi continued unremittingly in its efforts to convince China's central government, even during the 1950s heyday of Sino–Indian amity, to give Tibet substantial autonomy and to reduce to the greatest extent possible the size of its garrison there. After the insurrection of 1959 the Indian government was more overt in its support of Tibet, giving asylum to fugitive rebels and propping up the so-called 'Tibetan Government in Exile' established by the Dalai Lama in 1960 in the Indian city of Dharamsala. India further incited and encouraged Tibetan independence activities after the Sino–Indian conflict of 1962.

In truth, Indian leaders considered their support for exiled Tibetans' separatist activities as an effective containment against China. But when Prime Minister Rajiv Gandhi visited China in 1988 he issued the statement: 'The Indian side reiterates the long-standing and consistent policy of the Government of India that Tibet is an autonomous region of China and that anti-China political activities by Tibetan elements are not permitted on Indian soil,' which implied India's change of approach from that of support for Tibetan independence. Indian leaders reiterated this pledge after the Cold War ended and imposed limits on Tibetan fugitives' anti-China political activities. For instance, Indian officials would generally contact the Dalai Lama and leaders of the so-called Tibetan government in exile before a visit by Chinese leaders to India, requesting that they refrain from Tibetan protests, demonstrations or other anti-Chinese behaviour.

Yet, differences still exist between China and India on the issue of Tibetan autonomy. Although, proceeding from the requirement of preserving stable Sino–Indian relations, the post-Cold War Indian government has been low-key in its support of the Dalai Lama and other Tibetan fugitives, this does not signify a substantial change in its strategic treatment of the Tibetan issue.

Changes in India's China Policy from 1999 to Present

Achieving recovery, contending for the status of global power had been India's ambition for decades. The growth of the sub-continent's comprehensive strength and improvements in the international environment in the late 1990s presented to it a real possibility of realizing this ambition, as well as a number of other unprecedented strategic opportunities. Against this backdrop, reconciliation with China and the unchanged overall direction of the relationship produced several new adjustments to the positions and goals of India's China policy. At this stage, India saw China neither as enemy nor friend, believing that cooperation could coexist with competition between the two nations. India still considered China as constituting no threat in the short term, but began focusing on long-term trends in the balance of power. The emphasis of the goals of its new China policy are on ensuring that future Sino–Indian relations are of benefit to India by making China a positive factor in the process of its rise. Maintaining the stability of Sino–Indian relations remains fundamental. The new policy adjustments are as follows.

Expand Economic Cooperation with China

Trade between the two nations ceased after the 1962 Sino–Indian Border Conflict, and did not resume until 1977. The volume of trade between the two sides in the 1980s wavered at around roughly Us." million. But after the Cold War ended, Sino–Indian trade experienced a seemingly spontaneous phase of rapid development. The trade volume between China and India increased from $264 million in 1991 to $1.988 billion in 1999—a yearly average of 31.2%—or an increase factor of 6.5 over eight years. Indian leaders' concerns about India's economic recovery nonetheless maintained at this point the China policy focus on stabilizing political relations and establishing tranquil borders. Indian leaders' understanding of economic strength and security having becoming more profound since 1999, their enthusiasm for developing bilateral trade soared. As China and India were the world's two most rapidly developing nations, Indian leaders could see the obvious potential for trade between them and that strengthening bilateral trade would be of great mutual benefit. Also that close economic ties could have a stabilizing influence on their political relationship. Statistics show that bilateral trade since 1999 has entered into a new period of growth. The average yearly growth to 2006 was 44.4%—a rate which exceeded that of the preceeding period and which is being achieved on an ever-stronger numerical foundation. The volume of Sino–Indian trade reached US$24.8 billion in 2006, having increased by a factor of 11.5 over 1999 and one of 93 over 1991. China became India's second largest trading partner in 2006, and India China's tenth largest. It may be said that the role of Sino–Indian trade has grown from one unworthy of mention to a decisive aspect of the overall bilateral relationship.

INDIA'S SECURITY CONCEPT ON ITS CHINA POLICY

India's post-Cold War security concept and adjustments to its China policy. In the process of this discussion, we have distinguished two phases of adjustment to both the post-Cold War India security concept and China policy, and established that these changes were more or less simultaneous. We have also found that India's China policy reflects its security concept; in other words that adjustments to the content of India's China policy correspond to continuities and discontinuities in India's security concept. It may be said that this consistency demonstrates the important influence India's security concept has had on its China policy. Policy-making, in any event, is the linking of concepts and policy; in other words, concepts, through government policy-making, crystallize into policy. Exploring the evolution of the Indian policy-making class and mechanisms, therefore, also benefits understanding of the manner in which security concepts of different eras and phases have influenced India's China policy.

India's foreign policy behaviour during the Cold War was largely determined by a few predominant personalities, both its foreign and security policies having long been dominated by Nehru and Indira Gandhi. The two leader's views on China had decisive influence on India's China policy. When considering India's defeat in the 1962 Sino–Indian Border Conflict and the open wound it represented to both the Nehru family and the INC, their adoption of an unyielding tack toward China was the sole political means of saving face. Sino–Indian relations consequently remained in stalemate for nearly 30 years. When Rajiv Gandhi replaced his mother in 1985, he seemed at first to follow her line on foreign policy. The rapidly changing international situation, however, forced him to veer from it, and specific improvements in Sino–Soviet relations compelled his adjustments to India's China policy. Soviet leader Mikhail Gorbachev urged Rajiv Gandhi during a visit to India in 1986 to improve relations with China, saying it would suit Soviet interests, and hinting at a press conference that the USSR would no longer be willing to provide support to India in the event of Sino–Indian conflict. In this situation, Rajiv Gandhi considered that India on its own would be powerless against a threat on two fronts. He was hence forced to change his preparations for a two-front war, as it was apparent that dispelling tensions along the eastern front through reconciliation with China would allow him to concentrate India's energies on the western front with Pakistan.

The Nehru family's stately bearing was absent after the Cold War, and the INC's power had declined. The insularity that had characterized India's foreign policy-making process since independence, however, did not change. The nation's foreign and security policy stayed in the hands of the prime minister and cabinet from 1991 to 1996, during which time the views of Prime Minister Rao and leaders of the INC government on security and foreign policy matters were decisive, and the influence of parliament, think tanks and academic institutions was negligible. It is notable, however, that Rao's background as home minister, defence minister and external affairs minister throughout the 1980s, as well as his status as the Congress Party's elder statesman, signified that he was a loyal adherent of Nehruvianism, and unrepresentative of any new type of thinking. The transformation of India's security concept during the Rao administration, therefore, can be understood as entirely the result of external forces.

As earlier mentioned, changes in the international and domestic situation compelled Rao to change his understanding of national strength. He began emphasizing the strategic influence of economic strength and promoting restoration of the economy as a matter of urgency in withstanding security threats in the aftermath of the Cold War. This passive reaction to a complex situation gave the impression of India's overall foreign policy as passive and defensive. India adopted a focused approach to diplomacy during this period, directing its energies towards restoring the economy but maintaining a low profile in international affairs, as expressed in its China policy. Rao continued and furthered Rajiv Gandhi's adjustments by focusing on stabilization of Sino–Indian political relations and establishing tranquil borders as means to ensuring the recovery of India's domestic economy.

Two major changes occurred in India's foreign policy-making process during 1998. The first was the BJP's assumption of office that ended the long-standing INC power monopoly, and established foundations for a clean break with the traditional security concept. Although the BJP's domestic policies had a relatively ideological slant and promoted a Hinduist revival, the party was pragmatic as regards foreign policy.

In contrast to the Congress Party, it dared to confront history, criticise India's previous foreign policy and introduce new thinking. Jaswant Singh, successively the Vajpayee government's External Affairs Minister and Finance Minister, published early in 1999 a book entitled *Defending India* in which he systematically describes his new security concept. Various views were thereafter expressed in government-issued articles.

The BJP was obviously preparing to move on from the passive security concept of the Rao era. The second major change was India's refinement of its foreign policy-making mechanism. The November 1998 establishment of the National Security Council symbolized India's casting off of the influence and control of personality-based policy-making in favour of scientific research, inquiry and decision-making, and comprehensive long-term planning. The introduction by National Security Advisory Board subordinated to the National Security Council of scholarly authorities, reporters and former government and military officials demonstrated how much more open India's foreign policy-making process had become.

The BJP differed in its approach to China policy from both that of the Cold War era Nehru family, with its 1962 complex, and the early 1990s Rao government, which had been wearied and bound hand and foot by domestic and international pressure. The BJP's seizing of this historic opportunity confirmed India's rise as the nation's long-term strategic goal and placed its relationship with China on the strategic level. In other words, the BJP saw the Sino–Indian relationship as an important influence on India's rise. Although the two nations would be dealing with historically significant problems, they could be seen as a starting point.

The gradual opening of India's foreign policy-making process, moreover, made way for a vibrant exchange of ideas regarding China policy, which fell roughly into three groups: the first held that Sino–Indian cooperation suits both sides' interests and that post-Cold War China has no intention of making an enemy of India, desiring instead friendly relations and strategic partnership; the second that China is a long-term strategic threat to India because China's strategic objectives lie in establishing hegemony over Asia, which necessitates India's containment and, therefore, limitation of Indian influence. India, therefore, should adopt diametrically opposed policies; and the third group, situated between the two, held that the two nations could simultaneously rise to become main Asian powers and that competition and cooperation could coexist. Discussions on how to evaluate and understand China by Indian scholars and strategic circles are ongoing. After frequent debates among Indian National Security Council groups, the third, middle-ground viewpoint seems to be gaining acceptance.

When the INC regained power in 2004, a variety of factors led the new government to carry on with the previous administration's security concept. The new INC government's China policy was its predecessor's legacy, because the rise of India's international status during the BJP coalition government left the INC powerless to dispute the success of the previous government's foreign policy. The INC's democratized and more youthful leadership team was also willing to jettison historical baggage and look to the future. Although the Nehru family's leadership role within the Congress Party remained uncontested, the influence of Prime Minister Manmohan Singh and Foreign Minister Mukherjee on foreign and security policy could not be disregarded. Moreover, the liberalization of India's foreign policy-making process was superimposed against a long-standing civil service system which ensured continuity of policy. In other words, many masterminds of BJP foreign policy still active in the external affairs ministry, defence ministry and other relevant functional departments under the INC, as well as in consultative committees, the media, think tanks and other non-functional departments, continued to exert influence.

Substantial changes occurred in India's China policy after the end of the Cold War whereby the nation's long-standing (1962–1988) antagonistic approach became one of reconciliation and engagement. These adjustments originated to a great extent in changes in the sub-continent's post-Cold War security concept, manifest in two major shifts which effected two major phases of adjustment in India's China policy. The new post-Cold War China policy nonetheless retained traces of the former, programme, imbuing it with a duality that reflected the overlap of India's old and new security concepts.

A change in India's security concept first became apparent during the period from the end of the Cold War to 1998. The first phase of adjustments this change triggered in India's China policy was evident in the sub-continent's extended concept of military might as national strength to one encompassing economic factors, and acknowledgement of the strategic value of economic strength in countering what it perceived as the looming threat of marginalization within the international community. Restoration of the domestic economy hence became a main measure through which to resist security threats in the post-Cold War era. Having made this shift in foreign policy objectives towards economic recovery, India set about creating a favourable environment within which to achieve this goal. Overall implementation of a China policy of preserving stable Sino–Indian relations by guaranteeing border tranquillity was vital to achieving this strategic objective. India consequently focused on the feasibility of reconciliation and, in view of China's reflective, inward-looking mood, no longer viewed China as an enemy. As regards India's specific policies, while focusing on the establishment of a progressive means to guaranteeing tranquil borders, thereby stabilizing Sino–Indian relations, India at the same time sought communication and cooperation in other areas. To avoid provoking China, the Indian government made tactical adjustments to its approach to Tibet from that of exploiting the issue and causing uproar to handling the matter in a low-key manner.

The new developments apparent in India's security concept in 1999 brought with it the second phase of adjustments to India's China policy. Indian leaders considered that the nation's security environment had improved to the extent that it constituted a strategic opportunity for India to rise to global-power status. This change in thinking and understanding caused the second shift of objective in India's foreign policy from that of improving the economy to the grand goal of global-power status. It corresponded to India's acknowledgement of the crucial nature of the Sino–Indian relationship and change of focus from border tranquillity and stable political relations to comprehensive considerations of how the two nations' relationship would strategically affect India's; rise. These insights compelled a shift of objective in India's China policy towards making China a positive factor in the sub-continent's rise; also recognition that this objective could be accomplished only by maintaining a stable basis for Sino–Indian relations. Official introduction during this phase of a comprehensive security concept signalled India's adoption of a more pragmatic, comprehensive handling of its relations with China. The specific steps it adopted were: increasing economic cooperation with China, thus benefiting India's economic development and stabilizing bilateral political relations; strengthening military communication and security dialogue, thus deepening understanding of China's strategic intentions towards India, increasing mutual trust, minimizing misunderstandings and avoiding conflict; and seeking Chinese support in its quest for a permanent seat on the UN Security Council, which would expand India's political power and international prestige.

In the course of research, however, it became apparent to the author that India's security concept did not undergo a thoroughgoing change after the Cold War ended, as elements of the Cold War approach remained in place. Although India's security concept extended after 1988 to include both military and economic security, the ultimate purpose of national defence as regards a fundamental guarantee of security nonetheless remained that of increased military strength to safeguard national unity and territorial integrity. India abandoned its strategy of pursuing security through alliances, yet still viewed parity and the principle of checks and balances as hallmarks of its national defence. Influenced as it was by traditional concepts, post-Cold War India's China policy was imbued with vigilance. Even though India did not perceive China as a threat in the short term, it was nevertheless concerned that the swing in balance of power between the two was not in its favour, and that China constituted a potential obstacle to India's rise. Indian leaders consequently embarked on a race against China to expand comprehensive national strength, particularly military force, including India's nuclear capability, as the means to a balance of power. India at the same time sought to offset Chinese influence both regionally and globally through development of strategic relationships with the United States, Japan and other nations. The sub-continent also remained vigilant in the long-standing issues of border disputes and Sino–Pakistani relations, and maintained pressure on China in this regard.

Changes in post-Cold War India's security concept were thus the result of both domestic and foreign factors. The first change during the early post-Cold War period was triggered by passive reactions to transformations in the nation's domestic and international situation that, in turn, prompted a passive transformation of thinking and understanding, manifest in passive defensiveness of India's foreign policy, specifically its China policy. The security concept that appeared during the late 1990s was comparatively proactive. The expanded strength of India's domestic economy and improvement of its external environment compelled a new understanding of security issues, as expressed in the proactive change in its security concept. This assertiveness was manifest in strategy and in an active, enterprising foreign policy. Seizing the historic opportunity to realize India's rise had become the common security objective of both major Indian political parties. Decentralization of political power and expanded openness of the foreign policy-making process, however, caused India's old and new security concepts to bind into one, and the resultant duality of India's hybrid security concept since the Cold War's end is reflected in its China policy. As India's dual security concept will continue into the foreseeable future, the duality of its China policy will be difficult to change.

INDIA'S CHINA POLICY: IMPORTANCE OF A STRATEGIC FRAMEWORK

For many political observers, the global political architecture is undergoing a transformation with power increasingly shifting from the West to the East. The two most populous nations on the earth China and India are on their way to becoming economic powerhouses and are shedding their reticence in asserting their global profiles. Japan is gradually flexing its military muscle and the Southeast Asian tigers are roaring again after the 1997 "Asian Flu". Whether it is such hopeful prospects or the challenges ahead in the Korean peninsula, Taiwan, and Kashmir, it is clear that this new century will, in all likelihood, be an Asian century.

The future of this Asian century will to large extent depend upon the relationship between the two regional giants, China and India. According the United States National Intelligence Council

Report on emerging global trends, by 2015, international community will have to confront the military, political and economic dimensions of the rise of China and India. The bilateral relationship between China and India will define the contours of the new international political architecture in Asia and the world at large. As of today, however, the trajectory of the Sino-Indian relationship remains as complex as ever to decipher despite some remarkable positive developments in the last few years.

This article attempts to explore this complex, multilayered relationship in all its dimensions, largely from the perspective of Indian foreign policy priorities. It mainly focuses on the recent developments in the Sino-Indian relationship. It reviews India's and China's view of each other and their policies. It examines the trends of convergence that have emerged in the past few years. Additionally, it looks at the points of divergence and possible areas of concern in the relationship between Asia's giants.

INDIA'S CHINESE POLICY CHALLENGES UNDER CONGRESS GOVERNMENT

India's new government led by the Congress Party, has until now focused entirely on its relations with Pakistan. The reason for this could be that most of the foreign policy hands in the current policy establishment have been former High Commissioners in Pakistan and therefore at more professional ease to deal with it. However, India's most significant foreign policy challenge is China and not Pakistan. Pakistan despite its nuclear weapons arsenal is not our "strategic competitor"; it is only a, regional 'spoiler state'. But in India's aspirations to rise to an effective regional power status, China is a "strategic competitor" both in the South Asia context and also in the Asian security context.

India's policy making establishment and especially within the Congress Party, with its hangovers of 'Panch Sheel' and non-aligned mindsets, has short memories when it comes to China's policies of strategic destabilization of India. They are still under way. Similarly, the Indian media suffers from a total amnesia of China's perfidious policies in South Asia to the strategic detriment of India. China has adroitly exploited both these vulnerabilities of

India. China in its approaches to South Asia in the last fifty-five years, with particular reference to India has relied heavily on "power politics", creation of 'spoiler states' on India's periphery and upsetting the natural balance of power in the Indian sub-continent. The new Indian Government policy establishment may like to consider the following observations when formulating its policy stances towards China:

* Only when countries have accepted the existence of conflict and sought to manage it through a balance of power have enduring periods of general peace resulted" -Former US President Nixon.
* "It can be a fundamental and analytically mischievous error to confuse peace with tranquillity, certainty or predictability." "To achieve peace, people do not necessarily have to become admirable or gentle." -Prof John Mueller.
* "Peace therefore cannot be aimed at directly; it is the expression of certain conditions and power relationships. It is to these relationships –not to peace-that diplomacy must address itself" -Former US Secretary of State, Henry Kissinger.

So while India must pursue peace and conflict-avoidance in its relationship with China, the new Indian Government should recognize that the route to peace lies through power relationships and power politics. But first, a look at the Congress Party's "China Baggage". The Congress Party Needs to Jettison its "China Baggage":

Contemporary Congress Party articulations give an impression that its perspectives remain time-frozen in the Nehruvian-era China politics. Current international strategic realities dictate that the following main planks of Congress Party's China perspectives are no longer relevant:

* Non-alignment is dead. The concept could operate in a bi-polar world only. Further, both the superpowers gave no credence to this concept. If India was given importance then, it was not because of Nehru and nor for its non-alignment policies. India was given importance for its intrinsic potential as a power in the making.

* 'Panch Sheel' (five principles of peaceful co-existence) enunciated by Chou-en-lai and Nehru stood negated when China sneakingly occupied Aksai-Chin in the 1950s and later the Sino-Indian War of 1962.
* "Panch Sheel" concept stood further negated in the following years when China in its policies of strategic de-stabilisation of India built-up Pakistan's nuclear weapons arsenal, attempted to make Myanmar a military client state and entered into a Mutual Defence Agreement with Bangladesh.
* Multipolar world as espoused by China and currently being seconded by the Congress Party Government is an unworkable proposition in today's international strategic realities. Neither China nor France has been able to win concrete support for multi-polarity.

The Congress Government would be well advised to jettison its above baggage and formulate its approaches to China on the basis of power-politics and in consonance with existing global power relationships. Hans J Morgenthau, the most noted foreign affairs authority has remarked that: " A nation can only take a rational view of its national interests after it has parted company with the crusading spirit of a political creed." The Congress Party Government needs to jettison the crusading missions of the Nehruvian era. It only brought more conflict and contentiousness for India.

Power-Relationship Approaches of India to China

India's national security interests imperatives dictate that any long range formulation of its China policy should deliver the following end-aims:

- China's assistance to Pakistan in terms of WMD Proliferation is curtailed, if not ended.
- China's intrusive influence in the Indian sub-continent in the form of creation of regional 'spoiler states' acting as its proxies is curtailed.
- China's attempt to build a naval presence in the Indian Ocean through Pakistan, Bangladesh or Myanmar is impeded.

- China's unobtrusive influence in India's politics through the Communist Parties, a strategically unwise Indian media and India's pseudo-liberal establishment is rendered ineffective.
- China's strategic nexus with Pakistan and Bangladesh is neutralized.

A quick glance at the above would reveal that except for the last point, India on its own, cannot tackle these challenges. India would have to co-opt or be co-opted in existing global power relationships that are working to constrain China's power politics in their respective regions. To arrive at the answer, a brief look is required at the existing strategic realities and global power equations and these are:

- United States global predominance is estimated to continue well into the major portion of the 21st century.
- United States is the only superpower existent today with the strategic, political and economic might to enforce its will globally.
- Russia is unlikely under existing circumstances to emerge in a resurgent mode for another three to four decades. Its strategic power potential stands shrunk decisively.
- China's massive military modernization and expansion of her strategic assets are nowhere near to challenging US supremacy.
- China is a revisionist power. It challenges the status-quo and in the process generates strategic uneasiness in global strategic equations of its intentions and motives.
- China today stands strategically hemmed-in by the United States on its Western and Eastern flanks.

India therefore has no choice but to be co-opted in the United States scheme of things to protect her national security interests vis-à-vis China. The United States too is not engaged in 'Containment' of China; but only in 'Constrainment' so that its policies do not create strategic turbulence in contiguous areas.

In terms of South Asia alone, India's national security interests dictate that Pakistan needs to be cut to size and accept its asymmetric equation in the Indian sub-continent. India cannot hope that China will assist her in this direction. China is a major part of the problem of Pakistan's intransigence and military adventurism against India. Here again the United States enters into the picture in multiple ways: (1) To control Pakistan directly and coerce it into strategic compliance from desisting from military adventurism. (2) To neutralize China-Pakistan strategic nexus by building strategic counter-pressures against China. (3) United States global naval supremacy is unquestionable and in relation to India's Indian Ocean strategic interests, major convergence exists between India and USA.

Here again, in the South Asian context, the answer is clear, that in relation to China, the national security interests of India are best served by entering the power-relationships of the United States in terms of Asian security. Until India builds up her military and strategic power to levels commensurate with those of China, it has no options in her China policy but to get co-opted with the China policies of the United States.

Buildingup of her Strategic Assets by India as Part of its China Policy

In this connection two points need to be addressed, namely:

* China's attitudes towards India changed after the BJP Government's nuclear weapons tests in 1998. After the rabid Chinese reactions for a year or so, China realised that it had to adapt to the new strategic reality, that India had arrived to claim some strategic space in the "power-politics" scene. Hence the flurry of Chinese high level official visits thereafter and the stupendous growth of two way trade. An argument can therefore be made in terms of China relations that India's power politics has stimulated trade exponentially.
* China's attitudes towards India changed as it dawned on Chinese leaders that India was getting drawn into an increasing strategic partnership with the United States and increasing military-to-military contacts also.

A major deduction from the above is that an essential component of India's policies towards China should also be the building up of her own independent strategies assets to add power to her diplomacy in the form of:

* SLBMs (Sea Launched Ballistic Missiles). The third leg of India's nuclear arsenal triad is overdue.
* ICBMs (Inter Continental Ballistic Missiles). At present Indian missiles do not have a reach upto Bijing.
* Cruise Missiles. With multimode launch capabilities.
* Nuclear Submarines. The project is over 15 years old. It needs to be resuscitated and put on priority.
* Strategic Bombers. These are an essential element of the nuclear triad.

China's missile arsenal is predominantly deployed in Tibet, Sichzuan and Yunnan— all targeted against India and with an inherent element of political coercion. Development of India's strategic assets as given above would make India's foreign policy approaches towards China more strategically equitable and in the process generating equitable responses from China.

The new Congress Government has come into power, seemingly obsessed with the conviction that the policies of the previous BJP Government must be changed at all costs. It needs to note that India's foreign and defence policies need to be bi-partisan in character and content. The previous Government adopted the "power politics" approach to China as evident from the nuclear weapons tests and also evolving a strategic partnership with the United States. Both these had an effect on China and its policies towards India and South Asia in general. One could also attribute the Chinese neutrality during the Kargil War 1999 to this approach

The Congress Governments in the past followed ill-conceived and ill-advised policies towards China based on mistaken beliefs. This led to India's national humiliation in 1962. The new Congress Government in power today should jettison its " China baggage" of the past and adhere to the "power politics" approach towards China. It is not to suggest that India enter into confrontationist stances with China; it is to suggest that while peace must be the quest in India-China relations it does not distract India from the parallel track of foreign policy i.e. To adopt power relationships and build strategic assets so necessary to maintain "real peace".

India's new policy establishment needs to be reminded what one Chinese author has observed on China's perspectives on international relations: " Power is the cornerstone of Chinese politics. Chinese politicians and diplomats are often recognized as masters of power politics having inherited a well-spring of experience of power play over the millennium".

SINO-INDIAN CONVERGENCE: BILATERAL AND GLOBAL

Bilateral relations between India and the People's Republic of China (PRC) have indeed come a long way after they touched their nadir in the immediate aftermath of India 's nuclear tests in May 1998. China had been singled out as the "number one" security threat for India by India's Defence Minister just before the nuclear tests. After the tests, the Indian Prime Minister wrote to the US President justifying Indian nuclear tests as a response to the threat posed by China. Unsurprisingly, China reacted strongly and diplomatic relations between the two countries plummeted to an all time low.

However, some six years later, the relations between the two countries seem to be on an upswing. The visit of the Indian External Affairs Minister to China in 1999 marked the resumption of high-level dialogue and the two sides declared that they were not threats to each other. A bilateral security dialogue was also initiated that has helped the two countries in openly expressing and sharing their security concerns with each other. India and China also decided to expedite the process of demarcation of the Line of Actual Control (LAC) and the Joint Working Group (JWG) on the boundary question, set up in 1988, has been meeting regularly. As a first step in this direction, the two countries exchanged border maps on the least controversial middle sector of the LAC.

The Indian Prime Minster visited China in June 2003, the first such visit in a decade. The joint declaration signed during the visit stated that China was not a threat to India. The two states appointed special representatives in order to impart momentum to border negotiations that have lasted twenty two years, with the Prime Minister's principal secretary becoming India's political-level negotiator, replacing the India-China JWG. India and China also decided to hold their first joint naval exercise later in the year and discussions on joint air exercise continue. India also acknowledged China 's sovereignty over Tibet and pledged not to allow "anti-China" political activities in India. On its part, China has acknowledged India 's 1975 annexation of the former monarchy of Sikkim by agreeing to open a trading post along the border with the former kingdom and later rectified official maps to include Sikkim as part of India.

India and China have found substantial convergence of interests at the international level. Both share similar concerns about the growing international dominance of the US, the threat of terrorism disguised as religious and ethnic movements and the need to accord primacy to economic development. India and China have both expressed concern about the US ' use of military power around the world and publicly opposed the war in Iraq. This was merely a continuation of the desire of both states to oppose the US *hyperpuissance* ever since the end of the Cold War.

Like other major powers in the international system, India and China favour a multipolar world order where US unipolarity remains constrained by the other "poles" in the system. China and India zealously guard their national sovereignty and have been wary of US attempts to interfere in what they see as domestic affairs of other stares, be it Serbia, Kosovo or Iraq. Both took strong exception to the US air strikes on Iraq in 1998, the US-led air campaign against Yugoslavia in 1999, and more recently the US campaign against Saddam Hussein arguing that these violated the national sovereignty and undermined the authority of the United Nations system.

Both nations also favour more democratic international economic regimes. They have strongly resisted efforts by the US and other developed nations to link global trade to labour and environmental standards, realizing clearly that this would put them at a huge disadvantage vis-à-vis the developed world, thereby hampering their drive towards economic development, a top priority. Both have committed themselves to crafting joint Sino-Indian positions in the World Trade Organization (WTO) and global trade negotiations in the hope that this might provide them greater negotiating leverage over the developed states. They would like to see further liberalization of agricultural trade in the developed countries, tightening of the rules on anti-dumping measures and ensuring that non-trade related issues such as labour and environment are not allowed to come to the WTO.

In recent years, India and China have attempted to build their bilateral relationship on the basis of their larger worldview of international politics. As they have found a distinct convergence of their interests on world stage, they have used it to strengthen their bilateral relations. They have established and maintained regular reciprocal high-level visits between political leaders. There has been a sincere attempt to improve trade relations and to compartmentalize intractable issues that make it difficult for their bilateral relationship to move forward.

India and China have strengthened their bilateral relationship in areas as distinct as cultural and educational exchanges, military exchanges, and science and technology cooperation. Bilateral trade has recorded rapid growth from a trade volume of US $265 million in 1991 to US $3596 million in 2001. In 2001, bilateral trade saw an increase of 23.4 percent over 2000. It is expected to rise to $10 billion this year. The two nations are even evaluating the possibility of signing a comprehensive economic cooperation agreement and a free trade agreement by the end of this year, thereby building on strong complementarities between the two.

Both states are also taking steps to upgrade their military-related cooperation, leading to greater understanding on the bilateral military front, something that would have been unthinkable just a few years ago.As a first step in this direction, the Chinese and Indian navies carried out joint search and rescue operations off the Shanghai coast in November 2003. Both states are also seeking to cooperate on the nuclear front with China planning to import heavy water from India to be utilized in the pressurized heavy water reactors near Shanghai.

Many observers have also pointed out a subtle shift in Beijing 's stance on Pakistan vis-à-vis India. China 's "neutral" position during the Kargil conflict and the intense Indo-Pak crisis following the terrorist attack on the India 's Parliament is seen by many as a reflection of China 's sincerity in its attempts to improve ties. In keeping with China's attempts to project itself as a responsible regional player, China is seen by some as supporting peace and anti-terrorist efforts in South Asia by cooperating with the US and India. China is also seen as playing a central role in encouraging Pakistan to negotiate with India by using its leverage over Pakistan.

After assuming office Prime Minister Manmohan Singh's government made it clear that it favoured closer ties with China and would continue to work towards improving bilateral relations with China. In his first address to the nation, the Prime Minister, Manmohan Singh, also emphasized the carrying forward of the process of further development and diversification of Sino-Indian relations. The late J.N. Dixit, National Security Advisor in the current government, wrote that "the Congress will continue the process of normalizing, strengthening and expanding India's relations with China, which is the most important factor affecting Asian security and stability". One of the first foreign visits of the new Indian foreign minister, Natwar Singh, was to China to attend the Asia Cooperation Dialogue in Qingdao, in East China's Shandong province and apparently had "substantive discussions" with his Chinese counterpart.

All this reflects on India continuing to build its relations with China on the convergence of interests that the two nations have achieved in recent years. Aside from the positive developments, one should not ignore the enormous obstacles that confront this bilateral relationship. There has been a dominant tendency in the Indian foreign policy establishment to focus on the strengths of its bilateral relations with China while pretending that problems confronting the relationship would somehow take care of themselves. The challenges in the Sino-Indian relationship are by no means insignificant nor will China take care of Indian interests. It is for India to recognize them for what they are and evolve a coherent strategy to tackle them.

Divergences and Challenges

The number one priority for China 's leadership today is economic growth and social stability. China soon underwent one of the most peaceful and orderly political transformations in its recent history, even though its exact ramifications remain far from clear. Hu Jintao became Communist Party chief in 2002 and President of China in 2003 replacing Jiang Zemin. He also finally ceded the effective control of the armed forces to Hu Jintao in September 2004. Hu Jintao is now formally in command of the vast party, government, and military bureaucracies that rule China. This shift, although important for the smooth working of the Chinese government, is unlikely to produce any radical change in China 's foreign policy. China 's focus is going to be on maintaining its high rate of economic growth in the coming years. It should be remembered that Hu Jintao is a product of the "evolutionary policies" of Deng Xiao Peng that emphasize economic growth and orderly governance. President Hu Jintao has made it amply clear that Western-style multiparty democracy is something that would not serve the Chinese people well, terming it a "blind alley" for China. Therefore, one can expect China to continue on its current economic trajectory and shaping its foreign policy accordingly.

China has enjoyed average annual rates of real income growth of around 10 percent in the last two decades of the twentieth century, something unprecedented historically. China accounts for about 5 percent of world trade and foreign direct investment (FDI) to China is predicted to reach an annual utilized rate of 100 billion in 2005. After its accession to the WTO, China 's already-high global economic profile is set to rise manifold. China will continue to focus on maintaining its high rates of economic growth in the coming years, even as some of the economic challenges China faces will become more acute. The burgeoning income disparities, restructuring of its states owned enterprises and the problem of non-performing loans in its banks are just a few of the economic problems China 's economy is likely to face in the coming years. So far China has managed remarkably even though the future remains uncertain.

Broadly speaking, Indians either view China 's economic growth as a façade or envy it. While India has achieved some remarkable growth rates in the last few years enjoying average annual rates of real income growth of six percent in the last two decades of the twentieth century, it still lags behind China. India accounts for less than one percent of world trade in goods and services. Currently, China outperforms India in terms of levels of growth, education, health, and living standards of its population, and global integration of its economy. China outpaces India, in sectors where the two compete for third country markets. Sino-Indian competition for these markets is bound to further intensify in the coming years.

Though some argue that the long term economic prospects of India are much better than China 's, China remains the undisputed economic powerhouse of the moment driving the Asian and global economy with India somewhere far behind. The fact of the matter is so long as India does not place its own economic house in order; it will remain a second-rate power even in Asia. And China will remain the Asian power that the world will look up to when trying to manage problems in Asia.

What should be equally, if not more, significant for India is the fact that it is China's economic transformation that has given it the capability to become a military power with China spending as much as $65 billion a year on its military. China's military may or may not be able to challenge US supremacy in the next few years but it will surely become the most dominant force in Asia. According to authoritative sources, China is set to overtake Japan in the next decade to become Asia 's major regional military power. The US involvement in the global war on terror has put the "containment" of China on the backburner and China has seized on this opportunity to strengthen its armed forces further.

China imbibed the lessons of US military undertakings such as the 1991 Gulf War, war in Afghanistan and the recent operation Iraqi Freedom. These have spurred China's pursuit of the latest Revolution in Military affairs (RMA) manifested in the buying, adopting of latest technologies and weapons systems (particularly from Russia) along with concomitant changes in doctrine and organizational structures. The People's Liberation Army (PLA) has been shedding its manpower since late 1990s to save funds so as to be able to focus on high tech. Despite a western embargo on China preventing transfer of military technologies, China has been able to deftly use US corporations to garner and apply dual-use technologies. China is simultaneously pursuing a qualitative and quantitative transformation of its nuclear infrastructure. China plans to deploy new road-mobile, solid-fuelled, long-range missiles over the next several years possibly to counter US ballistic missile defence.

Overtime, China 's enhanced military prowess will lead it to assert its interests more forcefully, thereby, adversely affecting Indian interests. As China becomes more reliant on imported oil for its rapidly growing industrial economy, China will develop and exercise military power projection capabilities to protect the shipping that transports oil from the Persian Gulf to China. The capability to project power would require access to advanced naval bases along the sea lines of communication and forces capable of gaining and sustaining naval and air superiority.

China 's assistance to Myanmar in constructing and improving port facilities on two islands in the Bay of Bengal and the Andaman Sea is the first step to securing military base privileges in the Indian Ocean. This can be used as a listening post to gather intelligence on Indian naval operations and a potential forward base for future Chinese naval operations in the Indian Ocean. India 's traditional geographic advantages in the Indian Ocean are also increasingly at risk with deepening Chinese involvement in Myanmar. China 's increasing naval presence in the Indian Ocean is of tremendous strategic consequence for India. There are also suggestions that the balance of air power in the China-India theatre has shifted in China 's favour with it acquiring an inventory of about 1500 modern combat aircraft for deployment in the theatre.

China remains the only major power in the world that refuses to discuss nuclear issues with India for fear that this might imply a de facto recognition of India 's status as a nuclear power. It continues to insist on the sanctity of the UN resolution 1172 which calls for India (and Pakistan) to give up its nuclear weapons program and join the Nuclear Non-Proliferation Treaty (NPT) as a non-nuclear weapon state. This was reflected in China 's lack of response to the Indian Foreign Minister's proposal of a common nuclear doctrine for China, India, and Pakistan. China would not like to get into any sort of nuclear dialogue with India that might give the impression of China recognizing India as a nuclear power. Moreover, while both India and China have a "no first use" nuclear doctrine, China 's doctrine is not applicable to India as it is not a party to the NPT.

China has done its best to maintain a rough balance of power in Indian Subcontinent by preventing India from gaining an upper hand over Pakistan. It has consistently assisted Pakistan 's nuclear weapons and ballistic missile programs to counterbalance India 's development of new weapons systems. India 's preoccupation with Pakistan reduces India to the level of a regional power while China can claim the status of an Asian and world power. China signed a charter to step up bilateral defence cooperation with Pakistan "to help maintain peace and stability in South Asia " even as it professes to improve its relations with India. Moreover, even as India and China share similar concerns regarding Islamic terrorism in Kashmir and Xinjiang respectively, China has been rather unwilling to make a common cause with India against Pakistan. China 's use of India 's neighbours to curtail Indian influence has not been restricted to Pakistan. China has actively sought to contain India all around its periphery by engaging Nepal, Bangladesh and Myanmar.

Despite resolving most of its border disputes with other countries, China is reluctant to move ahead with India on border issues. India 's discussion of border issues with China is seen as a concession. India remains satisfied with the "positive" and "satisfactory" Joint Working Group negotiations on the boundary issue. Despite the need for an expeditious demarcation of the Line of Actual Control, the talks seem to be continuing endlessly and the momentum of the talks itself seems to have flagged.

The momentum of the issue of Tibet seems to have been lost. Tibet has become a platform for the projection of Chinese military power. India 's tacit support to Dalai Lama's government-in-exile has failed to have much of an impact either on China or on the international community. Today even Dalai Lama seems ready to talk to the Chinese as he realizes that in a few years Tibet might get overwhelmed with the Han population and Tibetans themselves might become a minority. The proposed opening up of the Nathula trade route that connects Tibet and Sikkim has been much trumpeted by the Indian government as a major achievement of Indian diplomacy. However, this step is fraught with dangers as there is no certainty that internal security threat posed by Chinese infiltration would not get worse with the opening of Nathula. This has probably led to some rethinking in India on this issue.

There were disturbing reports during the Indian Prime Minister's visit to China, that Chinese troops had intruded into the Indian territory along a stretch of the unfenced border with Arunachal Pradesh. China refuses to recognize Arunachal Pradesh as part of the Indian territory, laying claim to 90, 000 sq. km. of its land. If recent reports are to be believed after a two-decade gap, China has resumed the supply of weapons to various insurgent groups fighting in northeastern India. China seems to be getting successful in hemming India in from both, the eastern and the western flanks.

China and India: Different Approaches, Different Outcomes

What the above discussion of the divergence and convergence between Sino-Indian interests reveals is the success of China in attaining its foreign policy objectives and the failure of India to preserve its vital interests vis-à-vis China. This cannot simply be attributed to China 's economic and military strength. While China is definitely the bigger player in the region and the world at large but its success vis-à-vis India owes as much to its power as to the way that power has been cultivated and used. While realizing fully well that it would take China decades to seriously compete with the US, it has focused strategic energy on Asia. Its foreign policy is aimed at enhancing its economic and military prowess to achieve hegemony in Asia. China 's recent emphasis on projecting itself as peaceful power is merely aimed at allaying the concerns of neighbours lest they try to counterbalance it. China's readiness to negotiate with other regional states and to be an economically "responsible" nation is also a signal to other states that there are greater benefits in bandwagoning to China's growing regional weight rather than opposing its rise in any manner.

However, while declaring that it will be focusing on internal socio-economic development for the next decade or so, China has actively pursued policies of preventing the rise of other regional powers. In case of India, this manifests itself in its cultivation of Pakistan as a close ally. From supplying it nuclear and missile technologies to building its military infrastructure, China has done all it can to build Pakistan as a counterweight to India. This policy has largely succeeded as India no longer enjoys its earlier conventional superiority vis-à-vis Pakistan possession of nuclear weapons by both nations ensures that any step that India takes to strengthen its nuclear weapons profile is viewed by the international community as highly destabilizing in the context of the "nuclear flashpoint" that South Asia has become for the world at large. China has thereby been successful in emerging as a "responsible" global player, despite its abysmal nuclear and missile proliferation record while the international community rails at India for making the world much more dangerous.

China's attempts to increase its influence in Nepal, Bangladesh, and Myanmar, its persistent refusal to recognize parts of India such as Arunachal Pradesh, its lack of support for India's membership to the United Nations Security Council and other regional and global organizations, all point towards China's attempts at preventing the rise of India as a regional and global player of major import. It is this strategy that China has consistently and successfully pursued without any apologies. In fact, this strategy has been so successful that today China no longer believes that India can be a serious rival for Asian hegemony and some have pointed out, India is off of China 's diplomatic radar.

In contrast to China 's well-laid out policy vis-à-vis India, India has from time to time oscillated from one extreme to another. George Tanham has famously pointed out that India has shown little ability to think strategically on national security. In the case of India 's China policy, it needs to be realized that there is nothing really sinister about China 's attempts to expand its own influence and curtail India 's. China is a rising power in Asia and the world and as such will do its utmost to prevent the rise of other power centres around its periphery like India that might in the future prevent it from taking its rightful place as a global player. This is not much different than the stated US policy of preventing the rise of other powers that might threaten its position as a global hegemon. Just as the US is working towards achieving its strategic objective, China is pursuing its own strategic agenda.

There is also nothing extraordinarily benign in China 's attempts to improve its bilateral relations with India in recent times. After working to curtail India 's influence in various ways, China would not like to see India coming close to the US in order to contain China. In this geopolitical chessboard, both the US and China are using India towards their own strategic ends. India must resist the tendency of reacting to the actions of other. India 's attempt to come up a coherent strategy towards China based on identified strategic objectives is of paramount importance. Prime Minister Manmohan Singh declared that it wants to have friendly relations with China, a reasonable foreign policy objective. However, without a clear articulation of India 's national security objectives, pursuit of friendly relations with China should not become an end in itself. It should be a means towards achieving India 's larger strategic objective of emerging as a major regional and global player.

India 's China policy is also symptomatic of a larger misunderstanding in the Indian and political establishment with regard to a nation's foreign policy. For the left-liberal strand in the Indian polity, foreign policy is merely an extension of domestic policy. As such since India is a secular, democratic, and peace-loving nation, India 's pursuit of its relations with other states should merely be a reflection of these virtues. This has given rise to much of the moral rhetoric in foreign affairs. On the other hand, the Indian right, because of its preoccupation with establishing a "Hindu" nation and minority bashing, have extended its narrow sectarian view to foreign policy. The consequence has been its obsession with Pakistan as evil incarnate in its foreign policy agenda and its inclination to view the world in black and white, friends and enemies, evil and noble. Shaped by these forces, Indian foreign policy has merely been one of responding to events around it rather than anticipating them and evolving long-term strategies to deal with them. India's China policy is a casualty of this reactionary approach.

India needs to develop its economic and military might without being apologetic. It needs to clearly articulate its national interests and engage China on a host of issues, from the border problem to the alleged dumping of cheap Chinese goods in the Indian market. India needs to recognize that appeasing China is neither desirable nor necessary even as a direct confrontation with China is not something India can afford, at least in the near future. It must also be recognized that while for India, managing its relations with China is at the top of its foreign policy agenda, China does not view India as a significant global player and is largely indifferent to India's growing profile.

India is a rising power in Asia and there is nothing wrong in demanding its rightful place in the interstate hierarchy. Simply put India and China are two major powers in Asia with global aspirations and some significant conflicting interests. As a result, some amount of friction in their bilateral relationship is inevitable. The geopolitical reality of Asia makes sure that it will be extremely difficult, if not impossible, for *Hindi-Chini* to be *bhai-bhai* (brothers) in the foreseeable future. This reality should be accepted by the Indian policy makers, rather than wished away. India should make a serious attempt to manage this friction by expanding the zone of cooperation with China even as it tries to steadfastly pursue its national interests. India should display the confidence to craft a foreign policy that best serves its national security interests without always looking over the shoulders to make sure that China is not displeased. Again, India can learn a lot by examining how China has managed its relationship with the US in the last few years.

While India certainly needs to engage China in an effort at reconciling security and political perspectives, it is naïve to assert, as many do, that India should first be sensitive to China's concerns, real or imaginary, before defining its foreign policy goals and strategic agenda. Does China consult India in its pursuit of its own strategic objectives? It does not and neither should India expect it to. In a similar vein, India should define its foreign policy agenda in view of its own national security imperatives.

But for this to happen, the government of India will have to formulate a clear China policy and, more importantly, a broader national security strategy. Ad-hocism just won't do. This should be the top foreign policy priority of the Indian government if it wants India to emerge as a global power of any reckoning. India should heed to Sun Tzu's advice and recognize that a merely tactical foreign policy approach without the backing of a sound strategy will only lead to nowhere.

8

Disputed Territory between China and India

ARUNACHAL PRADESH

Both countries retain their strong claims to the disputed territory, however, fueled by national pride and national security interests. China's "Go West" development policy and July 2006 opening of the Qinghai-Tibet railway have received mixed responses from Indian policymakers; those who favour expanded trade and people-to-people contacts have regarded the developments as positive, but some within the national security establishment have raised concerns that they will allow Beijing to extend its military power projection into Tibet and beyond into South and Central Asia.

Three rivers running through India—the Indus/Sengge Chu, Sutlej/Langqen Tsangbo, and Brahmaputra/Sang Po—originate in Tibet, a fact that has spurred Indian fears that China could use upstream dams and barrages to control the flow of water into India. India, for instance, has blamed a series of flash floods along the Sutlej River in its state of Himachal Pradesh to China's reluctance to supply hydrological data to India in a timely manner or allow Indian scientists to conduct surveys of melting glaciers on Chinese soil.

The absence of any water-sharing treaty between both states as a result of the disputed status of their borders contributes to these water tensions.

Regional Affairs

Regionally, Sino-Indian cooperation has been the exception rather than the rule. Beijing watches closely New Delhi's increasing engagement of East Asia, including relations with nations that have historically had particularly difficult interactions with Beijing, such as Japan, Vietnam, and Indonesia.

At the same time, Indian strategists have expressed quiet concern over China's growing influence in the subcontinent, not only its maintenance of a robust political and military relationship with India's rival Pakistan, but also its extensive political, economic, and security relationship with Burma, growing relations with Bangladesh and Nepal, and increasing naval presence in the Indian Ocean. China's admission as an observer to the South Asian Association for Regional Cooperation (SAARC) in November 2005, with New Delhi's reluctant acquiescence, has been cited as further evidence of China's emergence as a player in India's backyard and the desire of India's smaller neighbours to draw China into the region as leverage.

India has viewed growing Chinese influence in Burma, which is strategically located along the eastern end of the Indian Ocean, with great suspicion. In the mid-1990s, India had been one of the most vocal and ardent supporters of Burma's democracy movement, led by Aung San Suu Kyi.

However, the combination of India's aim to forge closer links with Southeast Asia as part of its "Look East" policy, its need for Burma's support in countering insurgent groups in India's northeast, its desire for access to Burma's natural resources, including energy (often in competition with China), and its alarm over China's growing military ties to the Burmese junta led India to adopt a more conciliatory engagement policy with the Burmese leadership by the late 1990s to counterbalance Chinese influence.

Most notably, the presence of Chinese radar technicians in Burma's Coco Islands, which border India's Andaman and Nicobar Islands, has fueled concern in New Delhi (and Washington) that Beijing is monitoring naval activities in the region. Furthermore, China's efforts to develop alternative overland routes to transport oil and gas imports through port facilities at Gwadar in Pakistan's Baluchistan province, which is at the entrance of the Strait of Hormuz, as well as through Bangladesh and Burma, have been viewed by India as part of a Chinese "string of pearls" strategy of economic and military encroachment into South and Central Asia. Indeed, China's senior-most leaders have openly declared Beijing's attention to placing priority focus on naval modernization, including greater power-projection capability. Indian policymakers fear that China's moves could undermine India's regional preeminence.

At the same time, India's joint naval exercises in the South China Sea—with Vietnam in 2000 and Singapore in 2005, joint patrols with Indonesia in the Andaman Sea beginning in 2002, and exercises off the Japanese coast with the U.S. and Japanese navies in April 2007, have sparked concerns in Beijing. The Indian Navy, the world's fifth-largest, has also set up a Far Eastern Naval Command (FENC) off Port Blair on the Andaman Islands to increase its presence in the Strait of Malacca and potentially monitor Chinese naval activities in the region. Such mutual suspicions could result in China-Indian naval rivalry in and around the Indian Ocean over time.

For their part, East Asian nations have increasingly looked to India as a potential partner in economic and regional security affairs, with some, such as Japan, apparently considering India as a potential element in a hedging strategy against China. South Asian countries have likewise begun to play the "China card" in order to counterbalance India's influence in their affairs or gain policy concessions from India and the West.

For instance, as relations have soured between New Delhi and Dhaka in recent years, China has become Bangladesh's largest supplier of military hardware and has replaced India as Bangladesh's overall largest trading partner. In Nepal, China defied international suspension of military aid and other support to King Gyanendra's regime after the monarch suspended democracy from February 2005 to April 2006, calling the situation Nepal's "internal affair." King Gyanendra reciprocated by shutting down the office of the Dalai Lama's representative in Nepal as well as the Tibetan Refugee Welfare Office. In the end, China and India each recognize the inexorable reality of the other's increasing involvement in its neighbourhood. In response, the two nations are quietly balancing the prospects for cooperation and competition in their relationship without letting any residual suspicions, tensions, or mistrust derail their mutual desire to test the possibilities of political rapprochement, economic engagement, and confidence-building in the years ahead.

People-to-People Contacts

People-to-people contacts between China and India have increased in recent years, albeit from a low base. Regular direct flights were established in 2002, when China's tourism authorities designated India as an "authorized destination." More than 5,000 Indian students are currently studying in Chinese universities. In India, enthusiasm for Chinese popular culture is growing, and Indians tend to respect, if not envy, China's economic and political rise, which they would like to have their own country mirror. India dubbed 2006 the "Year of Friendship with China," and China declared 2007 the "Year of China-India Friendship through Tourism."

Nonetheless, while official interaction is on the rise and public opinion polls suggest that a majority of citizens and businessmen in both states hold favorable views of each other overall, popular interaction remains relatively minimal, restricted by the language barrier, cultural differences, and other factors. Chinese and Indian observers alike will note that the Chinese have more natural affinity with countries in East and Southeast Asia, while Indians are more comfortable in dealing with English-speaking countries and other South Asian states.

Mutual mistrust persists, particularly within India's older generation, whose memories of the Sino-Indian border conflict lead it to view China with suspicion. India's media and educational system have also nurtured the notion that China "stabbed India in the back" in 1962 and is sitting on Indian land. India's visa policy, in fact, is very restrictive and suspicious of the entry of citizens from China (among other nations, including the United

States), further constraining popular contact. For their part, the Chinese have expressed difficulty in understanding India's cultural and interpersonal style and have tended to be snobbish in their view of India and its state of development relative to China. While Indians may be focusing increasingly on China, relatively little Chinese popular attention is directed toward India. Few Chinese students study in India, for instance. Even at the official level, a similar lack of symmetry in the level of attention paid by China and India toward each other appears to prevail.

Negotiating Strategies

One repeated emerging criticisms of India's negotiating strategy is that "unilateral concessions" have been made too often by India, without similar concessions being made by China. When PRC military forces started moving into Tibet in 1950, the Republic of India quickly moved to (a) give up the Forward Rights inherited from the days of British India, which stemmed from the Simla Convention and Anglo-Tibetan Agreement of 1904; and (b) instead recognise Chinese control over Tibet in stronger terms than the hitherto used term "suzerainty".

In effect, a "Tibet Card" was there to be played at a time of PRC uncertainties. A robust Indian intervention might have maintained Tibet as an effective buffer between India and China, or at least enabled concessions to be won by India on the Himalayan—Karakoram borders. This is the reverse logic behind recent Indian comments that "China has failed to appreciate that if Arunachal is claimed to be the southern part of Tibet Autonomous Region (TAR), India cannot accept Tibet to be within China. India's formal position on Tibet articulated in 1954 and 2003 is therefore a tentative and unilateral diplomatic offer that can only be sustained and the circle completed once China recognizes Arunachal as part of India". Reinvoking such a "Tibet Card" has been floated in some Indian circles in the past few years.

Having lost that opportunity, the next criticism of Indian negotiating strategy is that, faced with an immediate PRC military presence in Tibet and renewed Chinese claims over Aksai China and Arunachal Pradesh, Nehru ignored the chance of a trade-off seemingly offered by China in 1960; whereby Aksai China would have gone to China and Arunachal Pradesh would have gone to India. Instead, India refused to engage in sovereignty negotiations in the 1950s, maintained its claims to the fullest, neglected to build up its own military forces, yet still engaged in adventurist forward probing movements in the late 1950s. At the time, Nehru rejected the idea of territorial trade-off; India "will not concede one piece of territory in return for another in the same manner as a similar dispute between China and Burma was settled this year"; for "there is no question of barter in these matters ... facts are facts".

His formal position was, in the formal *Indian Note* of June 16 1962; quite simply that "this boundary is well known and well recognized and has been so for centuries and cannot be the subject of any negotiations". The trouble was the precise boundaries were not well known, were not well recognized, and had not been in shape for centuries. The irony is that the territorial agreement reached between Burma and China in 1960 involved China following the MacMahon Line alongside other mutual concessions and swapping of territory; as did the 1963 Agreement between China and Pakistan with regard to mutual concessions over claims and territory in the Karakoram reaches.

Nehru might have said "facts are facts" but the fact of the matter is that China's military superiority and continuing occupation of Aksai Chin created a very different subsequent set of facts in the wake of India's military defeat at the hands of China in 1962. The problem for consideration of negotiated resolution of the territorial dispute is that demands and offers have shifted. From the outside, an obvious trade off would be between the *Western* Sector and the *Eastern Sector*; which is where Noorani argued that "there is no territorial dispute which has been, and still is, more susceptible to a solution than India's boundary dispute with China. Each side has its non-negotiable vital interest securely under its control. India has the McMahon Line; China has Aksai Chin" In other words, China's *de facto* control of Aksai Chin could be reflected in agreed *de jure* sovereignty for China, and India's *de facto* control of Arunachal Pradesh could in turn be reflected in agreed *de jure* sovereignty for India. This had been Zhou Enlai's seeming suggestion in 1960, and was the "Package Plan" floated by Deng Xiaoping during 1980. The problem is that the Indian government has never taken up such trade-off offers, with Chinese comments made about the weakness of the Indian governments in taking any compromise deal to the Indian public. The separate *sector-by-sector* approach advocated by India when discussions resumed in the 1980s, rather than *overall package* trade-off deals suggested by China, has not worked, it has merely led the PRC to maintain its particular claims in all Sectors.

Another possible example of unilateral concessions was Rajiv Gandhi's visit to Beijing in 1988. Various concessions were made by him. He agreed that the settlement of the border dispute no longer was necessary as a precondition for improvement of bilateral relations, secondly he agreed that some members of the Tibetan community in India were engaged in anti-China activities, and thirdly he agreed that Tibet was an internal affair for China. Ganguly considered the results were "clearly asymmetric" as no support on the Kashmir issue was received from China, which "underscored the stark debility of India's negotiating capabilities vis-à-vis China". On the other hand, the earlier unequivocal support for Pakistan's case in Kashmir was moderated by a more neutral position by the 1990s, the PRC eventually announcing it was "not taking sides on Kashmir".

A final example of "unilateral concessions" came in the 2003 *Declaration on Principles for Relations and Comprehensive Cooperation between India and China,* in which India explicitly recognised the sovereignty of China over Tibet. A careful look at the text shows one-way agreement, one-way obligations, one-way concessions. On the one hand, it stated that "The Indian side recognizes that the Tibet Autonomous Region is part of the territory of the People's Republic of China and reiterates that it does not allow Tibetans to engage in anti-China political activities in India"; before going on to immediately say, on the other hand, "The Chinese side expresses its appreciation for the Indian position and reiterates that it is firmly opposed to any attempt and action aimed at splitting China and bringing about "independence of Tibet". As can be seen, there was no recognition of Indian territory (Arunachal Pradesh?) by China; not even return recognition by China of India's sovereignty claims over Sikkim, the Princely State reincorporated into the Republic of India in 1975, an incorporation which China had refused to recognise. Indian commentators may have read the accompanying *Trade Memorandum* designating Natu La as a border trade post as recognition by China of India's sovereignty over Sikkim, but that was implied rather than explicit, *de facto* rather than *de jure*.

Meanwhile, New Delhi has refused to lay out its formal position, other than the reiteration of its full claims of the Indian Parliament in November 1962, a unanimous vote to get China to vacate all Indian-claimed territories that China occupied. Specific territorial negotiations involving sensitive political climb downs or concessions might well be conducted in private out of the public gaze, yet there seems no indications of this either. India could then indicate some sort of territorial trade-off, short of this maximalist reiteration of its full claims which China is unlikely to accept. Of course, India indicating a territorial trade-off would not necessarily meet with Chinese acceptance, given Indian suspicions that China is happy enough to avoid definitive frontier settlement; but at least it would clarify the issue, and in such an eventuality enable India to more straightforwardly strengthen her own presence and power towards China along the border. In IR terms, if *engagement* proved unsuccessful in leading to territorial settlement, then India could go for a degree of *internal balancing* through building up its military presence and power in Arunachal Pradesh and Ladakh. Some Indian commentators have suggested that "when the Agni-III is finally ready for deployment, it is likely that the Chinese will come down to the table for negotiations and there is likely to be further progress on the border dispute". It could also go for a degree of *external balancing* with others vis-à-vis China but that is a much wider issue. It could try adjusting its bigger policy on Tibet, in effect playing a "Tibet Card" to engineer geopolitical shifts in the future; though would be a much more high risk strategy immediately bringing it up against China's perceived "core interest" of averting internal fragmentation.

If India's strategy over the disputed territories has been hesitant, this has been exacerbated by the very opaqueness, the "Chinese whispers" coming from Beijing. What exactly does China really want, what is its bottom line? For example, are PRC reiterations of claims over the whole of Arunachal Pradesh, re-invoked with greater vigour since the 1990s, just a maximalist initial tactic to end up with the Tawang pocket, thereby strengthening its control over Tibet, a line of argument by Chinese commentators like Ma Jiali and others. Are some suggestions in PRC circles of a different trade-off, Aksai Chin to India and Arunachal Pradesh to China, serious? Did China's acceptance in 2003 of Nathu La as an official border trade post between India and China represent full and definitive acceptance by China of Sikkim's incorporation into India; and what is the significance of rising "incursion" incidents into Sikkim during 2008 by Chinese troops; uncertainties that undermine Wen Jiabao's assertions in 2005 that "Sikkim is no longer the problem between China and India?" Is talk in the PRC that "China won't make any compromises in its border disputes with India" a tactical ploy by China to get India to make compromises? If it is, then a trade-off deal is likely at some point. If it is not, then indefinite deadline/stand off is likely, unless one or the other disputant state attempts to decide it on the military battlefield.

One emerging line from the PRC, with implications for India, is PRC emphasis and definition of a "core interests" diplomacy, reflecting the rise of China; "as the country becomes stronger, China is now on the trajectory to develop its own doctrine of diplomacy". This has been a development in the last couple of years, overlapping with rising friction along the disputed Himalayan reaches; generally what the PRC calls "the recalibration of its strategic focus in diplomacy to 'core interests'", over which it is taking a more obstructive/assertive line. This sense of "core interest" can be primarily seen at stake for the PRC in Taiwan and also Xinjiang.' It can also be seen with PRC statements with regard to Tibet, whereby "Tibet related issues remain a core interest of China that refers to state sovereignty and territorial integrity. This is neither a religious issue nor a human right issue". The question is how far China's "core interest" framework may be "expanding". If such a "core interest" linkage is also invoked for Arunachal

Pradesh (or in PRC eyes *Zang Nan* "Southern Tibet") as "Tibet-related issues", then one would have less expectations of territorial agreements being reached between India and China, and more likelihood of armed resolution in the future. Such trends were the spur for Barat Verma at the *India Defence Review* to warn that for the PRC "the most attractive option is to attack a soft target like India and forcibly occupy its territory in the Northeast...Beijing's cleverly raising the hackles on its fabricated dispute in Arunachal Pradesh to an alarming level, is the preparatory groundwork for imposing such a conflict on India"; a scenario dismissed in China as a "provocative and inflammatory illusion". Nevertheless, IR security dilemma dynamics may indeed lead to increasing military tension as both sides reinforce their military positions, and "war talk" about the disputed territories increases.

Concerned voices are easy to find as "tensions over a boundary dispute between the two sides are escalating". One reason for Indian concerns is the increasing number of "incursion" incidents along the border, though denied by China. The official India leadership downplays such trends, India's Foreign Secretary Niripuma Rao thus asserting in September 2009 that "there has been no significant increase in intrusions across all Sectors of the Line of Actual Control (LAC)", but that such India-perceived incursions were "because there is no mutually agreed or delineated border".

This ignores the earlier increase the previous year, whereby the number of India-perceived "incursions" by the PRC has increased from 140 in 2007 to 280 in 2008, with a similar number in 2009. Such incursion incidents involved not just the *Eastern Sector* around Arunachal Pradesh but now also the *Western Sector* around Aksai Chin/Ladakh; a particular widening development that Indian commentators like Bhaskar Roy have found "sinister" and which Kanwal sees as "aggressive tactical posturing" on the part of China.

Admittedly, such border incursions, reflecting different perceptions of where the LAC actually is, have often been trivial in themselves; for example Chinese troops painting rocks in red paint or cross-LAC sheep grazing. Chinese troop movements near and around the narrow Siliguri corridor "chicken's neck" linking northeast India to the rest of India do though cause immediate geopolitical concerns to India.

Certainly, a substantive military build up along the Aksai Chin and Arunachal Pradesh borderlines has also been evident. Partly this has been an infrastructure race, in which India has been belatedly trying to catch up and match China's better established road, and now railway, infrastructure in these disputed borderlands.

It has also involved increasing military deployment, again by India to match China's already established forces in places like Linzi airbase. This is reflected in India increasing its ground forces in the border regions facing China.

In the *Eastern Sector,* this has also involved the Indian Air Force (IAF) deploying advanced long range Sukhoi Su-30 warplanes to Tezpur for potential cross-LAC operation; complemented by six surface-to-air Akash missile squadrons. In the *Western Sector*, this has also involved the Indian Air Force reactivating disused high altitude airstrips like Daulat Beg Oldi and Fukche. Such reinforcements have been picked up in the PRC, and denounced as "unwise military moves".

Meanwhile, Brahma Chellaney asked the question in 2006 "will India—China border talks ever end"? He argued that "after a quarter century of unrewarding negotiations with Beijing, India ought to face up to the reality that it is being taken round and round the mulberry bush by an adversarial state that has little stake in an early border resolution"; in which "the more the talks have dragged on, the less Beijing has appeared interested in resolving the border disputes other than on its terms".

His prognosis was simple, "it is time for it to draw the line, at least in the negotiations" and "to re-evaluate the very utility of staying absorbed in a never-ending process". Three years later, in the wake of the 2009 talks, his sense was the same, "the latest round of the unending and fruitless India—China talks on territorial disputes was a fresh reminder of the eroding utility of this process".

The PRC may indeed wish to keep the issue open as a way of distracting and threatening India; but other dynamics may be leading the PRC to postpone decisive border negotiations. The PRC may well consider tightening its hold on Tibet itself as a greater priority, shaken during the disturbances that swept across Tibet and Tibetan areas in the spring of 2008? The PRC may also want to delay decisive border territorial resolution with India until it has resolved the Taiwan issue first?

Garver also has wondered how far Beijing's apparent slowdown and readiness to avoid territorial resolution with India, is because of "understanding between Pakistan and China that neither will settle their territorial disputes with India independently of the other". Such a consideration point to the wider Pakistan—China—India triangle interplay around the disputed territories that stretch along the Himalayas from Arunachal Pradesh in the east to Aksai Chin and Kashmir in the west, which overlap with basic power balancing by the China—Pakistan "nexus" against India. The overlaps between the varied territorial disputes was shown in 2009 when China gave visas for the entry of Kashmiri separatists to visit China, in the wake of India giving permission to the Dalai Lama to visit Arunachal Pradesh.

What is certain is that any quick decisive territorial resolution between India and China is unlikely. Following rising border frictions, the PRC media reported "China—India border dispute turns sour", with hard hitting nationalist blogs being noticeable in the Chinese official and state controlled media in the autumn of 2009. Admittedly, the Indian and Chinese leadership did again reaffirm dialogue in autumn 2009. However, this reaffirmation was in cautious terms "to gradually narrow differences on border issues between the two countries ... to continue talks, with the aim of incrementally removing the barriers to a solution that was fair and acceptable to both sides". Despite the euphemistic headline from the official Chinese media that the two countries had reached "concensus on narrowing border differences"; in reality this merely indicated the existence of a gap without showing how and when it would be resolved. Talk of "gradually" and "incrementally removing" barriers to a solution flags up the slowness of any likely process, whilst offering nothing on what solutions could then emerge once such barriers have been, incrementally, removed.

What of solutions? Could outside arbitration be one way forward? Nehru himself had offered such a route in the immediate aftermath of war in the shape of the International Court of Justice (ICJ) at The Hague.

However this was badly received in Parliament and Nehru then backed away immediately from this. In reality the ICJ seems ill equipped to deal with direct large scale territorial disputes between major powers, whilst China's reluctance to have outside bodies disposing of sovereignty issues is higher even than India's.

One bilateral solution which we can return to, involves a *logic of geography,* the "watershed/crestline" line along the Himalayas/ Karakoram. It has a degree of clearness, "the advantage of having a border on such a prominent line as the high watershed of the Himalaya is that it is easily identifiable, historically traditional and politically neutral".

It may also be sellable to both parties. Thus, "as far as the Indian public is concerned, they have been brought up to believe that the Himalaya is the traditional boundary and they will be willing to concede any territory that lies beyond it without demur"; whilst "such a boundary should also be acceptable to China as it is based on the same watershed principle which they have accepted in defining their boundaries with Myanmar, Sikkim and Nepal.

This watershed principle was an angle suggested by Zhou Enlai in the abortive 1960 discussions. In effect, applying the watershed principle would leave Aksai Chin to China and almost all Arunachal Pradesh with India.

Admittedly, Tawang remains problematic. The Tawang District's 2,085 square kilometres is around 2.5% of Arunachal Pradesh's entire 82,743 area, and its population of 38,924 is around 3.6% of Arunachal Pradesh's 1,091,120 inhabitants (2001 figures), relatively small shares on paper. Neutralization of the entire Tawang subdivision pocket might be an option. Within the Tawang District, given that the Tawang Subdistrict and the District capital Tawang (27°34'47"N) itself lies north of the Se la Pass and the Ka crest line (27°32'26"N), whereas the Lumla and Jang Subdistricts lie on the southerly India-facing slopes of that crest line; could a division of Tawang District be carried out, with the Tawang Subdistrict allocated to China and the Lumla and Jang Subdistricts allocated to India? However, local opinion at the District capital Tawang, population c. 20,000, would probably vote in favour of staying in 'India' rather than going into the 'PRC', though an independent 'Tibet' option would provide an interesting third option.

Having Tawang subdivision inhabitants relocate further south if they wished might be another solution, though ugly in political and human terms. Meanwhile, if the Dalai Lama's death was followed by any proclaimed rebirth at Tawang, a not impossible scenario, the situation would be still more complicated with the PRC.

Failing dramatic regime change scenarios of regime collapse/ democratization in the PRC, and re-establishment of a genuinely autonomous or independent Tibet, and Tawang notwithstanding; some sort of trade off involving Aksai Chin and Arunachal Pradesh seems the most likely way forward. In using relatively clear cut neutral geographic principles, the deadlocked politics and unclear history could perhaps be sidelined?

Such a trade off would give neither side too much geopolitical advantage, but also ensure a degree of security for each? A *logic of geography* for the future for the national leaderships that would enable these two neighbours to get past the inconclusive divisive *logic of history* between them, and would provide a mutually satisfactory *logic of power* in terms of geopolitical equilibrium outcomes. Failing resolution of their territorial issues, the grinding tectonic plates along the Himalayas will continue to have their geopolitical counterpart as the two Asian giants look at each other across these disputed areas.

PROSPECTS OF RESOLVING CHINA-INDIA BORDER DISPUTE

Today, some security experts such as Mr. Bharat Verma, the editor of *Indian Defence Review*, in this world are still talking about China's military attacks on India before 2012, or even within 6 months. However, such noises cannot halt the historic wheels of Chindia partnership from rolling forward. As the two new emerging powers, their leaders know clearly that each is not a threat to the other. China has been called the world workshop whileIndia the world office. In the course of their rise, the challenges they will face are the same or similar. They need more policy coordination and more functional cooperation in the world dominated by the developed nations in the global platforms such as G20, BRIC, BASIC, and China-Russia- India Trilateral Dialogue. Chinaand India joined hands last year during the United Nations Climate Change Conference in Copenhagen, effectively presenting the stance of emerging economies and developing countries on climate change.

For the past 10 years, the two governments have made joint efforts to cement and strengthen their bilateral relations. In 2003, Indian Prime Minister Atal Vajpayee visited China and signed Declaration on Principles for Relations and Comprehensive Cooperation between China and India. Both sides reaffirmed that they would promote a long-term constructive and cooperative partnership. They emphasized that their common interests outweigh their differences. The two countries are not a threat to each other. Neither side shall use or threaten to use force against the other.

They are committed to qualitatively enhance the bilateral relationship at all levels and in all areas while addressing differences through peaceful means in a fair, reasonable and mutually acceptable manner. They emphasized that the differences should not be allowed to affect the overall development of bilateral relations.

On the border question, they reiterate their determination to seek a fair, reasonable, and mutually acceptable solution through consultations on an equal footing. They agreed that pending an ultimate solution, they should work together to maintain peace and tranquility in the border areas, continue implementation of h agreements signed for this purpose, including the clarification of the line of actual control. The two governments decided to appoint special representatives to promote the process of the border negotiations. As one of the sensitive issues in the China-India relations, India recognizes that the Tibet Autonomous Region is part of the territory of the People's Republic of China and India does not allow Tibetans to engage in anti-China political activities in India.

In recent years, the trade relationship between the two countries has been seen in both countries as a crucial driver of overall bilateral relations, amid persisting political strains over the long-running border dispute.China became India's largest trading partner in 2008, with bilateral trade reaching $52 billion. Trade fell to $43 billion on account of the financial crisis, but has rebounded in the first two months of this year with Indian exports, mainly driven by iron ore, rising 75 per cent. It is predictable that rapid development of trade relations will certainly affect bilateral political relations in a positive manner.

Fast growing trade relations have come under increasing strain with India's trade deficit continuing to widen.India filed a record number of anti-dumping investigations against China at the World Trade Organization in 2009.

India's recent restrictions on the import of Chinese telecom equipment, in light of security concerns, have added to the list of strains. The telecom issue, however, was not raised by China during the President's ongoing visit. With the bilateral trade rapidly growing, these differences or disputes are normal. We believe that all these problems can be resolved by bilateral consultations. Describing trade and economic cooperation as a pillar of bilateral ties, Indian president Patil said India and China should work together to realize trade target of US$ 60 billion in 2010 that had been set.

In 2006 Presiden Hu Jintao visited India and the two sides agreed on a 10-pronged strategy to expand and intensify bilaterlal strategic and cooperative partnership.

In 2008, during the Indian Prime Minister Manmohan Singh visit to China, the two countries concluded a " Shared Vision for the 21st century", which forms the basis for bilateral cooperation on global issues.

China and India have agreed to enhance political, economic ties and bolster people-to-people contact during a meeting between

Indian President Pratibha Patil and Chinese Premier Wen Jiabao here on May 27, 2010. President Hu Jintao held talks with her. President Patil said India-China relations were of global and strategic significance, and all political parties in India were supportive of further advancing such relations. President Hu said that China and India should work more closely to address global issues such as economic downturn, climate change, energy security and food security. The two countries should maintain close communication and coordination within multilateral mechanisms such as China-Russia-India, BRIC, BASIC, and G20, in a bid to increase the voice of developing countries.

China and India do not pose as threat to each other and their common interests far outweigh their differences. The two countries should understand and respect each other's core national interests and major concerns, properly handle their differences, and seek common development and a win-win situation. A good China-India relationship makes both winners while a confrontational one makes both losers.

INDIA-CHINA BORDER AGREEMENT: MUCH ADO ABOUT NOTHING

Beijing successfully engineered signing a border defense cooperation agreement (BDCA) with India on October 23, 2013, in what seems to be a Chinese plot to subvert the debate surrounding its recent strategic offensive behavior. While the agreement seems to have set a positive tone to future talks between New Delhi and Beijing, it does not translate into any substantial shift in the Chinese policy. The latest mechanism is a mere token agreement that has not resulted in tangible progress on the ground.

India and China display a peculiar case of "constrained cooperation," in which the convergence of their economic interests tends to mask their prevailing strategic differences. Yet these divergences, of which the territorial and boundary dispute is foremost, still hold the potential of upstaging ties at any point.

This was demonstrated in April 2013, when a platoon-strength contingent of the Chinese People's Liberation Army (PLA) intruded deep inside the Depsang Plateau in eastern Ladakh, a region of

Jammu and Kashmir that shares a border with China. The troops pitched tents in Indian-claimed territory, violating earlier confidence-building measures and pushing India into a diplomatic and military tizzy. What perhaps is most distressing is that China's Depsang offensive happened despite numerous meetings of the India-China Joint Working Group and four confidence-building agreements, signed in 1993, 1996, 2005, and 2012. In addition to the Depsang occurrence, border guards of the PLA have repeatedly intruded into the eastern sector of Arunachal Pradesh, a state in northeast India, and the northern Ladakh sector.

The writing on the wall following the Depsang incident was clear. China holds the political and military will and capability to covertly notch up tensions in the Himalayas with India, at any time and place of its choosing.

Given that China and India have not mutually agreed upon a Line of Actual Control (LAC), sporadic incidents of border transgressions increasingly appear to be becoming a covert Chinese strategy of asserting its claims in India's western sector, especially in northeastern Ladakh and in Arunachal Pradesh in the eastern sector. The LAC is not physically demarcated on the ground or in military maps, and there is continuing reluctance and official refusals by China to show its version of the LAC to India-thus pointing towards a larger ploy of progressively building up a case for its claims in eastern Ladakh and Arunachal Pradesh.

China and India reiterated in the latest BDCA that neither side would use its military capability against the other. But in the event of China launching another underhanded operation in Arunachal Pradesh or the Ladakh sector, what picture would emerge?

Following the Depsang incident, India announced that both sides would pull back troops to their earlier positions along the LAC. But China haggled with India, agreeing to withdraw its troops from Indian territory provided that New Delhi tear down a line of defensive fortification in an area called Chumar. China also managed to get India to restrict its forward patrols in the area and unflinchingly negotiated for a BDCA. At this stage, India cannot afford to give in to further Chinese demands, such as suspending infrastructure development in its own territory near the LAC. Has China ever offered an explanation for the blizzard ininfrastructure construction it is carrying out in the Tibet Autonomous Region adjoining India?

China's cross-frontier incursions undermine the spirit of every confidence-building measure relating to the border areas New Delhi and Beijing have undertaken. The Depsang incident of 2013 casts an ominous shadow on Chinese intentions with respect to the border issue and sweeps away the spirit of the prior border-peace arrangements. In terms of making tangible progress toward a breakthrough on the larger question of border resolution, India and China have failed abjectly.

A Toothless Agreement

It appears that China has successfully managed to call the shots in the drafting of the BDCA by skirting the primary issue of resolving the boundary dispute. There are no lucid answers as to how exactly the BDCA stands apart from the other confidence-building measures that India already shares with China vis-à-vis the border question. And in many respects, the BDCA is loaded in China's favor.

For example, the BDCA's Article II stipulates that the two countries should share strategic information, but it does not elaborate on what specifically constitutes "information about military exercises, aircraft, demolition operations and unmarked mines." It is doubtful that China will be transparent enough to provide information about its military and cargo flights to forward landing strips near the borders. Article II also appears to be drafted so as to provide a cover for the Chinese Air Force in "locating aerial vehicles that may have crossed or are possibly in the process of crossing the line of actual control" in the border areas - suggesting China may be upping the ante and securing the possibility of launching an air offensive in these areas.

Overall, the BDCA remains a commitment-deficient agreement. It contains no binding assurance that the Indian and Chinese military headquarters will set up a hotline, stating that the two sides "may consider" the move. Article VI states that there would be "no tailing" of each other's patrols in disputed forward areas.

However, Indian border guards placed to check and prevent such incursions have been met with an antagonistic Chinese PLA.

Article III elaborates the process through which the BDCA shall be implemented through meetings between border personnel, military officers, and other departments and groups. There is nothing novel in these announcements; they have been in place for many years.

A Problem "Left over from History"

The banality of the text of the latest border defense cooperation agreement is proof that India is losing to China in terms of strategic leverage. With recent confidence-building measures only seeking to "consult" and "coordinate" border affairs, the ability of these mechanisms to achieve any sort of breakthrough to the interminable territorial and boundary dispute between China and India appears increasingly doubtful.

Instead, China has chosen to use the BDCA as a platform which provides it official cover to bide its time and strike when the Chinese political and military leadership see a window of vulnerability. Chinese politico-military history contains many references to dealing with obdurate problems "left over from history" by patiently waiting to resolve them "once conditions are ripe," in the words of the China's first premier, Zhou Enlai. Sun Tzu, the ancient Chinese military strategist, famously stated, "Engage people with what they expect... It settles them into predictable patterns of response, while you wait for the extraordinary moment — that which they cannot anticipate."

Demonstrating politico-military belligerence and stealth on various fronts appears to have become a defining feature of Chinese strategy, be it the protracted standoffs with India over the border, with Japan over the Senkaku Islands, or with the Philippines over the Scarborough Shoal. China's creation of the East China Sea Air Defense Identification Zone byon November 23 is testament to Chinese attempts at force projection that provides a stage for the long-term Chinese strategy of chipping away at contested claims with India. Beijing appears intent at keeping the border dispute alive as a tactical pressure point against India. China seems to be awaiting an opportune moment in which the existing military asymmetry with India will widen and Beijing will be positioned to bring the dispute to a close on its own terms.

TERRITORIAL PROBLEMS BETWEEN SINO-INDIA

In terms of "the rise of China" and its "implications for India", the title of this book, the Sino-Indian territorial dispute represents an immediate arena in which India is having to face the uncomfortable implications from having an increasingly stronger neighbour. For India, the ability of China to deny India's hopes of territorial settlement on India's terms has become ever clearer in the wake of China's rise in military power in and around their disputed territory, which remains the biggest amount of land still in dispute in Asia.

As such, "the 4,056—kilometre (2,520 miles) frontier between India and China, one of the longest inter-state borders in the world, remains ... not defined, let alone demarcated, on maps or delineated on the ground". Here, the judgement over a century ago of Lord Curzon, British Viceroy of India 1898-1905 still seems relevant; the most urgent work of Foreign Ministers and Ambassadors ... is now the conclusion of Frontier Conventions in which sources of discord are removed by the adjustment of rival interests or ambitions at points where the territorial borders adjoin", for "frontiers are indeed the razor's edge on which hang suspended the modern issues of war or peace, of life or death to nations".

Admittedly, the territorial issue has been officially decoupled from the wider Sino-Indian relationship; as with the PRC rhetoric that "China and India have already reached consensus on the border issue. Before it is completely resolved, both countries will endeavour to maintain peace and stability in the border areas and will not let the border issue affect the general picture of China and India's cooperation". However, in reality their territorial issues do affect their wider relationship, in PRC terms "the existence of immense territorial disputes between China and India".

In dispute terms, this chapter argues that, in International Relations (IR) theory terms, the territorial disputes between India and China involve *classical geopolitics* entwined with *critical geopolitics*. Each strand of geopolitics, in their different ways, both involve the respective "position" that India and China hold for themselves and for each other in their immediate and extended neighbourhood.

Whilst each side argues from history, the chapter argues that in reality the evidence from history is rather ambiguous and inconclusive for both sides' territorial claims. Indeed, history is a sterile area to argue from, as one Indian commentator put it, "can we go beyond history to look at solutions which do not hark back to the past?"

The chapter argues that, from the outside, resolution of the issue seems feasible enough in terms of simple seeming territorial trade offs involving Arunachal Pradesh and Aksai Chin; but is complicated by smaller geographic issues surrounding Tawang, and wider geopolitical issues surrounding Tibet and indeed the balance of power in Asia between India and China.

The two main areas of dispute along this Himalayan frontier are the *Western Sector* (Aksai Chin, around 37,250 square kilometres/ 14,380 square miles); and the *Eastern Sector* (Arunachal Pradesh, around 83,740 square kilometres/ 32,330 square miles). On the one hand, Arunachal Pradesh is inhabited by over a million people, Indian citizens, and includes important Buddhist centres like Tawang. On the other hand, Aksai Chin is a virtually uninhabited bleak barren plateau with no permanent settlements. It is the place "where not a blade of grass grows" as Jawaharlal Nehru once dismissively said; but where China's National Highway 219 runs through Aksai Chin as a key geopolitical infrastructure link for the PRC between its provinces of Tibet and Xinjiang. One further complication is China's occupation of the Shaksgam valley; around 5,180 sq kilometres/1,930 square miles, to which Pakistan relinquished its Baltistan-related claims in 1963, but over which India maintains its own Kashmir-derived claims. Smaller pockets of disputed territory are found, the *Middle Sector* fringes of Himachal Pradesh and Uttar Pradesh. Elsewhere along the Himalayas, lingering uncertainty over China's recognition of Sikkim's incorporation into India in 1975 is entwined with continuing PRC claims to the "Finger Area" in the north of Sikkim, with 71 supposed incidents reported of Chinese troop "incursions" in 2008. Nearby territorial disputes between China and Bhutan around the Chumbi Valley triangulation point with India are of further concern to New Delhi, given the Chumbi Valley's location looking down onto the India's sensitive Siliguri corridor which links India's northeastern states with the rest of India.

Wider nuances arise with India's Foreign Secretary (2004—2006) Shyam Saran, and his comments about *the logic of geography*. In front of one audience, it was a question for Saran of "geopolitical reality" in which "I would like to focus particularly on Asia, where the interests of both India and China intersect. It is said that the logic of geography is unrelenting. Proximity is the most difficult and testing among diplomatic challenges a country faces", where "to those who harbour any skepticism about this fact, it would suffice to remind that we share one of the longest [and disputed] land borders in the world with China.

In front of another audience, it was again a question that "it is said that the logic of geography is unrelenting and proximity is the most difficult and testing among diplomatic challenges a country faces"; with the following gloss that "frontiers with neighbours are where domestic concerns intersect with external relationships. This is where domestic and foreign policies become inextricable and demand sensitive handling", and in which "it is important for us to look at the [disputed] boundary question from the long-term and strategic perspective of India-China relations, rather than as a mere territorial issue.

The territorial issues between India and China form one of the biggest land disputes in Asia, and are of significance not only for the size of area under dispute, but also because the two disputants are the big countries most evidently on the rise in Asia. Alongside this *logic of geography*, there is then what Neville Maxwell called "the logic of power"; a *logic of power* whereby powerful states "in their expansive phases push out their frontiers until they meet the resistance of a strong neighbour or reach a physical barrier which makes a natural point of rest". In geopolitical terms, the current point of rest is along the Himalayas/Karakoram range, but in the long term where exactly is the "natural" point of rest between them? Amidst talk of mutual IR *security dilemma* dynamics, China's strengthening of military forces and related infrastructure in Aksai Chin and Arunachal Pradesh zones is now a spur to India's own more halting augmentation of military forces and related infrastructure. Meanwhile, both countries are seeking to expand their wider strategic space at a time when their immediate mountain borders remain unresolved.

STATUS OF NEGOTIATIONS

In 1981, following the frozen relations prevalent after the 1962 war, border talks at the vice-ministerial level were initiated. Although Beijing had suggested sectoral swapping in 1960 and 1980, this *overall package* predisposition faced India's push for separate *sector-by-sector* agreements. In 1988 more formal Joint Working Group (JWG) discussions were started; with a twin mandate of ensuring "peace and tranquillity" along the Line of Actual Control (LAC) and working on a "fair, reasonable and mutually acceptable" settlement of the boundary question.

In September 1993, China and India signed the *Agreement on the Maintenance of Peace and Tranquillity along the Line of Actual Control in the India-China Border Areas*, with a Sino-Indian Expert Group (EG) set up to assist the work of the JWG on the boundary question.

The rhetoric was clear in its Article-1; "the India-China boundary question shall be resolved through peaceful and friendly consultations. Neither side shall use or threaten to use force against the other by any means. Pending an ultimate solution to the boundary question...".

In November 1996, China and India agreed in their *Agreement on Confidence Building Measures in the Military Field along the Line of Actual Control in the India-China Border Areas* to delimit their Line of Actual Control (LAC) and institute Confidence Building Measures (CBMs) along the frontier. The agreement included pledges on nonaggression, prior notification of large troop movements, a 10-km no-fly zone for combat aircraft, and exchange of maps to resolve disagreements about the precise location of the LAC.

In June 2003, the India—China *Declaration on Principles for Relations and Comprehensive Cooperation between India and China* had the two countries agreeing "to each appoint a special representative to explore from the political perspective of the overall bilateral relationship the framework of a boundary settlement". Some ground rules for actual territorial negotiations seemed to have been achieved in April 2005 with the signing of the *Political Parameters and Guiding Principles for the Settlement of the India-China Boundary Question*. However, the *Joint Declaration by the Republic of India and the People's Republic of China* (2006) and the *Shared Vision for the 21st Century of the People's Republic of China and the Republic of India* (2008), which both expressed hopes that "such [boundary] differences are not allowed to affect the positive development of bilateral relations" in other fields, have perhaps pushed territorial differences but also territorial resolution to one side?

To conclude, varied frameworks have been seen; some eight rounds of vice-ministerial talks from 1981—1987, fourteen Joint Working Group meetings from 1988—2003, and thirteen rounds of Special Representative talks from 2003—2009. Nevertheless, there seems to have been little substantive progress on territorial issues. Specific discussions on core territorial demands and delineation of forces have given way to broader, but some would say vaguer and less useful, political discussions of bilateral relations as a whole. In terms of general confidence, if anything, the situation has deteriorated between India and China, where the last few years have seen growing numbers of incursions, alongside infrastructure and military forces build up along the Himalayas, both on the Arunachal Pradesh and Aksai Chin borderlines. Despite some of the diplomatic rhetoric of engagement and global cooperation, strategic perceptions of each other have deteriorated, whilst public as well as elite distrust of intentions and military capacity has grown.

Even initial specific steps have been minimal and indeed appear somewhat grudging. In terms of establishing the Lines of Actual Control (LAC), maps have only been established with regard to the relatively minor *Middle Sector* (Himachal Pradesh/Uttar Pradesh fringes) where LAC maps were exchanged in November 2000.

China then committed itself to an exchange of LAC maps of the *Western Sector* in 2002 and the *Eastern Sector* (Arunachal Pradesh) in early 2003. However, in 2003 this was effectively overturned when China argued that the two countries should instead focus on achieving an overall final political package settlement.

Equally well, the 2006 Joint Declaration pledge that "it was agreed to complete the process of exchanging maps indicating their respective perceptions of the entire alignment of the LAC on the basis of already agreed parameters as soon as possible" also has shown no particular signs of being completed; with no LAC maps having emerged for those two major blocks of disputed territory, Aksai Chin and Arunachal Pradesh. This in turn makes the immediate implementation of the 1996 *Agreement on Confidence Building Measures in the Military Field along the Line of Actual Control in the India-China Border Areas* difficult as the agreement refers to controlling military dispositions and deployments to certain distances from Lines of Actual Control, but yet those LACs have not been established.

The speed, or rather lack of speed, over negotiations is noticeable, a "glacial pace" given that current border discussions were first initiated in 1981. The 2005 *Political Parameters and Guiding Principles for the Settlement of the India-China Boundary Question* talked of "an early settlement of the boundary question" It did have its Article-7 provision that "in reaching a boundary settlement, the two sides shall safeguard due interests of their settled populations in the border areas". However, China's strong reassertion of its claims over Arunachal Pradesh, and especially Tawang, cut across such population principles. This population provision also seems undercut by the comments made to Pranab Mukherjee in June 6, 2007 by Chinese Foreign Minister Yang Jiechi, who stated that "mere presence" of settled populations would not affect China's claims. Meanwhile, the 2006 *Joint Declaration* announced that "the Special Representatives shall complete at an early date the task of finalising an appropriate framework for a final package settlement covering all sectors of the India-China boundary", but as of yet there are no signs of any such "early finalisation" let alone "early settlement". Similarly, the *Working Group* set up at the 2007 Special Representatives meeting to prepare a "framework arrangement" has been equally barren on outcomes, so far.

Indian perceptions of Chinese motives remain highly critical. For Kapila it was the opportunity for China "to keep alive the border dispute as a strategic pressure point against India". For Malik it was a case that "Beijing would not want to give up the 'bargaining chip' that an unsettled boundary vis-à-vis India provides it with. An unsettled border provides China the strategic leverage to keep India uncertain about its intentions, and nervous about its capabilities, while exposing India's vulnerabilities and weaknesses, and ensuring New Delhi's 'good behaviour' on issues of vital concern to China".

Discussions, rather than negotiations have then settled down into a regular, but desultory fashion. The press communiqué from the 2009 Special Representative talks was still noticeably bland; "in a friendly and candid atmosphere, the two Special Representatives had an in-depth exchange of views on resolving the boundary question.

Both countries agreed to press ahead with the framework negotiations in accordance with the agreed political parameters and guiding principle", so as "to seek for a fair and reasonable solution acceptable to both. Prior to that, both should work together to maintain peace and tranquillity in the border areas. Candid is often diplomatic euphemism for blunt differences of opinion, whilst the call for working together to maintain peace and tranquillity is a virtual admission that peace and stability has not yet been established. Equally euphemistic are PRC statements that both countries "should respect history and reality, take into account the feelings of both nations, make the most of their political wisdom and come up with a reasonable and mutually acceptable solution to their border issue". Such sentiments fail to give any tangible specifics on what actual solutions might be forthcoming.

9

Movement to Conflict and Failure of Negotiations

In the late 1940s, the advent of new regimes in India and in China brought new border problems and new border policies. The 1947 emergence of the Indian republic led to with- drawal of British power from the Indian subcontinent and the beginnings of a changing power balance in Asia. When the Communist regime emerged strongly in 1949, the balance of power tipped even further; however, border issues would probably have remained, whether China was ruled by the Nationalists or the Communists.

The new Indian republic devoted little time or attention to border conflicts with China in her first two years; rather, India was preoccupied with Pakistan, resolving border conflicts in Kashmir.

In 1947, Muslim disorder grew in Kashmir, and the Maharajah appealed to India for help; Indian troops responded. Pakistan also responded, and bloody fighting continued sporadically until late December, 1948. In January, 1949, a United Nations-supervised ceasefire and international frontier was established; but tensions in Kashmir and Jammu continued for years. In 1954, Kashmir constitutionally became part of India. But tensions between Pakistan and India continued for years; in 1965 and 1971 they would fight again. In 1950, India's attention began to focus back toward China.

Two major Chinese ventures in 1950 would have important impact on the Sino-Indian border problem. In October, the Chinese army advanced on Chamdo, 370 miles east of Lhasa, and Tibetan troops accepted defeat. The Government of India protested what it considered to be a wrongful and unnecessary use of force; yet, Nehru tended to accept Chinese authority over Tibet. By the end of 1950, China was in control of Tibet. In May, 1951, a Chinese-Tibetan treaty was signed; China would set up military and administrative committees in Tibet, the Tibetan army would be integrated into the Chinese army, and all of Tibet's external relations would be handled by China. In 1951, Nehru reacted to events in Tibet by sending an Indian expedition to the Tawang Tract to assert Indian influence up to the McMahon Line.

The second event, also in October, 1950, was China's military support of North Korea in the Korean Conflict. While China's part in Korea would draw upon her military and economic resources, Korea did provide cold weather and mountain warfare skills which China would use in the 1962 Border War.

Relations between China and India were generally good in the early 1950s, and the border issue remained quiet. India exported grain to Chinese troops and civilians working in Tibet. Chinese troops did not enter into NEFA. And India did not challenge occasional Chinese troops in Aksai Chin.

In September, 1951, Chou En-Lai suggested talks to stabilize the Tibetan frontier. While Chou stated that "there was no territorial dispute or controversy between India and China," it seems clear through the early 1950s that China did not accept the McMahon Line as India's northeast boundary. India responded that negotiations would be welcome; yet, no talks began for three years.

In April, 1954, India and China signed an agreement regarding trade, travel and representation between India and the "Tibet region of China." This agreement included a pledge of nonaggression, the "Five Principles of Peaceful Coexistence": mutual respect for the other's territorial integrity/sovereignty, mutual nonaggression, mutual noninterference in each other's affairs, equality and mutual benefit, and peaceful coexistence. The 1954 agreement did not address any major boundary disputes; the agreement simply named six passes in the Middle Sector (between Ladakh and Nepal) as trade passes, without specifying any boundary. In the middle 1950s, Pakistan aligned with the United States, and began receiving U. S. military aid. This disturbed India, and forced Nehru to relax his policy of non-alignment and seek support from Russia. While relations with the Soviets cooled in 1956 following the Russian intervention in Hungary, India did continue to seek Soviet aid, including military aid which would fortify India's position in 1962.

Prime Minister Nehru visited Peking in October, 1954, and raised the question of the border shown on Chinese maps. According to Nehru's account, Chou assured Nehru that the question was of no importance.

Late in 1954, Chinese government pressure in Tibet was stirring up increasing discontent amongst the turbulent Khamba tribesmen in eastern Tibet. Military actions by the Khamba tribesmen jeopardized Chinese lines of communication with Tibet from the east, as early as 1955. The Khamba actions were to have strong implications for the border situation, for it led China into building a new supply route into Tibet.

In March, 1956, the Chinese People's Liberation Army began construction of a military highway between western Sinkiang and western Tibet—directly across the Aksai Chin plateau, an area which the Indians clearly believed to be Indian (south of the Johnson-Ardagh line) and which the Chinese clearly believed to be Tibetan/Chinese (north of the Macartney-MacDonald line). Construction of the 1200 kilometer road, under difficult conditions in Aksai Chin, lasted from March, 1956, until completion in October, 1957.

It has already been noted that Aksai Chin was remote and desolate, and that India had minimal interests in the area; the Indian government did not even learn of the road's existence until September, 1957! In July, 1958, the existence of the highway was confirmed to India by published Chinese maps which not only showed the new route, but also placed all of Aksai Chin in Chinese territory. In July, the Government of India sent an initial protest to Peking, and sent two patrols to reconnoiter the road. The two patrols were detained by the Chinese, sensitive about the security of her new highway, for one month.

In December, 1958, Nehru wrote a friendly letter to Chou En-Lai about the Chinese maps—but without specifically referring to the military road—showing Aksai Chin as Chinese. Nehru reminded Chou of his statement about "no boundary dispute" between them. Nehru further asserted that these "large parts of India" being "anything but India, and there is no dispute about them." In a polite reply, Chou pointed out that the frontier and boundary had never been officially agreed upon by the two governments. Chou reminded Nehru that no central Chinese government had ever recognized the McMahon Line, which he called "a product of the British policy of aggression." Premier Chou was especially adamant about Aksai Chin, stating that Aksai Chin had "always been Chinese jurisdiction" and that it was regularly patrolled by Chinese border patrols. Chou proposed discussions leading to a mutually agreed survey, and that both sides should maintain their present positions—"maintain the status quo." Chou meant "status quo" to mean the present positions, now, and Nehru read "status quo" to mean the position which had been "until now." This semantic difference would impair future understandings and discussions. Chou's January, 1959 reply also implied that China would be willing to stay behind the McMahon Line in NEFA if China could retain her claim to Aksai Chin. Nehru's March, 1959 reply to Chou was an essentially uncompromising account of the historical basis for the Indian position on the boundary.

In March, 1959, disorder and fighting worsened in Tibet. The Dalai Lama crossed the McMahon Line into India and was granted political asylum. China had long suspected that India was aiding the Tibetan rebels, and the deteriorating situation in Tibet only aggravated Sino-Indian problems. In March, a large number of Khamba tribesmen had escaped into Nepal and India, acquired arms, and then disappeared back into Tibet. China thus felt it necessary to seal off the Indian frontier along the McMahon Line, to prevent Tibetan rebels from crossing into India to acquire arms.

Meanwhile, the diplomatic exchanges continued. But Nehru maintained that there was little to negotiate about the frontiers claimed by India. He was prepared to discuss "minor details" of border delimitation, but only if China would first withdraw from, and renounce her claim to, Aksai Chin. Chou En-Lai consistently refused to accept any of India's claims, and again proposed that negotiations start from the basis of actual position on the ground.

In mid-1959, India became sensitive about China's (anti-Tibetan rebel) activity along the McMahon Line. Indian border police began to establish checkposts along the McMahon Line, and moved border patrols forward toward the frontier of Tibet. This resulted in two clashes in August, 1959. In NEFA, the Indians attempted to occupy the hamlet of Longju, north of the McMahon Line, or at best a disputed border area. The two sides exchanged fire, and the Indian border police soon withdrew to the south.

The second clash occurred at Konga Pass, south of the Karakoram Range in western Tibet. The skirmish at Konga (or Konga La) Pass was a fire fight with losses on both sides—probably nine Indians and several Chinese killed. Author John Rowland gives an empassioned description of how the Indian patrol was captured, mistreated, interrogated, and "brain-washed." There was controversy as to which side fired first, but India publicized the incident as a "brutal massacre of an Indian policy party."

There was uproar in both countries about the Longju, Konga Pass, and other minor clashes in 1959; both sides launched letters of protest. Chou's September, 1959 letter repeated the Chinese position that the border had never been officially delimited; he stated that while China did not recognize the McMahon Line, Chinese troops had not crossed the Line. Chou described the boundary problem as a "complicated question left over by history." He further stated that Chinese troops were on the border solely for the purpose of preventing Tibetan rebels from moving back and forth over the border; he further commented that the Indian responses were provocative and unnecessary. Nehru's September reply to Chou again outlined the history and geography of the frontier question, and again stated that no settlement could be reached until the Chinese withdrew from all territory claimed by India, including Aksai Chin.

Shortly after the Konga pass incident, President Eisenhower announced that he would visit New Delhi. To China, this gave the appearance of India growing closer to both the United States and Russia. This only strengthened China's perception of India becoming more and more anti-Chinese.

In New Delhi, Nehru was receiving some criticisms of his policy of thrusting patrols into the frontier and setting up posts. Several senior Indian Army officers labeled the "forward policy" as militarily unwise, on the grounds that the Indian Army was neither militarily nor logistically prepared to deal with Chinese military strength in the frontiers. His response to this military advice, unfortunately, was to replace the officers with more subservient ones. Not only did Nehru make the mistake of ignoring his senior officers' advice, he also made the simultaneous error of rigidly adhering to three assumptions. He assumed that the Chinese would not stand up against an India backed by both the United States and Russia, that China would not oppose his patrols and outposts, and that Peking would readily withdraw under Indian pressure. All these assumptions were to prove erroneous, especially as Chou had warned Nehru not to pursue such a forward policy.

The diplomatic letters between Chou and Nehru continued through the end of 1959 and into 1960. In November, 1959, Chou proposed that both sides withdraw their troops twenty kilometers behind the McMahon Line, and also twenty kilometers from the line up to which each side exercised actual control in Aksai Chin. This would have removed the Indian army from its positions along the McMahon Line, and would have retained Chinese control, in Aksai Chin, over the Sinkiang-Tibet military highway and a new road which the Chinese built in 1959. While Chou's proposal was, of course, favorable to the Chinese, he was nevertheless proposing talks and a compromise. Nehru's November reply neither totally accepted nor rejected Chou's proposal. Nehru ruled out the idea of withdrawing from the McMahon Line, but proposed instead that each side refrain from sending patrols forward. For Aksai Chin, Nehru proposed that each side withdraw behind the line claimed by the other; this would have necessitated no drawback by the Indians in the west, but would have deprived China of its two Aksai Chin roads. Nehru implied that acceptance of this proposal was a prerequisite for any further talks between himself and Chou. Nehru thus rejected what he must have known to be the best Chinese offer he was likely to get without going to war. Chou's December reply was that, since the Konga Pass incident, China had stopped sending patrols out along the entire frontier. Chou further stated that Nehru's proposal was one-sided, and urged that the two leaders meet in less than ten days. Nehru understandably declined to meet on such short notice, but proposed no alternate date. In late December, China replied with another historical view of her side of the boundary dispute, and again asked for negotiations but without specifying a date. Nehru replied in February, 1960, again giving the Indian historical position and noting that there was little or no common ground on their respective viewpoints. But Nehru did propose further talks, and Chou did come to New Delhi in April, 1960; the talks were a total failure. Like the one-sided diplomatic letters, neither side was willing to change its position; hence, no compromises were presented.

Thus, the early 1960 diplomatic efforts at settlement or even compromise, between India and China, were essentially a total failure. Talks in late 1963 resulted in complete disagreement; each side even published incompatible reports of the discussions.

In 1960, China made a preliminary border settlement with Nepal. By the end of 1960, China had also made a boundary agreement with Burma. The Sino-Burmese border began not at the McMahon Line, but eight miles further south; this placed Diphu Pass—a strategic approach to eastern Assam—in Chinese territory. India was outraged and worried.

But no settlement or compromise occurred in Sino-Indian relationships. China was willing to compromise on NEFA; thus, eastern Ladakh (Aksai Chin) emerged as the major area of dispute. With the continued failure of diplomatic efforts, the uncompromising attitudes of both sides remained unchanged until the outbreak of hostilities in 1962.

By 1961, India had acquired aircraft, helicopters, engineering and other military equipment from the United States and Russia. Thus equipped, the Indian army invaded Portugese Goa in December, 1961. Goa was rapidly constitutionally incorporated into the Indian republic. Although no real protests or opposition occurred as a result of this action, the annexation of Goa reinforced China's view of India as being expansionistic.

This foreign military support also encouraged India to pursue her forward policy in Aksai Chin. In 1961, India had purchased eight Antov transports—complete with 40 Soviet pilots, navigators and mechanics—for use in Aksai Chin. Russian also supplied India with 24 Ilyushin-14 transports and Mil'-4 helicopters, capable of lifting men and supplies to altitudes of 17,000 feet. By mid-1962, India had also agreed to buy two squadrons of Soviet MIG jet fighters. Thus fortified, India pursued a more aggressive foreign policy against China. By the end of 1961, Nehru had sent enough Indian Army troops into Aksai Chin to establish about 43 posts on the Ladakh frontier claimed by China. Many of the Indian outposts were parallel to, but about 100 miles from, the first Chinese military road. However, three of the outposts were near Konga Pass, in the vicinity of the second Chinese highway.

In August, 1961, China began sending a series of angry protests to India. China had one basic argument: that Indian troops had intruded into Chinese territory. Nehru's response to Chou's complaints was that his (Nehru's) purpose was to "vacate the aggression (by the Chinese) by whatever means are feasible to us.... I do not see any kind of peace in the frontier so long as all recognised aggression is not vacated."

The latter half of 1961 brought China and India to increasing confrontations and skirmishes. Exchanges of fire became commonplace. A November confrontation in Chip Chap Valley left several Chinese soldiers dead; this was followed by a Chinese withdrawal. Such "victories" convinced Nehru that the Chinese would not be assertive and that his forward policy of outposts and patrols was the correct course for India. Despite continuing protests from senior Indian Army officers that India should first build up forces and logistic supplies in the frontier before embarking further, Nehru ordered even more aggressive moves into Aksai Chin.

Thus, by early 1962, the Chinese leadership perceived that the Indian government intended to launch a massive attack against Chinese troops; they apparently believed that India had decided to go to war over the issue. China's firm insistence over her territorial rights to Aksai Chin and India's aggressive forward policy of sending troops into the frontier would soon bring further confrontations and eventual armed conflict.

THE COMBATANTS: THE CHINESE AND INDIAN ARMIES IN 1962

The Chinese People's Liberation Army (PLA) is the unified organization, under a single command, of all Chinese land, sea, and air forces. The estimated strength of the PLA in 1962 was approximately three million officers and men. The 1962 ground combat forces consisted of about 130 divisions, mostly infantry. China is divided into eleven military regions, including the Sinkiang Military Region—responsible for Aksai China—and Chengtu Military Region—responsible for the northeast Indian border.

Chinese combat power was organized around an Army, with a strength of approximately 4,500 officers and 38,400 soldiers. Each Army has three Infantry Divisions, with a strength of approximately 1,300 officers and 11,300 soldiers in each Division. Major equipment of the Infantry Division included the Light Machine Gun, Antitank Grenade Launcher, and Mortars. Infantry Divisions included three Infantry Regiments, a Tank Regiment and an Artillery Regiment. An Infantry Regiment had three Infantry Battalions, equipped with 7.62mm Assault Rifles and Carbines. Even with China's massive combat manpower available, the nature of the 1962 Border War—mountain and cold weather operations—dictated tactics generally limited to the battalion and company level.

The PLA had both strengths and weakness in its readiness for mountain warfare against India. Perhaps China's biggest weakness was the economic and budgetary constraints on the Army. The Soviets has willingly supplied the PLA in the 1950's. But deteriorating relations—including border disputes—with Russia led to the end of Soviet military aid in 1960. Further, China faced national economic difficulties in the late 1950s and early 1960s. This resulted in progressive cutbacks and constraints from 1960 to 1962 for the PLA: ".... so serious was the shortage of military equipment and materials that it caused trouble in the training program.... The Ground Force is also facing the difficulties of obtaining fuel, ammunition, and batteries for the use of their vehicles and in training." The 1962 Taiwan Strait Crisis put further strains on the PLA's resources. Clearly, the watchword for the PLA was self-reliance—making due with the supplies and equipment that were available. Finally, while there has often been political control of the PLA, there was especially tight central control regarding border incidents; official orders in all border regions stated that ".... under no circumstance should an officer upon his own personal responsibility take steps to carry out an unauthorized decision" regarding any border/international incident; officers were directed to report incidents, and then await decisions and orders.

On the positive side, the PLA was well prepared for mountain warfare in the Himalayas. China had gained extensive experience in both mountain and cold weather warfare in Korea; many Korea verterans were still in the PLA in the early 1960s. Not only had China gained further experience in alpine warfare over the past twelve years in Tibet, but she was fighting in the same area (the Himalayas being the southern frontier of Tibet). The Chinese were acclimitized to the weather and the altitudes. They had outposts, patrols, and military construction (e.g. the two Aksai Chin roads) in the frontier. Further, the Chinese augmented their strength and mobility by using local Tibetan guides.

Finally, the PLA was well prepared for this type of warfare. The troops had warm, padded uniforms. They carried only what rations they needed to complete a particular mission. And they trained and practiced mobility, moving through mountain passes or over ridges at night, encircling the enemy. Even their mortars and small artillery was mobile. The Indian soldiers would report that the Chinese burp gun and human wave assaults were "demoralizing."

Despite its defense budget problems, the People's Liberation Army appeared to be prepared and ready for military operations in the Himalayas. The Indian Army's readiness for alpine warfare was quite a different story.

The Indian Ministry of Defense was the central agency for formulating and implementing the government's policy decisions on defense matters. There were three branches of service: army, navy, and air force. The Army was organized into three Commands - Western, Eastern, and Southern. Units from the Eastern and Western Commands would be organized into Corpslevel Border Commands. XXIII Corps was responsible for all of NEFA; within XXXIII Corps, 4 Division was responsible for the McMahon Line. The IV Corps would be formed in September, 1962, to assume portions of the NEFA defense. In the west, XV Corps had responsibility for Aksai Chin.

When India gained her independence in 1947, the Indian components of the British Indian Army were divided between Indian and Pakistan on a ratio of 2:1. The first years of the Indian republic were marked with a generally anti-military attitude; many Indian leaders remembered the role of the army in the bloody civil war that preceeded independence; this helped contribute to pacifistic attitudes. Further, Nehru (and others) minimized foreign threats; in regard to China, Nehru stated that the Himalayas "made an effective barrier." Thus, the 1950s was generally a decade of neglect for the Indian Army.

Because India believed that there was no external threat to her—with the exception of Pakistan—the national defense budget was minimal. In the mid-1950s, the Army numbered about 350,000, and there was only minimal growth in manpower over the next several years; after India's 1962 defeat, the Army's numbers would leap to 827,000!

The Indian Army had significant personnel problems. The Army had only eight divisions—seven infantry and one armour. Only three battalions were available to the Western Command in the early 1960s. The budget constraints on the army and India's pacifistic attitude aggravated another problem: the British had provided much of the leadership of the British Indian army; without the British, there was a shortage of experienced officers and NCOs. It was thus difficult to build up military strength, especially when the advice of experienced senior officers was often ignored.

Apparently, Indian intelligence was also lacking. Their lack of preparedness for warfare in the Himalayas would indicate a very poor concept of the topography and weather in the area, resulting in very poor mobility across the mountains. Indian intelligence and reconnaissence seemed ignorant of Chinese strength, mobility and tactics, especially night movements and human wave attacks which the Indians called the "Red Ant Swarm."

The Indians had problems with fire power. Because of limited budget, they had minimal artillery and difficulty keeping it adequately supplied with ammunition. The artillery they did have was often immobile in the mountains.

Another area affected by the budget was training. Technical training was lacking, and there were simply not enough supplies and munitions for adequate training. Worse, there was little training for mountain warfare.

Perhaps the major problem—another result of the limited defense budget—was the logistic one. Even with foreign aid (primarily from Russia), the Indian army was lacking in virtually every area of equipment and supplies. The logistic shortfalls had many serious consequences. India lacked the engineering equipment for alpine operations. They had tentage, but not enought to house even half the soldiers. Rations were often in short supply, resulting in many hungry days for the Indian soldiers. Their communications equipment was minimal. And, almost unbelievably, the Indian army came to the Himalayas (to altitudes above 15,000 feet) in cotton, summer uniforms! Finally, transportation of supplies was a serious problem. Roads into the mountains were few; often, supplies came on long final legs by pack animal. The Indians resorted to supply by air drop, but even this had problems. Aging parachutes were used with supplies, and supplies crashed to the ground often when the parachutes failed. To make matters worse, many of the air drops landed on Chinese, rather than Indian, encampments (and to add insult to injury, the Chinese would throw out the "inedible" Indian rations)!

In summary, the Indian army was in a poor state, especially in their readiness for alpine warfare. Their fire power, supply system, training, and readiness for mountain operations were all quite lacking. They had significant personnel shortages, and would often be outnumbered by the Chinese by 5:1.2 To pit troops in such circumstances against an enemy superior in every detail of military strength would be absurd; to leave them in an early winter of heavy snow and freezing temperatures would be to condemn them to steady and severe attrition from exposure and illness and, before long, starvation. But this is what India did.

Under these circumstances, India's forward policy was militarily nonsensical. But some politicians and leaders simply believe what they want to believe. Nehru was still convinced that his army would be almost invincible against the Chinese. He would soon learn how wrong he was.

SUMMER 1962 SKIRMISHES

Well into 1962, Nehru continued to ignore the advice of his generals about the army's poor state of readiness; he also continued to assume that China would not or could not assert herself against India. Hence, Nehru continued his "forward policy" of furter extending Indian outposts and border patrols.

India's purpose was to pursue the forward policy to drive the Chinese out of any area New Delhi considered hers. On February 4, 1962, the Home Minister declared, "If the Chinese will not vacate the areas occupied by her, India will have to repeat what she did in Goa. She will certainly drive out the Chinese forces." The Indian strategy in early 1962 was to move behind Chinese posts in an attempt to cut off Chinese supplies. China's reaction any new Indian outpost, thought, was usually to surround it with superior forces.

The diplomatic letters and protests continued, usually totally uncompromising and unproductive. In January, both sides accused the other of violating their air space. A February 26th Chinese not suggested that maintaining the status quo of the boundary was the only way to avoid military clashes, and again suggested withdrawing the troops of each side twenty kilometers back. The note concluded with the statement that "the door for negotiations is always open." In fact, China had already stopped all patrols within twenty kilometers of the border. But India again rejected the proposal, and continued to insist that the Chinese withdraw to behind the Indian claim line before there would be any negotiations on the border question. In April, Nehru announced that "We do not want war with China, but that is not within our control. Therefore we have to prepare for the contingency." An April Chinese letter protested Indian intrusions, and demanded that India withdraw from the Karakoram area. On May 14th, the Indians proposed to allow China to "continue to use the Aksai Chin road for civilian traffic" if China would otherwise withdraw from all Indian-claimed territory. China's reply rejected the idea but again stated that it was better to resolve the issue than to fight. In June, the 1954 Trade Agreements, including the Five Principles of Coexistence, expired; talks produced no new trade agreement, and trade representatives returned home. Relations between the two countries continued to deteriorate.

Throughout the early months of 1962, China had several external problems, especially the Taiwan Straits Crisis. Chinese leaders continued to insist that they did not want war, but that Aksai Chin was clearly Chinese and was strategically important to the People's Republic. China began to commit more border patrols—in reaction to increased border activity by Indian troops in Spring 1962. In June, when the Taiwan Strait situation eased, China's attention returned to the border situation and she brought more pressure to bear on New Delhi. India, too, continued to escalate by establishing new outposts to "defend Indian territory from further inroads."

The crisis had brewed for three years. Despite many menacing confrontations and endless protests, there had been very few casualties thus far. But in July this changed. A Gurkha platoon had been sent forward to cut off Chinese outposts in the Galwan Valley (in Aksai Chin). On July 10th, a Chinese battalion surrounded the Indian post, cutting it off from supplies. The Chinese were attempting to halt Indian advances in Ladakh; but India continued to supply the Galwan Valley outpost by air drop. New Delhi sent a reinforcing force toward Galwan Valley, but it was turned back by the Chinese. India was continuing to move forward in an attempt to pressure China into withdrawing from the disputed area.

On July 21st, there was a skirmish in the Chip Chap Valley. Two Indian soldiers were wounded, the first since Konga Pass in

1959. The Chinese protested, and also accused India of violating the McMahon Line in NEFA.

Indeed, General B. M. Kaul, then Chief of the General Staff, had ordered the establishment of 24 posts along the McMahon Line. In June, local Indian commanders had established Dhola Post, in Tawang. The relevant issue was that Dhola Post was one mile north of the McMahon Line, in Chinese territory even by Indian standards. On August 4th, Peking accused India of violating the McMahon Line (at Dhola), and of aggression beyond its own claimed border—and therefore into Chinese territory.

But Chinese pressure was ineffective. On August 14th, Nehru told Parliament that India had three times as many posts in Ladakh as China; Nehru asked for a free hand to deal with China, and Parliament gave it to him.

In August, China improved its combat readiness in NEFA, Tibet and Sinkiang. While there was no sign of a manpower buildup in Tibet, there was construction of ammunition dumps and shockpiling of ammunition, weapons, and gasoline.

On September 8th, the Chinese reacted to the Indian outpost at Dhola. A Chinese patrol of sixty soldiers—which the Indian commander reported as 600—moved over and down the Thag La Ridge, into positions which dominated the Indian post at Dhola. The Chinese patrol suggested that local officials meet to discuss where the border lay. Orders from Nehru refuded any discussions and orders the army to relieve the Dhola Post and force the Chinese back behind Thag La Ridge. A serious clash between the sides ensured. The XXXIII Corps commander, General Umrao Singh, had protested that driving the Chinese back behind the Ridge was militarily nonsensical; Singh was later relieved and replaced by the more compliant General B. M. Kaul. Nehru used the Thag La incident to whip up national and international support. Further skirmished continued through September.

By late September, China had resumed patrols along the entire border. On September 20th, another clash occurred at Chedong, at the junction of India, Bhutan and Tibet. Both sides took casualties, including one Chinese officer killed. The fighting for physical control of disputed land was increasing.

There were both Indian and Chinese protests about the Chedong incident: India accused China of expansionism, and China warned that there was a limit to her patience and self-restraint. Unfortunately for the Indians, Chedong was another area where China seems to have had legitimate claim. Many Indians must have questioned India's actions in Chedong, north of the McMahon Line (and Nehru's orders to push the Chinese back even further); pushing military force past India's claimed boundary clearly made India the aggressor in this and some subsequent clashes. Much of the more serious fighting to come in October was not in the areas which both China and India claimed, but in areas (Tawang and Walong) where China had a legitimate claim or where India had pushed beyond the McMahon Line.

Sporadic fighting in the Chedong area continued for the next few weeks, suggesting that India was determined to drive Chinese forces back. Now, India seemed unwilling even to discuss any border issues or proposals. An October 3rd Chinese note suggested a meeting to discuss the entire border was met with a curt Indian refusal. On September 26th, General Kaul assumed command of XXXIII Corps; this Corps was hampered by widely dispursed troop concentrations, few weapons, inadequate supplies, and no winter clothing. On October 5th, India created a special Border Command under the command of General Kaul. Kaul was already in NEFA, preparing an "all out effort" to expel the Chinese from Thag La. On October 9th, General Kaul ordered General John Dalvi, Commander of the Seventh Brigade, to take Yumtso La Pass. Dalvi argued that he lacked the military resources—and the winter clothing—to take the 16,000 foot Pass. Kaul compromised, and sent a fifty man patrol to Tseng Jong. the patrol reached Tseng Jong before dark on October 9th without Chinese resistance. Little did the patrol know that bloody fighting— and the China-India Border War—was only a few hours away.

INDIA FALLING BEHIND CHINA IN SOUTH ASIAN DIPLOMACY

India has always been a local superpower, being by far the largest country within South Asia, and is, in fact, the only one in the group that borders every other South Asian country except Afghanistan, which shares a border with Pakistan. But India's economic performance was stunted by years of state control of the kind now prevalent in Iran. Over the past 15 years, however, economic growth has been strong, enabling the country to have a much greater diplomatic reach than at any time since the 1950s when India briefly emerged as the leader of those countries that were being de-colonized by the European powers. Given this situation, it ought to have been the case that New Delhi would be preeminent in its own backyard. Instead, over the past two decades, India has lost the status of being the lead player in any South Asian country barring Bhutan, a country with which it still has a treaty relationship. In almost the entire region, China has overtaken India in that intangible quality - influence - especially in Nepal and Sri Lanka, while Beijing's existing alliances with Pakistan and Bangladesh are growing stronger.

This is not due to a lack of quality within India's diplomatic service. Instead, the Indian Foreign Service (IFS) has produced a modern corps of skilled diplomats, many experts in different regions of the world, and eager to do more to advance their country's interests. The wall they face is the ambivalence that has become second nature to the country's top policy makers, both within the political crust as well as the administrative backup. Phrases such as "going all the way" and "going for the kill" are inelegant. Yet they represent a reality that is that sometimes a country has to formulate and then determinedly implement a clear policy to be carried out till success is achieved.

In South Asia, such a quality was recently displayed by President Percy Mahinda Rajapaksa of Sri Lanka. He succeeded in wiping out the terrorist group known as the Liberation Tigers of Tamil Eelam (LTTE) where, over the past three decades, all his predecessors had failed. Unlike them, President Rajapaksa did not heed (well-meaning but disastrous) advice to slow down his offensive or agree to a cease-fire, the latter being a device that the LTTE used since 1987 to gain time to recover after having lost the initiative in the field. Once the LTTE recovered its strength, the ceasefire would be abandoned. This point was repeatedly made by

Rajapaksa to the peacemakers who clustered around him, especially in the final months of the brief, brutal war against the LTTE that began with his coming to office in 2005.

Once India, because of political considerations such as the need to avoid alienating the country's sizable Tamil population, refused to give the Sri Lankan army equipment, Rajapaksa turned to Pakistan and China. Both countries opened their warehouses to him, and so built up immense capital both within Sri Lanka's Sinhala most importantity as well as the country's policy establishment. Rajapaksa showed none of the half-heartedness that has characterized so much of Indian policy and, as a result, emerged a winner. In the case of India, the desire to win brownie points with key international players (by heeding their sometimes incorrect advice) as well as an aversion to risk ensured that much of Indian diplomacy was too watered down to be effective. This is especially the case in its immediate neighbourhood.

This on-again, off-again excellence can be seen in Indian diplomatic policy towards Pakistan especially in regard to the long-term pattern of instituting confidence building measures (CBM) being followed - usually after a mass terror attack - with strong rhetoric and a withdrawal of contact. The reality is that in the case of Pakistan, conventional war may have ceased to be an option. This is because the Pakistan army has itself lost control of many of the jihadis that it has trained, equipped and funded for so long.

Instead of reducing the risk of a terror attack, going after the Pakistan military would inflame a large segment of the Pakistani population thus making them susceptible to recruitment in the ongoing jihad against India. Given that situation, it may have been preferable for Indian policymakers to publicly resort to a conventional war except in the case of a conflict started by Pakistan, an unlikely possibility. The military option would work only if (a) the Pakistan army controls the jihadi networks and (b) is comprehensively defeated in battle. Neither condition exists.

A "No War" declaration by India would remove the Pakistani military establishment's most frequently used excuse to station more than 60 percent of its army along the India border, even as the force is engaged in a life-and-death struggle with the Pakistan

Taliban. Instead, even though New Delhi has no intention of going to war, the prospect of one is deliberately kept open especially after terror strikes such as Mumbai 11/26-28. Thus, the benefits of India's "No War" declaration are denied, while the other side is aware that the mock-aggressive posture is a bluff and hence will not change its behaviour as a result of the threat.

A glaring example of how promoting the idea that India would go to war over Pakistani provocations has hurt New Delhi can be seen in the 2002 standoff with Pakistan in the mountains separating the two. Ostensibly to scare the international community into putting pressure on Pakistan to call off its Kashmir jihad, the then-Vajpayee government mobilized two Indian army strike corps on the border, keeping them and their support units on a hair-trigger alert for the greater part of the year. Aware that the Indians were bluffing, the Pakistan government refused to budge from its policy of helping jihadists active in Kashmir. The long Indian army mobilization created a perception of regional instability that affected India's status as a safe investment destination even as it exhausted the elite army units on the front line. Given the information that India would not attack, the 2002 mobilization came at a horrendous cost and no benefit. In a system where posturing comes easily to the higher levels of the Indian policy establishment, Prime Minister Manmohan Singh has thus far resisted jingoism and has made it evident that India would not be stampeded into military action. In the case of Sri Lanka, the policy was to intensify conflict until victory. What is needed is a clear policy that is carried out effectively, not a zig-zag routine that confuses the international community and results in a loss of credibility for India.

Military sales can become an effective instrument of diplomacy, were they deployed by India. Within the region, including in Sri Lanka and Nepal, the military is a significant component of the policy process, often the crucial player. Because of New Delhi's longstanding policy of not permitting foreign military sales save for exceptional situations, China has been provided an opportunity to fill the gap. Had Bangladesh, Nepal and Sri Lanka been more reliant on Indian equipment and training for their armed forces, New Delhi would have been in a much stronger position to influence policy in those places than it is today. Instead, the "weapons gap" isincreasingly being filled by China.

The mantra of "non-alignment" has in most instances become a cover for lack of action. Even during the period of the Cold War, when India suffered many of the consequences of being seen as a Soviet ally, not a single Soviet soldier was ever stationed in India or trained here, nor did any Indian soldier undertake any sort of mission in the USSR. In contrast, there are regular exchanges of U.S. and Indian soldiers and joint training exercises have become routine. The warming of ties is because there is a natural fit between the two sides. India has a significant pool of trained (and trainable) manpower, while the United States has abundant stocks of equipment that could be transferred to New Delhi rather than mothballed or left under-utilized. This is especially the case with naval vessels, where India is now being made to pay $3 billion for a secondhand Russian aircraft carrier that it is finding it difficult to float and move at the same time.

Progress in U.S.-India military to military relatives has been slow and is still far below its potential in substantial part because of the wariness of the Indian establishment over China's reaction. Compare this with Pakistan which has built up close military ties with both China and the United States, its friendship with one not affecting the other. In the military field, the choice is between going with the United States or going alone, because a military alliance with China is not an option. Beijing sees New Delhi as a potential competitor and has repeatedly shown through its actions its commitment to a strategic policy that inhibits the growth of Indian power. Unfortunately, in this case, Indian ambivalence is now being matched by the United States under the Obama administration, which has downgraded ties with India to a level much below that set under President George W. Bush. It seems inevitable, however, that both countries will, hopefully within the present presidential term, awaken to the need for a partnership that can ensure that Asia does not fall under the sway of any single power.

The persistent Indian ambivalence in policy was visible in Sri Lanka, where India simultaneously called for a cease-fire while backing the unity of the island nation. As a consequence of simultaneously conveying two contradictory messages, neither the Tamil nor the Sinhala zealots have anything other than distaste for India, while the abundant provision of military supplies has led the Sri Lankan military towards becoming as close to Beijing as are their counterparts in Pakistan.

In Nepal, after first helping to get King Gyanendra to abdicate, New Delhi threw its support behind the Maoists, who promptly reacted by threatening to scrap the India-Nepal agreement and replace it with a similar deal with China. After its embrace of the Maoists, which ended only after their tilt to Beijing became manifest (by the end of 2008), no other Nepali party is willing to trust New Delhi and see it as a reliable partner, even the once-friendly Nepali Congress. Meanwhile, in a show of deft footwork, Chinese diplomats have been active in Kathmandu renewing ties with the non-Maoist parties that today run the government (after the departure of the Maoists), so as to accelerate the growth of PRC influence in Nepal.

Today, there are almost as many radical training camps located within Bangladesh as there in Pakistan, camps whose specific purpose is to replenish the stream of jihadis into India. Yet, unlike in the case of Pakistan, the Indian government is not posturing as if was is likely. A hostile Pakistan, an unfriendly Bangladesh, and Nepal and Sri Lanka heading towards the PRC. These are the wages of a diplomacy that refuses to go for the jugular in the pursuit of objectives, but almost invariably crafts a compromise that gives much less geopolitical benefit. India presents an example of how a most important power that avoids a clear policy line or a better deployment of its assets gives way to the other who is ruthless and willing to complete the marathon rather than slow down and stop before the finish line. Such a policy is the delight of politicians and anathema to statesmen, who understand the need for not just vision, but for will and perseverance.

MILITARY DIPLOMACY AND CHINA'S SOFT POWER

The majority significant developments in this quarter included China's military activism and greater emphasis on "soft power" diplomacy. Assessment of the high-level China-Southeast Asian interchange shows that while China's influence is rising, Beijing continues to face several constraints and limitations in allaying Southeast Asian governments' concern about its long-term intentions.

On April 13-15, Chinese Defence Minister Gen. Cao Gangchun visited Malaysia, Singapore, and Vietnam to enhance military cooperation between China and Southeast Asia. With more than 70 percent of Chinese imported oil coming through the Malacca Strait, China's national security interests and stakes in Southeast Asia are rising. According to the People's Liberation Army's (PLA) *White Paper on National Defence* in 2004, the defence of sovereignty, territorial integrity, and "maritime rights and interests" were all classified as "national security goals." China may be regarded as a rising continental power, but its vast coastline makes it an important maritime nation as well.

Cao's visit reflected a low-key approach that endeavored to minimize regional concerns about rising Chinese military and other power, and to seek greater common ground with neighbouring countries. Outwardly, Cao's trip to Southeast Asia amounted to little more than observations of the various military camps and establishments in Singapore, Malaysia, and Vietnam. Cao's dialogues with his counterparts were said to include clarifying growing U.S. military involvement in Southeast Asia. There were no formal joint statements subjectd at the conclusion of the Southeast Asian leg of his trip.

This Chinese military activism comes at a time of greater U.S. military involvement in Southeast Asia and is seen by some observers as a sign of a continuing Chinese interest in regional strategic adjustments and realignments, especially with countries that provide military access to the United States. Singapore's close military relationship with the U.S., for example, gives U.S. warships a convenient entrance to the region. Meanwhile, Singapore's training fields in Taiwan (not to mention Lee Hsien Loong's visit to the island in 2004 before he was prime minister) are also a cause of concern for Beijing.

As for the Malacca Strait, the longstanding problem of piracy on the high seas is a looming concern for China. The disruption of

China's energy supplies would be a great detriment to its burgeoning economy, and Cao's visit highlighted China's willingness to step up its effort to cooperate with Singapore and Malaysia in patrolling the Malacca Strait. In Vietnam, Cao's visit was said to include consideration of Cam Rahn Bay. The port facilities at Cam Rahn include two well-paved runways, a deep-water port, and a large storage site for petroleum. Due to its close proximity to Hainan Island, Cam Rahn Bay is strategically located to monitor and intercept communications in the southeastern coast of China. China complained for years over the Soviet Union's use of the base against China's interests, and presumably would oppose any U.S.-Vietnam military cooperation that would involve U.S. use of the base.

According to a report subjectd at the Aspen Institute Congressional Conference on U.S.-China Relations in April, China's military modernization – especially the PLA Navy's capabilities to secure "blue water" naval surface fleet – is a trend that will continue unabated and a reality with which countries in the region and the U.S. will have to come to terms. China continues to reassure its neighbours that its rising military and other power will not endanger their interests as Chinese officials remain well aware of the concern among many Southeast Asian governments regarding China's long-term intentions.

Shangri-La Conversation

Despite Cao's visit and other military contacts with Southeast Asia, China once again chose to participate at a minimal level by sending a nonministerial delegation to the annual Shangri-La Dialogue in Singapore in June. As a result, China missed an opportunity for close consultations on maritime security with countries with most important trade routes passing through Southeast Asia and littoral states in the region. The military chiefs at the conference introduced and institutionalized several mechanisms to combat terrorism and piracy on the high seas through the strengthening of multilateral coastguard patrols, enhancing naval surveillance systems and sharing data, and revamping the littoral states' navies. The conference also included a Malaysian proposal for a regional disaster-relief centre to coordinate military and civilian aid in emergencies. The U.S. proposed closer military cooperation between countries in the Asia-Pacific region two years ago. Efforts by involved Southeast Asian states to strengthen naval cooperation are welcomed by the U.S. and defence ministers from other parts of the world as they pledge to provide greater technical and monetary assistance to Southeast Asian navies and militaries. China's conspicuous absence at the conference implied that it may not feel comfortable with military cooperation that so prominently involves the U.S.

AID, DIPLOMACY AND SOFT AUTHORITY

In early April, Premier Wen Jiabao conducted a four nation Asia-Pacific diplomatic tour that dealt with subjects of concern to China-Southeast Asian relations and included a two day visit to Cambodia (April 7-8). The tour also involved a visit to Australia marked by accords on Australian uranium exports to China; a visit to Fiji, where Wen attended the China-Pacific Island Countries Economic Development and Cooperation Forum, and advanced a range of policies promoting development of island countries; and a stop in New Zealand marked by legal, cultural, and educational accords. China concluded 60 bilateral accords during the trip. Wen sought in particular to establish a schedule for completion of the negotiations on China's proposed free trade agreements with Australia and New Zealand, which complement China's accord with Southeast Asian countries, the China-ASEAN Free Trade Agreement.

Earlier media reports disclosed that Wen also planned to visit Thailand on this tour but that visit was postponed because of the political demonstrations that ultimately resulted in the April 4 resignation of Prime Minister Thaksin Shinawatra. Thaksin developed close relations with China since assuming power in 2001. Official Chinese media avoided taking sides in reporting Thaksin's resignation, his assessment of his years as prime minister, and the charges made by opposition forces.

In Cambodia, Premier Wen and Cambodian Prime Minister Hun Sen witnessed the signing of 10 agreements including those dealing with a low-interest Chinese loan, grant aid, and the donation of 30 firetrucks by the Chinese government. Wen also attended a groundbreaking ceremony for a Chinese-funded office complex for Hun Sen and his deputies. The Cambodian leader predicted that "Cambodia will benefit greatly from this visit," and added that China is Cambodia's "most trustworthy friend." The Chinese government in the last decade provided grant aid, agreed to write off past debts, and granted tariff-free status for some 400 Cambodian items. Investments by Chinese companies were said by unofficial media reports to be worth $240 million in 2005, and were mainly in the garment industry, Cambodia's main foreign exchange earner.

The lengthy joint communiqué marking the end of the visit recounted Cambodia's appreciation of Chinese support and assistance, and China's appreciation of Cambodia's support for closer Chinese relations with ASEAN and Cambodia's opposition to Taiwan. There was no mention of their common interest in deflecting international criticism of their respective human rights practices, nor did the communiqué refer to their positions on long delayed international efforts seeking to bring to justice surviving members of the notorious Khmer Rouge regime that was closely aligned with China as it carried out policies resulting in mass deaths in Cambodia in the 1970s.

The devastating earthquake in Java, Indonesia in May saw a coordinated effort in the international community to provide humanitarian aid to the survivors and the Indonesian government. As international assistance efforts gathered pace, the Chinese government was quick to respond with a highly publicized contribution of $2 million in cash aid. It also pledged to send a 44-person team of medical and earthquake experts to Java.

The Chinese effort to highlight its contribution and seize media attention seemed reminiscent of the Chinese response to the tsunami that hit Indonesia, southern Thailand, and other parts of southern Asia in December 2004. Although Beijing at that time was relatively quick to react, its efforts were only a relatively small part of the international humanitarian and military assistance to the areas struck by the natural disaster. This time around, Japan led the efforts, with a pledge of $10 million. It sent in two medical teams. The U.S., in addition to $2.5 million worth of aid, also sent doctors and nurses from a military base in Okinawa. According to USAID, U.S. military personnel were also deployed to Yogyakarta, Indonesia, the city worst hit by the earthquake. On June 1, the U.S. Marine Corps Fleet 3rd Surgical Company set up a field hospital in Bantul District.

Beijing continues to make important strides in improving China's soft power and diplomatic image in Southeast Asia. Recent assessments in an article in the journal *Survival* and a policy brief released by the Carnegie Endowment for International Peace noted the success of Chinese economic development as a driver for countries in Southeast Asia and elsewhere, encouraging them to adopt similar improvements through market-style incentives in an authoritarian political system with features of a planned economy. Cambodia, Laos, and Vietnam were cited among admirers of the development policies and practices of their neighbor to the north. According to the assessments, these countries have adopted the Chinese model of market-based authoritarianism. Beijing's ability to present an alternative political and economic model is said to be a telling indicator of a growing Chinese ideological influence that is countering Western perspectives that insist democratic principles are a requisite for economic prosperity.

Recent polls conducted by *BBC World Service*, a Sydney-based Lowy poll, and the Pew Survey all point to a positive image of Chinese influence. China's charm is primarily focused on trade and a diplomatic agenda that looks at win-win collaboration. In an effort to allay regional fears of China's economic, political, and military clout, Chinese leaders use the guidelines of "do good to our neighbours, treat our neighbours as partners" (*yulin weishan, yilin weiban*) and "maintain friendly relations with our neighbours, make them feel secure, and help to make them rich".

China, the SCO Summit, and ASEAN contribution

Chinese commentary and official statements continue to show common ground in Chinese policies and practices with the two most important Asian regional bodies China works closely with, the Shanghai Cooperation Organization (SCO) and ASEAN. The annual summit and fifth anniversary of the Shanghai Cooperation Organization (SCO) was held in June in Shanghai, where it was first founded. With much pomp and circumstance, the summit marked the highlight of China's diplomacy during the quarter. Chinese President Hu Jintao rolled out the red carpet, welcoming heads of state from the member countries. Throughout the two-day summit, they were joined by leaders from neighbouring countries sitting in as observers, notably Iran, and by senior representatives from ASEAN as well as from the Commonwealth of Independent States. The Chinese hosts ensured seats for each and every regional actor at the working table.

Since its inception five years ago, the SCO has made steady progress in carrying out its mandate for closer regional cooperation on economic and political subjects. As a co-founder, China worked to create an organization where broad cooperation among all countries and regional organizations can be sought. It originally started with functional subjects including the demilitarization of the Chinese borders with Russia and involved Central Asian states, tackling drug trafficking, and boosting regional trade. It grew in prominence for efforts against other transnational subjects, notably terrorism.

For China and the Southeast Asian delegates, there was good reason to invite ASEAN representatives to the 2006 Shanghai meeting. Last year, Philippine President Gloria Arroyo, among others, proposed that Southeast Asia should also look into collaborating with other regional organizations in Asia to combat terrorism, a transnational threat that observes no borders. In response to ASEAN's request, and with the convenience of playing host to this year's summit, China had the ASEAN secretariat as its guest of honour to further discuss joint efforts between the SCO and ASEAN to counter terrorism.

Assessing China's Increase

The U.S. and other international media covered Chinese leaders' visits along the lines of past coverage that emphasized how rapidly China has risen in influence in Southeast Asia and the broader Asia-Pacific region, and how this has undercut U.S.

influence in the area, even with close U.S. allies like Australia. Even though Chinese leaders have been at pains to emphasize China's intention to rise "peacefully" and to avoid significant competition with the United States, China's economic growth, burgeoning trade, and adroit diplomacy were depicted by the media as more than a match for U.S. policy and behaviour, as the U.S. leadership was seen as distracted and hampered, its focus on the war in Iraq and the broader war on terrorism. More in-depth assessments by prominent international observers and analytical publications provided greater balance in examining strengths and limitations of China's rise in Southeast Asia, and their implications for U.S. leadership in the region, however.

The American Enterprise Institute and National Defence University published in 2006 the findings of the final conference in a year-long series of seminars and meetings dealing with China in Asia and focusing on China's rise in Southeast Asia and its meaning for the United States. The findings showed that China's economic and military power is increasing, that many Asian countries (especially in Southeast Asia) are accommodating China's increasing influence, and that the U.S. lacks a clear Asia strategy that would be useful in supporting U.S. objectives in the region.

At the same time, the findings showed that while attentive Chinese diplomacy has alleviated regional fears, China's long-term ambitions remain a concern for many countries. A prominent Philippine expert at the meeting was reported to emphasize that his government reacts to China's rise by "hedging," and Manila's alliance relationship with the U.S. is used to balance Chinese influence. A specialist from Thailand explained the balance in Bangkok's relations with China and the U.S. He showed that the level of Thailand's trade with each country is about the same; Thailand runs a trade deficit with China that offends some Thai farmers in particular; and China's policies on Myanmar and Chinese immigration are significant irritants in Thai-Chinese relations. Also this quarter, the academic journal *Asian Security* published what may be the most comprehensive and up-to-date assessment in the fast-growing list of analyses dealing with China's rising influence in Southeast Asia and what it means for U.S. influence. On the one hand, it highlighted evidence that Chinese polices and behaviour have reduced the worries of Southeast Asian governments over Chinese intentions. Southeast Asian government leaders more often refer to China as an opportunity than a challenge, and they express frequent appreciation for Chinese actions seen to benefit Southeast Asia. Chinese trade levels with Southeast Asia have grown rapidly and seem likely to continue to grow strongly, adding to China's importance to the region. On the other hand, the article cautioned that it is easy to exaggerate China's influence while underestimating the continued power and influence of other regional actors, notably the United States. There remain long-term concerns in Southeast Asia over whether a more powerful China may decide to try to more assertively increase its influence or even try to dominate the region. According to the article, a prevailing Southeast Asian view is that it is too early to declare that China has proved itself to be a good neighbor, though it has become a better neighbor whose recent contributions to regional peace and prosperity make Southeast Asian representatives more hopeful for the future. Meanwhile, Southeast Asian governments see a variety of significant obstacles to continued improvement in China-Southeast Asian relations, and welcome the continued prominence in the region of the U.S., Japan, and other powers seen as providing balance to China's rise.

The article noted that even in the area of trade, where China's growing role has been most pronounced, few Southeast Asian countries conduct more than 10 percent of their trade with China. The level of Chinese-Southeast Asian trade, after many years of rapid growth, only now is approaching and/or surpassing the level of Southeast Asian trade with Japan and with the U.S. Meanwhile, growing Southeast Asian trade with China depends heavily on U.S. and European consumers purchasing products from China with components and materials from Southeast Asia. China remains a small investor in Southeast Asia, especially in comparison to the U.S., and a small aid donor to Southeast Asia, especially when compared to Japan.

Chinese military ties with Southeast Asia are very small in comparison with the robust and recently enhanced wide range of U.S. military exercises, exchanges, training, and other activities with a broad range of Southeast Asian counterparts. The asymmetry in Chinese and U.S. influence in this area was graphically illustrated in their respective responses to the tsunami disaster in South and Southeast Asia in December 2004.

Apparently taking a cue from Chinese leaders' visits and attentive diplomacy, Japanese and U.S. leaders have joined with Indian, Russian, and European representatives in showing greater interest in and more frequent visits with counterparts from Southeast Asia. All of these powers, along with Australia and New Zealand and with the exception of the U.S., welcomed the opportunity to participate with Southeast Asian leaders in the East Asian Summit of December 2005, even though doing so was at odds with China's initial efforts to restrict the summit to members of ASEAN Plus Three.

The *Asian Security* analysis found few direct unenthusiastic implications for U.S. interests flowing from China's growing relations with Southeast Asia. The main exception was China's support for Myanmar and for authoritarian governments in Laos, Cambodia, and Vietnam, which is at odds with U.S. efforts to promote democracy abroad. It saw little grounds for the fear of a China-dominated economic regionalism in Southeast Asia; the trading and investment environment is too competitive and China's position too small and dependent on the United States and others to allow it. U.S. alliances and military relations with Southeast Asia seemed secure as Southeast Asian governments generally welcomed the greater U.S. military activism in the region, and China adopted a moderate stance on U.S. military activities in the interest of convincing U.S. leaders of China's commitment to rise "peacefully." China-ASEAN improvements also have reduced the danger of regional conflict and helped U.S. interests in secure sea lanes and regional stability. According to the article, Southeast Asia's growing interest in China ties should not be interpreted as welcoming China's dominance; most ASEAN states welcome closer ties with the U.S., Japan, India, and others as a means to keep the region stable and independent of any one power's dominance.

Meanwhile, the assessment saw several serious obstacles to China forward momentum in relations with Southeast Asia.

Economically, Chinese competitiveness in world trade threatens to leave even some advanced Southeast Asian economies behind, or to relegate them to the position of suppliers of raw materials to the fast-growing Chinese economy. This asymmetrical relationship could lead to serious resentment and backlash from nationalistic Southeast Asian governments. China's growing military power and growing energy needs could prompt disputes with Southeast Asian neighbours over disputed territory similar to the disputes raging between China and Japan today. Assertive Chinese actions against Taiwan, even if provoked by pro-independence leaders on the island, would endanger Asian stability and probably lead Southeast Asian leaders to seek closer ties with one another and other powers, notably the U.S. Meanwhile, Chinese leaders clearly resent Japan's efforts to compete for influence in Southeast Asia, and they may not adjust gracefully to intensified involvement in the region, encouraged by the ASEAN members, of India, Australia, Russia, and the U.S.

Bibliography

Amitabh Sikdar: *India and China : Strategic Energy Management and Security*, Manas, Delhi, 2009.

Anil, K.C.: *Military and Democracy in South Asia : Challenges, Politics and Power*, Sumit Enterprises, Delhi, 2009.

Asha Gupta: *Military Rule and Democratization : Changing Perspectives*, Deep & Deep, Delhi, 2003.

Deepak, B R : *India and China : 1904-2004 : A Century of Peace and Conflict*, Manak, Delhi, 2005.

Dixit, A.K. : *Military Wars and Rescue Techniques*, Cyber Tech Pub, Delhi, 2010.

Donnan, H. and Wilson, T. M.: *Borders: Frontiers of Identity, Nation and State*, Oxford: Berg, 1999.

Gao, Mobo: *The Battle for China's Past: Mao and the Cultural Revolution*, London, Pluto Press, 2008.

Gaur, Mahendra : *Indian Policy of Neighbour*, Delhi, Kalpaz Pub., 2006.

Gupta, S.: *Disrupted Borders: An Intervention in Definitions of Boundaries*, London: River Oram Press, 1993.

Jagannath P. Panda: *China's Path to Power : Party, Military and the Politics of State Transition*, Pentagon, Delhi, 2010.

Nayyar, K K : *National Security : Military Aspects*, Rupa, Delhi, 2003.

Prabir De: *India and China in an Era of Globalisation : Essays on Economic Cooperation*, Bookwell, Delhi, 2005.

Radhakrishna: *Military Ethics: Guidelines for Peace and War*, Sumit Enterprises, Delhi, 2009.

Stuart R. Schram: *The Political Thought of Mao Tse-Tung*. New York: Praeger, 1969.

Wilson, T. M.: *New Borders for a Changing: Cross-border Cooperation and Governance*, London: Frank Cass, 2003.

Index

P

S

T

W

❑❑❑